THE ARAB HERITAGE

The Arab Heritage

By

Philip K. Hitti, Giorgio Levi Della Vida
Julian Obermann, Gustave E. von Grunebaum
Nabih Amin Faris, John L. LaMonte
Henry L. Savage, Edward J. Jurji and
Richard Ettinghausen

Edited by Nabih Amin Faris

NEW YORK
RUSSELL & RUSSELL INC
1963

REISSUED, 1963, BY RUSSELL & RUSSELL, INC.

BY ARRANGEMENT WITH PRINCETON UNIVERSITY PRESS

L. C. CATALOG CARD NO: 63-8362

PRINTED IN THE UNITED STATES OF AMERICA

To the memory of my best friend

PURNENDU NATH CHAKRAVORTY

1905-1942

PREFACE

One of the features of the Summer Seminar in Arabic and Islamic Studies, held at Princeton University every third year, is a series of lectures by eminent specialists in Semitic philology and other subjects contiguous to the Arabic and Islamic fields. The interest aroused by these lectures extended beyond the members of the Seminar and attracted a number of other scholars and cultivated lay men and women from the metropolitan area and the neighborhood. Several individuals expressed the wish that these lectures be compiled and published in book form, so that their contribution might be shared by a wider circle of interested people who could not, of necessity, attend the Seminar.

The present book represents a popular adaptation of the majority of the lectures delivered at the third Summer Seminar, which was held in 1941. The demand for the publication of these lectures in book form seemed urgent enough in 1941. Now it is more impelling than ever. The present global war has made the Arab and Islamic world, from North Africa to the eastern limits of Persia (clumsily dubbed "the Middle East"), of major interest to the United Nations.

In the following pages the reader is introduced to the wealth and diversity of Arab history and thought, its cultural development and permanent contribution to the world, particularly the West.

In the introductory chapter, Professor Philip K. Hitti of Princeton University surveys the entire field of Arabic and Islamic Studies in the United States, as well as the importance of these studies, not only to the specialist but also to the man on the street, and their bearing on current events and the shape of things to come. Indeed, the statesmen who would be entrusted with the task of building a new order on the ruins of the old, and the common men and women whose hopes are linked with the outcome of the present conflict and with the kind of peace that will follow it, would find in this book the background which they need for a fuller understanding of the problems involved and the solutions required in the Arab and Islamic world.

The introductory chapter is but a threshold leading to the house, wherein the seeker is shown a glimpse of the wealth of Arab heritage. Professor G. L. Della Vida of the University of Pennsylvania treats of Arabia before Islam, of the states and cultures which arose in the Peninsula, and prepared the way for Muhammad and his mission. The so-called dark age of Arabia is illumined, the historical gaps are filled in, and a clearer picture of Arabia before the advent of the Prophet unfolds.

But Islam, whether as a state that has spread from the Atlantic to the confines of China, or as a religion to which one eighth of the population of the world now adheres, was in no way isolated from the states, cultures, and religions with which it came in contact during its formative years. In the third chapter Professor Julian Obermann of Yale University discusses at length these relationships, particularly with Judaism and Christianity, and shows as well the impact of Islam upon its two sister religions.

Another facet of Arab heritage, almost of equal importance in molding Arab thought to what Islam was itself, is Arabic poetry. No sketch of Arab heritage is complete without a statement in which the complexities, scope, and content of Arabic poetry are discussed. Professor Gustave von Grunebaum of the Iranian Institute addresses himself to this subject.

What type of person does Islam and Arab culture produce? What type of philosophy of life do they evolve? A concrete answer to these questions is to be found in the life and works of al-Ghazzāli, perhaps one of the most fascinating saints of Islam and certainly one of its most versatile thinkers. The present writer attempts to sum up the life and works of this great man, whose works have influenced Medieval Christianity, and whose life has been and still is a source of inspiration to many, within and without the pale of Islam.

As we approach the eleventh century we find Islam spread over the entire Near East and the Mediterranean basin. We also find two of the sister religions—Christianity and Islam—locked in battle on the fields and plains of Asia Minor, Syria and Palestine and even Egypt. It might be too easy to succumb to the temptation of viewing these wars, loosely described as the crusades, as a struggle between two religions; or to oversimplify matters and describe them as a conflict between two ideologies. Professor John L. LaMonte of the University of Pennsylvania reviews the whole problem, and sets forth in lucid style an evaluation which takes into consideration the religious as well as the political and economic aspects of these two hundred year wars, without losing sight of the personal and human factors involved.

These two hundred year wars resulted, among other things, in bringing the East and West closer together, in the exchange of ideas and ideals, and in the establishment of permanent cultural and commercial relations between Western and Southern Europe on the one hand and the lands of the Eastern Mediterranean on the other. Travelers from the East embarked upon journeys to the lands of the "infidels," and travelers from the West set out for the lands of the "Turks" and "Saracens." A picture of the East through the eyes of a fourteenth century "tourist" from the land of the "Franks" is reproduced, for the first time in English, by Professor Henry L. Savage of Princeton University. This is no curiosity, no quaint story from Medieval times, but a mirror reflecting the thought, customs, and lore of the two peoples, and foreshadows modern interrelations between the East and West.

The course of Arab scientific thought, the tributaries that fed it, and the areas into which it flowed, irrigating, as it were, their soil, and making possible the growth of ideas which later blossomed into experimental science and the industrial revolution, are traced by Dr. Edward J. Jurji of the Princeton Theological Seminary and Princeton University.

Religion, literature, culture and even science take palpable shape in the art of people, advertising their accomplishments and exposing their limitations. The unifying principles underlying Arab and Islamic art, the lines along which it developed, and the taboos which warped its growth, as well as an evaluation of its permanent contribution, are discussed by Professor Richard Ettinghausen of the University of Michigan.

The aim of this book, however, is not the particular, but the general. The life of al-Ghazzāli, for example, is not treated in order to record the biography of an individual Moslem, but to show the type of man Islam is capable of producing. Likewise, the picture of the Holy Land through the eyes of a fourteenth century traveler is of interest not because of what a medieval pilgrim thought and said, but for its wider implications in depicting the interchange of ideas between the East and the West.

Interest in current events and the desire to ensure a lasting and enduring peace and to promote genuine goodwill among the family of nations call for a thorough familiarity with the history of the different members of the human race, a sane knowledge of their way of life and methods of thinking, as well as a sober appreciation of their cultures. It is hoped that this book will serve, partially, this purpose, and will arouse the interest of the reader for further reading and study. The bibliographies, attached to each of the chapters should therefore prove helpful.

Because of conditions imposed by the present war, and the purpose for which the book is intended, it has been found necessary to eliminate, for the sake of economy, most footnotes, as well as certain quotations which enrich the text but the deletion of which does not affect its integrity.

Finally, I wish to thank the contributors, one and all, for their patience and cooperation. In particular, I wish to thank Professor Henry L. Savage for his helpful counsel; and last but not least, Professor Philip K. Hitti, without whose help this book would not have appeared.

N. A. F.

PRINCETON, NEW JERSEY

CONTENTS

Preface vii

America and the Arab Heritage, by Philip K. Hitti 1

Pre-Islamic Arabia, by Giorgio Levi Della Vida 25

Islamic Origins: A Study in Background and Foundation, by Julian Obermann 58

Growth and Structure of Arabic Poetry A.D. 500-1000, by Gustave E. von Grunebaum 121

Al-Ghazzāli, by Nabih Amin Faris 142

Crusade and Jihād, by John L. LaMonte 159

Fourteenth Century Jerusalem and Cairo through Western Eyes, by Henry L. Savage 199

The Course of Arab Scientific Thought, by Edward J. Jurji 221

The Character of Islamic Art, by Richard Ettinghausen 251

Index 268

AMERICA AND THE ARAB HERITAGE

PHILIP K. HITTI

OUR CULTURAL HERITAGE FROM THE ARAB EAST

The so-called Dark Ages held no blackout for the Arabic-speaking peoples and Moslem lands. Throughout a large part of that period the torch of culture and enlightenment was kept aflame from the confines of China in the east, through Western Asia, North Africa and southwestern Europe, to the shores of the Atlantic Ocean. Turanians and Iranians, Syrians and Aramaeans, Arabians and Berbers, Andalusians and Sicilians—Moslems, Christians and Jews—were making contributions of greater or less significance to science, philosophy, art and literature. The chief medium of expression was the Arabic tongue; the auspices were those of the caliphate, whether in Baghdad, Cairo or Cordova. Between the middle of the eighth and the early part of the twelfth century, the Arabic-speaking peoples held the intellectual supremacy throughout the civilized world.[1]

When shortly before the middle of the seventh century the Arabians under the banner of Islam burst forth from their peninsula upon an unsuspecting world and established themselves in the Fertile Crescent and its two adjacent lands, Persia and Egypt, they brought with them but one cultural asset, a love of poetry. Soon, however, they became the beneficiaries of and collaborators with the more cultured peoples whom they conquered and who were gradually Islamized and Arabicized. India provided its wisdom—literature, astronomy and mathematics; Persia its belles-lettres and art; but above all Hellenized Syria, Egypt and Asia Minor, where the intellectual legacy of Greece lay as the most precious treasure at hand, offered their philosophical, medical and other scientific lore. Hellenism thus became the most vital of all foreign influences in the new Arab life. In fourscore years

[1] On this consult George Sarton, *Introduction to the History of Science*, 2 vols. (Baltimore, 1927, 1931), *passim*.

after the establishment of Baghdad as the seat of the caliphate, the Arabic-speaking peoples were in possession of the major works of Aristotle, the leading Neo-Platonic commentaries, the mathematical and astronomical compositions of Euclid and Ptolemy and the medical writings of Galen and Paul of Aegina. These translations into Arabic, transmuted in no small degree by the Arab mind during the course of several centuries, were transmitted, together with many new contributions, to Latin Europe mainly through Moslem Spain, Arab and Norman Sicily and crusading Syria. They laid the basis of that canon of knowledge which lay at the bottom of the modern European renaissance. Transmission, be it remembered, is no less essential from the standpoint of the history of thought than origination.

But the Arabs were no mere translators, imitators and transmitters. Their period of translation, roughly from the middle of the eighth to the middle of the ninth century, was followed by one of creative production. In the humanities, particularly theology (including philosophy and law), philology and linguistics, they carried on as Moslems and Arabs, throughout their entire history, original thinking of varying intensity. In pure and physical science they excelled at certain times. Algebra and alchemy, as these two words indicate, owe their very origin and existence to the Arabs. The founder of algebra was the ninth century al-Khwārizmi, whose name gave us "algorism" and whose text was done into Latin in the twelfth century. With the translation were introduced into Europe the Arabic numerals, and such terms as "zero" and "cipher" were directly borrowed. In the meantime, other mathematical terms were translated from Arabic into Latin and used in their translated form, as evidenced by "surd" and "sine." In astronomy research workers in Spain and the East have left on the sky immortal traces of their scholarship and industry readily discerned by anyone who reads the names of the stars on an ordinary celestial sphere. Not only many star-names in European languages are of Arabic origin, such as Acrab, Algedi, Altair, Deneb, Pherkad, but a number of technical terms, including "azimuth," "nadir" and "zenith," are likewise of Arabic etymology. They testify to the rich legacy of Islam to modern astronomy. In geography and cartography the most distinguished name of the Middle Ages was that of al-Idrīsi, who graced the court of Roger II in Palermo and whose map places the sources of the Nile—supposedly discovered in the latter part of the nineteenth century—in the equatorial highlands of Africa. In the social sciences suffice it to mention the name of the fourteenth century ibn-Khaldūn, who may be considered the discoverer—as he himself claimed—of the true scope and nature of history and the founder of sociology.

The medical annals of medieval times are adorned by such illustrious names as al-Rāzi (Rhazes, died 923), the first to distinguish scientifically between measles and smallpox; ibn-al-Nafīs (d. 1288), who discovered the pulmonary circulation of the blood two and a half centuries before Servetus, usually credited with the discovery; ibn-Sīna (Avicenna, d. 1037), whose *Canon* recognizes the spreading of disease by water and soil and in the words of Dr. Osler "remained a medical bible for a longer period than any other work."[2] In their Latin translations the medical and other scientific works of the Arab authors were used in such early universities as Naples, Bologna and Paris, as well as in the medical academies of Salerno and Montpellier. Through them such words as "julep," "rob," "sherbet," "syrup" and "soda" found their way into European languages. In sciences auxiliary to medicine suffice it to note that chemistry developed out of alchemy and that the greatest botanist of medieval Europe was the Hispano-Moslem ibn-al-Bayṭār (d. 1248). "Alcohol," "alkali," "alembic" and "elixir" may be mentioned as evidence of Arab chemical influence. What is perhaps more important than any concrete scientific contribution that we may cite is the new spirit of inquiry and investigation and the method of observation and experimentation which were in-

[2] William Osler, *The Evolution of Modern Medicine* (New Haven, 1922), p. 98.

troduced or enhanced in Europe as a result of its contact with the East.

In philosophy ibn-Rushd (Averroës, d. 1198) became "the commentator"—or to quote Dante, "*che il gran comento feo*" —as Aristotle was "the teacher." The Averroist school flourished in Paris until the sixteenth century. Thomas Aquinas' *Summa Theologica* contains references to ibn-Rushd as quoted by his contemporary and fellow Cordovan ibn-Maymūn (Maimonides). The liberalizing, rationalizing influence over Christian Europe of these two philosophers—one a Moslem and the other a Jew and both writing in Arabic—helped to provide a common intellectual foundation for medieval philosophy. The thinkers of all three faiths began searching for a reconciliation between the revealed truth of the Scriptures and the truth as arrived at by philosophers, a *modus vivendi* between science and religion, faith and reason. Medieval philosophy could thus be viewed as one philosophy which happened to be written in Arabic, Hebrew and Latin.[3] It dealt with the same general problem, represented the same tradition and arrived at the same general conclusion.

In the realm of mysticism and the interaction between Islamic Sufism and Christian monasticism the recent investigations of Asin have served as an eye-opener to medievalists. Even more startling were his studies of the literary influence of Moslem poets and philosophers on Dante.[4] The most significant contribution of Arabic poetry, however, lay in the subtle influence it exercised by its form and ideas, whether or not accompanied by material borrowing. These elements served to liberate Western imagination from a narrow and rigid discipline.

In the fine arts the importance of Arab contributions has assumed new proportions in recent years. The researches of

[3] Harry A. Wolfson, *The Philosophy of Spinoza*, I (Cambridge, 1934), 10.

[4] Miguel Asín, *Islam and the Divine Comedy*, tr. H. Sunderland (London, 1926).

Farmer[5] and Ribera[6] in music have opened up new vistas before us. "Arabesque," "ogive," "guitar," "lute," "rebec" and many other terms serve to remind us of this abiding influence. In industry suffice it to note such words as "sofa," "mattress," "muslin," "satin," "atlas"; and in agriculture "lemon," "orange," "ginger," "rice," "cotton," "sugar." Paper, whose manufacture the Moslems learned from Chinese prisoners in Samarqand, was introduced by Arabs into Spain, where its first mill was established in the middle of the twelfth century. A philological reminder of this fact is English "ream," a loan-word from Arabic through Spanish and old French.

ARABIC, THE MEDIUM OF EXPRESSION FOR THIS CULTURE

The language in which this rich and varied culture is enshrined is the Arabic language. Its uninterrupted literature of thirteen centuries touches virtually on every theme of human thought and endeavor; there is hardly a subject within the whole range of human interest to which some part of this literature has made no contribution. Consider one discipline only, history. In his *Geschichtschreiber der Araber*, written in 1882, Wüstenfeld notes five hundred and ninety historians who flourished in the first thousand years of Islam. Leopold von Ranke observes that, leaving Latin aside, Arabic is the most important of all the languages of the world for universal history. Sapir, in his *Language*, lists it as the third among those which have had an overwhelming significance as carriers of culture. English and French are conspicuous by their absence from this list. Montgomery, in the *Haverford Symposium*, asserts that Arabic has had the most unique development and spread of all the tongues of the earth and that only within the last two centuries has English

[5] Henry G. Farmer, *A History of Arabian Music to the XIIIth Century* (London, 1929), and several articles in the *Journal of the Royal Asiatic Society*.

[6] Julian Ribera, *Music in Ancient Arabia and Spain*, tr. Eleanor Hague and Marion Leffingwell (Stanford University, 1929).

come to rival it. In a recent article Archer[7] declares that Arabic is a richer and more flexible tongue than Latin or Greek; no Western tongue can equal it in the variety of its forms and verbal nouns.

Of the Semitic languages Arabic is not only the best known but the most characteristic, the most copious and, in many respects, the most conservative. As such it holds a key position among all Semitic languages and is replacing Hebrew as the starting point for Semitic philology. The medium of daily expression for some fifty million people, it stands in marked contrast to its sister languages in the Semitic family which are dead or quasi-dead.

As the language in which the word of Allah was revealed, Arabic holds a unique place throughout the world of Islam. From one end of this world to the other, whatever may be the living speech of the people—Persian, Hindustani, Javanese, Malay, Chinese, Tartar, Hausa or (until recently) Turkish—the Koran is read and the prayers are recited in this "tongue of the angels" (*lisān al-malā'ikah*). Wherever and whenever the believers chance to meet—be it on a caravan route in the steppes of Turkestan, on the plateaus of the Sudan or in the bazars of Damascus, Algiers or Kazan—they are sure to greet each other with "*As-salāmu 'alaykum*" ("Peace to you!") and other familiar Arabic phrases, and to exchange Arabic clichés and koranic passages. No thorough mastery over the subsidiary languages of Islam, such as Persian, Turkish, Urdu and Swahili, whose vocabularies are permeated with technical, theological, legal and scientific loan-words from Arabic and whose scripts were borrowed from Arabic, is possible without some adequate acquaintance with this tongue. In his inaugural lecture Professor Paul Casanova of the Collège de France relates an anecdote about certain Turks who in an argument with an Arab sheikh told him that Arabs did not know what honor was. The sheikh retorted by asking them what the Turkish word for "honor"

[7] John C. Archer, "Our Debt to the Moslem Arab," *The Moslem World*, XXIX (1939), 259.

was, and when told it was *'ird* and assured that there was no other word, he exclaimed, "But this word is one of the oldest in our language!" Thus does this language stretch one mighty arm through the ages to connect with Assyro-Babylonian and Hebrew and another arm to reach all kinds of modern tongues and dialects of Asia, Africa and eastern Europe.

ISLAM, THE DOMINANT FAITH

Islam, the prevailing religion of this culture, is historically an offshoot of Judaism and Christianity, and of all faiths it comes nearest to being their next of kin. Its dogmas involve belief in God as one, the Koran as His uncreated work and Muhammad as His last messenger. The two remaining dogmas relate to the angels and the day of judgment. Its five pillars, on which the religious duties of the Moslem center, include the profession of faith, prayer (five times a day), almsgiving, fasting in the month of Ramaḍān and a holy pilgrimage to Mecca and Medina. Islam has been and still is a living force from Morocco to India and a way of life to some 250,000,000 people of all colors, nationalities and races. Its adherents represent about one-eighth of mankind. Of all religions it is the only one that can claim to have met Christianity and defeated it. By virtue of its simple theology and practical character it makes headway where Christian missions fail, and that in spite of the fact that it has no priesthood, no clerical hierarchy, no church. Around the name of its early followers gleams that halo that belongs to world conquerors. Within a century after their appearance on the international stage of history the Moslem people rose into the mastery of an empire extending from the shores of the Atlantic to the confines of China—an empire greater than that of Rome at its zenith.

The significance of this expansion to medieval history has been brought into a new perspective by the brilliant researches of the Belgian scholar, Henri Pirenne,[8] which reveal that the

[8] *Mahomet et Charlemagne*, 7th ed. (Brussels, 1935).

Moslem conquests were by no means a peripheral phenomenon but a decisive factor in European history. According to Pirenne's thesis the Roman Empire was not a European but a Mediterranean power: the sea was its main highway and bond of unity. The Teutonic invasions, traditionally credited with ending the ancient period of history, left that economic-cultural unit intact; but the Moslem invasions shattered it. The passing of the control of the sea into Arab hands interrupted the old international trade; the unit of European society shrank till it became merely the agricultural unit—large or small—possessed by the feudal lord. More than that, the advance of Islam into Europe and the Mediterranean severed the West from Byzantium and forced it to depend upon its own sources of strength. Chief among these was the Church; hence the ecclesiastical form which Western society took and the ensuing dependence of the people upon clerics. In the meantime the Church itself felt the need of a secular protector and found it in the Carolingian rulers. Thus arose the Holy Roman Empire. This thesis, with which Pirenne's name is associated, shifts the end of ancient times from the traditional latter part of the fifth to the middle of the eighth century, the transitional period being the Arab advance between A.D. 650 and 750. It makes the Arab invasions the major force behind the formation which medieval society assumed.

ARABIC STUDIES IN EUROPE

With all these claims—scientific, literary, linguistic, religious and historical—upon the interest of the educated man, one would think that the Arabs and their culture would have received a large measure of consideration in European learned and academic circles. But that is not the case. In Europe Oriental studies drew their inspiration from interest in the Bible. Starting with Hebrew they diverged in the middle of the last century—after the decipherment of cuneiform and hieroglyphic writings—into Assyriology and Egyptology. In the early stages the value of Arabic to the understanding of the Old

Testament, the significance of Arabia as the probable cradle of the Semitic family and the importance of the Arabians, especially the Bedouins, as the purest representative—linguistically and anthropologically—of that family, all that was not fully recognized. Now, however, we realize that parts of the Hebrew scripture breathe the atmosphere of the desert, that the Hebrews were first nomads, that they worshiped a North Arabian deity, and that their heritage of tribal life continued to be well marked after they had settled in the Promised Land.

Formal Arabic studies in Europe had not only a late but an unfavorable start. Throughout the continent and on the British Isles they were conditioned by missionary activity and interest and by world politics. The European as a rule wanted to study Islam either to convert its followers or to further imperialistic interests. Western chauvinism, religious zeal and sheer ignorance played their part. Long persistence of legends about Muhammad, the founder of Islam, hostile prejudice of Christians toward a rival and aggressive faith, and the unpleasant memories of the crusades, reënforced by the ever present fears of the growing power of the Ottoman Turkish Empire, militated against an objective or dispassionate—not to say sympathetic—study of Islam. Martin Luther held the opinion that the Turks constituted a punishment from God. He would "not read from Mohamet's Alkoran . . . , which openly permits murder, adultery, unchastity, the destruction of marriage and other shameful abominations and deceptions."[9] The first English translation of the Koran appeared in 1649, "translated out of Arabique into French. . . . And newly Englished, for the satisfaction of all that desire to look into the Turkish vanities."

The first European view of Muhammad maintained that he was a god worshiped by the Saracens. Gradually this naïve view gave way in favor of his being an impostor or false prophet, a view which virtually dominated public and learn-

[9] *D. Martin Luthers Werke,* XXII (Weimar, 1929), 150.

ed opinion until Carlyle, toward the middle of last century, tried to reinstate the Arabian Prophet as one of the heroes of the world. The first full-dress biography of Muhammad in English to become standard was that of Humphrey Prideaux, dean of Norwich, *The True Nature of Imposture fully Display'd in the Life of Mahomet* (1697). Prideaux' statement of Muhammad's two ruling passions: ambition achieved by imposture, and lust as exemplified by his sanction and practice of polygamy and his Paradise of sensual delights, continued to represent British view.

In the thirties of the seventeenth century, Oxford and Cambridge established their first chairs of Arabic; other universities followed, but hardly any apologist's voice was heard amidst the chorus of continued denunciation. To the Reverend Joseph White, professor of Arabic at Oxford, who in 1784 delivered the Bampton Lectures designed "to confirm and establish the Christian faith, and to confute all heretics and schismatics," Islam was an "audacious imposture." Such utterance serves to explain the view of a Dutch Arabist, Professor Veth, who, in his inaugural lecture delivered about a hundred years ago, pointed out how little the English universities had done for the study of Arabic and Islam and laid the blame for it on the preponderating clerical influences in these institutions.

Oddly enough, one of the earliest professorial pronouncements in English favorable to Islam came from another Dutchman, Adrian Reland, professor of Oriental languages at the University of Utrecht, whose two Latin treatises were translated in 1712. Reland quotes the advice usually given to students against the study of Arabic, "because 'tis not worthwhile (say many) to undergo so much Trouble and Fatigue, only to consult the Dreams and Ravings of a Fanatick." "But really," Reland goes on to say, "the *Mahometans* are not so mad as we think them."[10] It is interesting in this connection to note that in France the distinguished

[10] *Four Treatises concerning the Doctrine, Discipline and Worship of the Mahometans* (London, 1712), p. 12.

humanist Rabelais[11] (d. 1553) had before this time gone so far as to recommend the study of "Arabique," putting it on a par with Hebrew, Latin and Greek.

Gibbon, who knew no Arabic, left Muhammad where he found him—an impostor dominated by ambition and lust. Scouting the idea that Muhammad was superior to the common herd in ability, Southey in his introduction to the *Chronicle of the Cid* (1808) gives him no credit for the spread of Arabic and Moslem institutions. "This is the nadir of opinion concerning Muhammad in English literature."[12] Not until the early part of the eighteenth century did English authors begin to approach Islam from a sympathetic point of view. Among these was Ockley, whose *History of the Saracens* appeared in 1718, and Sale, whose translation of the Koran with its "Preliminary Discourse" was published in 1734.

Since the beginning of the twentieth century a sane scholarly view of Muhammad and Islam has been gaining ground and Arabic studies have been increasingly promoted. The flourishing condition of such institutions as the School of Oriental Studies (University of London) and the École Nationale des Langues Orientales Vivantes, Paris, may be cited in evidence. These schools, however, are designed to equip men for foreign service. Our own Department of State has in recent years made use of the Paris school for this purpose. In 1937 England gave £17,000 for promoting Oriental studies, France £25,000, Italy £12,000 and Germany a large but unspecified sum.

This, however, does not mean that English literature on Islam is now what it should be. In the Hibbert Lectures, a series avowedly devoted to a sympathetic exposition of the major religions of the world, Mohammedanism is the only one that receives a rather harsh treatment, and that from none other than the late incumbent of the chair of Arabic at Oxford, Professor Margoliouth. Evidently our Christian

[11] In his "Lettre de Gargantua à Pantagruel."

[12] Byron Smith, *Islam in English Literature* (Beirut, 1939), p. 156.

scholars find it easier to comprehend and interpret entirely new and alien religions, like Buddhism and Hinduism, than cognate ones like Islam. The *Encyclopaedia Britannica* assigns to the life of the Saxon nun Hrosvitha, who in her distant Germany heard of Cordova and styled it "the jewel of the world," twice the space assigned to 'Abd-al-Rahmān III, under whom Cordova took its place as the most cultured city in Europe. *Cambridge Medieval History* allots about fifty pages out of over five thousand to the entire story of the Arab civilization in Spain. European textbooks in history are on the whole written from the national, provincial, point of view, and hardly ever give the Arabs their rightful place. Scholarly interest in America may be gauged from the fact that James Harvey Robinson, whose *Medieval and Modern Times* was until recently probably the most widely used textbook of its kind, devotes ten pages of over eight hundred to Islam and its followers, whom he calls "Mohammedans" (a term to which they prefer "Moslems") and hangs this section as a tail to a chapter entitled "The Monks and their Missionary Work."

IN AMERICA

Islamic studies, Arabic included, have not been hitherto seriously cultivated in the United States. It is true that, following the European precedent, a few leading universities have for decades maintained chairs in Semitic languages and literatures but the incumbents generally occupied themselves with the pursuit of Hebraic studies and Assyriology. Arabic courses, when offered, were treated as subsidiary to Hebrew and contributory to Semitic linguistics, rather than as their cornerstone. Until a few years ago nowhere were Arabic courses given for their own sake and as a key to the further investigation of Islamic culture. Even Egyptology had an earlier and more auspicious start in America. In a symposium on Semitic studies in America held by the American Oriental Society in 1888, it was stated that less than ten years prior to that a student at Harvard offered a thesis on an Arabic subject which had to be sent to "the sole and only Arabic teacher in the country, Professor Salisbury at Yale,"[13] a Sanskritist. In his presidential address at the annual meeting of the American Oriental Society in 1922, Nathaniel Schmidt,[14] himself a Semitic scholar, surveyed Oriental studies in Europe and America without making a single reference to Islam or its study in America. On a similar occasion in 1938, Professor Waterman, also a Semitist, delivered his address entitled "Oriental Studies in the Present World Picture,"[15] in which neither the word "Islam" nor "Arabic" occurs. The same could be said of the presidential address of Professor Theophile J. Meek, entitled, "The Challenge of Oriental Studies to American Scholarship," which was delivered in 1943 before the Oriental Society.[16]

That Oriental studies in American institutions should start with Hebrew and center on it and on closely allied subjects is easy to understand in view of the relation of Hebrew to the Bible and to Judaism and Christianity. Besides, Hebrew, Aramaic and Assyrian are relatively limited in their vocabulary and literature. Mastery over them does not entail the difficulties involved in establishing control over Arabic with its copious vocabulary, complicated grammar, multicolored literature, and long history of development.

Then the Americans inherited to a certain extent European political and religious prejudices against Islam. An inflated sense of racial superiority and intellectual complacency made the study of any culture other than European-American seem like a condescension. Tourists' letters, travelers' stories, sensational films, fantastic novels, careless utterances of public men, ignorant statements by the press, clerical interests and missionary reports—all these contributed to the increase of alienation and decrease of respect. In their zeal to arouse interest in and solicit support for their

[13] *Hebraica*, V (1888), 91.
[14] *Journal of the American Oriental Society*, XLIII (1923), 1 *seq.*
[15] *Ibid.*, LVIII (1938), 403 *seq.*
[16] *Ibid.*, LXIII (1943), 83-93.

work, missionaries, often unconsciously, painted Islamic society in dark colors or overemphasized its inferior character.

From the standpoint of the student three deterrents to the study of Arabic and other Islamic languages have stood in the way: the exaggerated difficulties inherent in their acquisition, the absence of proper incentive and the lack of academic tradition. In the atmosphere of a modern American campus, a serious study of such subjects, it must be admitted, sounds artificial, lacking in immediacy, too far removed from its natural or proper setting. As for the difficulties of acquisition they are no doubt enhanced by the method of teaching which, following the German procedure, does not use the inductive system and treats Arabic as a dead language. Little heed is paid to pronunciation and accentuation and the entire living modern literature is treated as nonexistent. Memorizing the paradigms and acquiring the rules of grammar by rote is not only detrimental to interest but to the capability of establishing real mastery over the language. In the experience of the writer lack of knowledge of English grammar (or any grammar), characteristic of American students, constitutes one of the primary difficulties to the understanding of Arabic grammar. There was a time when students of theology were required to study Hebrew and students of the humanities were grounded in Latin and Greek, but now theology has gone "practical" and classical studies are considered outmoded. The modern American student of a foreign language thus starts with a handicap: ignorance of linguistic vocabulary and of philological concepts. Nevertheless there is no reason why Arabic should not be taught to him as English would be taught to a foreigner.

The absence of proper incentive is a more serious situation, which can, however, be remedied at many points. The global and totalitarian dimensions of the present armed conflict have forced upon academic and governmental authorities the consciousness not only of the desirability but of the absolute necessity of cultivating the Oriental studies, hitherto considered the specialty of the erudite few. All of a sudden we were confronted with the inescapable fact that control of Oriental languages and knowledge of the cultures they represent has become a matter of as vital importance as the production of tanks, guns and airplanes. Not only for the successful prosecution of the war is training in these disciplines necessary, but for the establishment of peace and for the subsequent period of reconstruction. Its need will be enhanced rather than diminished in the new world order that follows. Mushroom-like, several courses in colloquial Arabic and other Islamic languages have sprouted on the campuses of many institutions of higher learning. Of what permanent value such courses may prove remains to be seen. At least they will tend to create a precedent and make up in part for lack of academic tradition.

Hitherto the typical Semitist has isolated himself in his graduate department, which—like all other graduate departments—is watertight, ministering to the intellectual needs of a few select candidates for the doctorate and carrying on his own researches unmindful of the fact that his discipline can and should serve to enlarge the academic horizon of the undergraduate body and interpret the present-day world order to the intelligent layman outside the university walls. Like all specialists he left the results of his researches to the popularizer, who is often a vulgarizer, and to the propagandist. Nor should the Arabist be content with book knowledge. Unless supplemented and vitalized by the personal experience which results from trips to the Orient, contacts with native scholars in Asia and Africa and exchange of students and teachers between the East and the West, such knowledge tends to lose its spark of life. To be a student of the Moslem world is not enough; one has to be a student *in* the Moslem world. Now, fortunately the number of native scholars in the East trained in the Western method of scientific research, whose intellectual companionship will be congenial to an American orientalist, is annually on the increase.

Our studies will remain anemic and ineffective unless they are given a wider base in popular esteem and pushed down to the undergraduate level. A committee composed of members of the American Oriental Society interested in Arabic and Islamic studies conducted four years ago a survey under Professor Obermann and the writer which revealed that only ten universities in the United States offer courses in Arabic language and that the courses are almost wholly on the graduate level. These are given at California, the Catholic University of America, Chicago, Columbia, Harvard, Johns Hopkins, Michigan, Pennsylvania, Princeton and Yale. Among the theological seminaries, not surveyed by the committee, Hartford takes the lead; among the colleges, Dropsie stands out. The committee recommended that steps be taken to make the several Arabic-Islamic fields serviceable not only to Semitics but also to linguistics, Romance languages, philosophy, fine arts, history of religion, comparative religion, anthropology, history of medicine and history of science. Graduate students specializing in any of these fields will find a "no man's land" between their chosen specialty and Arabic or Islam which they will do well to explore and occupy. Not only is it no man's land but it is virgin soil, full of promise and potential productivity. At present there is hardly an American scholar who can do justice to Spanish-Islamic civilization from both sides of the fence, hardly a specialist in the crusades or medieval culture or Byzantine history who is equally at home in both Oriental and Occidental sources. The committee further recommended that undergraduate schools at such colleges and universities as offer Arabic and Islamic courses in their graduate departments should be persuaded, first, to introduce a general culture course on the Near East and, secondly, to list Arabic as an elective for upperclassmen. In Princeton we have for years been offering a popular senior course entitled Ancient and Medieval Semitic Culture, the second half of which is devoted exclusively to the history of the Arabs. The committee urged the desirability of bringing about a better use of facilities extant in this country, particularly through the publication of catalogs of manuscripts and lists of printed books dealing with the several disciplines in this field. The largest collection of manuscripts, the Robert Garrett Collection in the Princeton University Library which numbers over ten thousand titles, has been only partially cataloged in two volumes, one for the Arabic and the other for the Persian and Turkish. Among the book collections that of the New York Public Library is probably the most important. The committee also urged that advantage be taken of existing facilities at a given university to invite Arabists and Islamists from other institutions to give public lectures or to serve as part-time visiting professors. Our university authorities should become convinced that no liberal education to a modern or future American student could be considered complete without some adequate acquaintance with the history and literature of the Arab and Moslem world and its contribution to Western thought and life. If, in the recent words of President Roosevelt, the defense of Turkey is essential to the safety of the United States in time of war, surely the study of the history, literature and religion of the Turks can no more be considered esoteric in time of peace.

Nor should infiltration be confined to academic and learned strata. As far as possible we should seek to establish points of contact between our studies and the varied aspects of the life of the community. Here we will do well to take a leaf from the book of Soviet orientalists whose studies, in the words of Graves "have lost some of the stigma of esotericism which they formerly possessed."[17] Through our lectures, writings and activities in the learned or other societies we should stimulate a wider interest even among amateurs, at least amateurs in the etymological sense of the term. Here is a whole area of potential friendly interest not fully exploited. The necessity for cultivating this area will increase as the sources of private income to universities decrease or dry up. Until the number not only of professional students and members of academic bodies but of those who take up the

17 "Some Notes on the Oriental Studies in the Soviet Union," *The American Quarterly on the Soviet Union*, II (1939), 95.

study of a language for the love of it is vastly increased, it is not possible for intelligent knowledge to become widespread and for support to become public. Both the late Sir E. Denison Ross and Sir Thomas W. Arnold of the School of Oriental Studies, University of London, recognized the importance of this fact.[18] Herein lies no small part of the value of the work done by the Iranian Institute of America and by its New York exhibition of Persian art in 1940. In figurative words, we should be able to coin the boundless treasures entrusted to our care into useful currency without debasing their sound metal. One may start as a dilettante but need not remain such. Sir William Jones, founder of the Asiatic Society of Bengal; George Sale, translator of the Koran; Edward William Lane, translator of the *Arabian Nights* and compiler of the *Arabic English Lexicon*; Sir Charles Lyall, author of several works dealing with Arabic poetry, all these and others began their scholarly careers with only a dilettante's interest.

That there is a new trend in American Semitic scholarship in favor of Islamic studies is evident from a number of recent events. In 1935 the University of Michigan established a chair of Islamic art, the first of its kind in the history of American education. In 1936 the James Richard Jewett chair of Arabic was endowed at Harvard by a gift of $210,000. The last three appointments to Semitic chairs in America—Princeton, Columbia and Pennsylvania—have been received by Arabists. The Library of Congress added to its staff in 1938 a consultant in Islamic archaeology and art. The American Oriental Society, meeting in New York in 1940, devoted a session to Islamic discussion—an unprecedented procedure, within the knowledge of the writer, in the history of any American learned society. The practice has been continued since.

In 1937 a committee of the American Council of Learned Societies made a survey of American higher education and came to the unanimous conclusion that of all the under-

[18] *Bulletin of the School of Oriental Studies*, I (1917), 2, 115.

worked fields Arabic and Islamic studies were the ones that should be most encouraged. The committee pointed out that there was no place in America where adequate training in Turkish languages could be secured and that almost as serious was the lack of facilities for studying medieval and modern Persian. This need has since been partially met by a new appointment to its faculty by Princeton University. The Council now includes among its committees one devoted to the promotion of Arabic and Islamic studies. The work of Sarton—a historian of science—as editor of *Isis* and author of *Introduction to the History of Science* may be singled out as a factor of major significance in itself and in giving impetus to this trend. The success of the Summer Seminar in Arabic and Islamic Studies held in Princeton in 1935, 1938 and 1941, which attracted an average of about thirty advanced scholars from fields to which Islam is peripheral, attests to this same tendency. These budding scholars were on the whole not Semitists but historians of Europe and the Near East, medievalists, Byzantinists, historians of science, students of fine arts, philosophy, religion and political science, and others who have become convinced of the necessity of acquiring some competence in the Arabic-Islamic phases of their respective fields of specialty.

The association of "Arabic" and "Islamic" is misleading to the extent of leaving out of account two entire blocks of literature: the Judaeo-Arabic and the Christian. In the Judaeo-Arabic field notable contributions have been made and are still being made by American scholars; but the Christian literature, introduced into Europe in the seventeenth and eighteenth centuries by al-Ṣahyūni (Sionita), al-Ḥāqilāni (Ecchelensis), al-Samʿāni (Assemani) and other Maronite Lebanese scholars of Rome and Paris, and in more recent times championed by Graf in Germany, Mingana in England and Cheikho in Beirut, has been thus far entirely ignored by American scholarship. To Brockelmann this literature simply does not exist. Specialization in this field requires knowledge of Syriac, Coptic, Ethiopic and to a less extent Armenian. Most of the contemporary Arabic literature, be it remembered, is the product of Christian authors, whether in Syria, Lebanon, Iraq, Egypt or New York.

IMPORTANCE OF THE CONTEMPORARY WORLD OF ISLAM

Those to whom the "here" and the "now" in education has special appeal should realize that regardless of the present emergency the contemporary world of Islam offers a most attractive and fertile field of investigation. This world lies athwart the great international highway of trade and transit connecting three historic continents. For the last century and a half it has been a storm center of European diplomacy where the high game of politics has been incessantly, though not always edifyingly, played. At the outbreak of the first World War almost the entire Arab Asia was a part of the Ottoman Empire. Witness the change since then! Most of the Arabian Peninsula is now under two independent potentates: the Imām Yaḥya in the south and ibn-Su'ūd in the north. Iraq, after a period of tutelage as a mandate of Britain, is today a sovereign power under an Arab king in Baghdad, once the seat of Hārūn al-Rashīd. Its boy king is a grandson of the war-famed Faysal, a scion of the Prophet Muhammad. Syria and Lebanon, which at the conclusion of the first World War were put under French mandate, have been finally acknowledged independent republics by the great powers, including the United States, in 1943 to 1944. Egypt, which aspires for the intellectual and spiritual headship of Islam, enthroned in 1936 its youthful king as the first independent sovereign of a free state. Through marriage ties its royal house has been brought close to the imperial family of Iran. The dramatic and forcible reforms of Kamālist Turkey, whose Islam has become subservient to radical nationalism and secularism, are influencing to some extent Iran and to a less extent Iraq. The three are now linked within the Oriental Entente, to which Afghanistan also belongs and to which Su'ūdi Arabia is being drawn. All these national states have been seeking admission to membership in the Western comity through various doors.

At the end of the nineteenth century pan-Islam was the rising phenomenon on the distant horizon. Its exponents on the intellectual side were Jamāl-al-Dīn al-Afghāni and the mufti of Egypt, Muhammad 'Abduh. Patronage came from the sultan caliph of Turkey, 'Abd-al-Ḥamīd, who saw in the political unity of the Moslem world an effective weapon against European aggression. The death knell of this movement was tolled in 1916, when the Sharīf of Mecca rose in insurrection against the Turks, and the Arabic-speaking peoples espoused the doctrine of nationalism on the latter-day Western pattern. As late as the turn of the twentieth century Arab nationalism was still nebulous. At present not only have the various Arab lands achieved partial or full independence but they have launched a pan-Arab movement designed to give more pronounced expression to the community of ideals and cultural elements among them. The rise of these vitalized, rejuvenated Arab states on the ruins of the defunct Ottoman Empire is one of the most significant developments of the post-war Near Eastern history.

This national political effervescence in the Arab East—itself, no doubt, a ripple in a world-wide wave—is but a manifestation of a process of intellectual and spiritual renaissance that has been going on among the Arabic-speaking peoples for the last sixty years or so. That the movement is basically intellectual has been demonstrated in the recently published *Arab Awakening* by George Antonius. Those who sounded the first clarion call to unity, freedom and independence were poets and belletrists—not politicians and statesmen—most of them trained in the American institutions of the Arab East.

The main stimulus producing the awakening has been contact with the West, including commercial and other economic relations, migration to the United States, educational and missionary activities and the Arabic press, which owes its origin to the invasion of Egypt by Napoleon. Lebanon, because of its predominant Christian population, proximity to the sea and the progressive character of its people, has been the main center of this stimulation. It is significant that this, the smallest of all the Arabic-speaking states, was the first to proclaim itself a republic and that under the French in 1920. The United States of America—and this may come as a surprise to most Americans—has been the main source of stimulation. In New York City alone there are today more Arabic presses run by Lebanese than throughout the Arabian Peninsula. The New York presses are linotype, those of Arabia are hand presses. A large part of the intellectual leadership of Arab society has been provided by graduates of the American University of Beirut, founded in 1866 and probably the most influential American institution of learning outside the United States. Through the press, platform and school the ideas of the most progressive thinkers, not only in English but in French, too, have been made accessible in the original or in translation to the Arabic-speaking reader. Several of the masterpieces of German and Italian literature are now equally available. In brief, the Arab society is passing from medievalism to modernism, all in a couple of generations and under our very eyes.

On the destructive side the process involves the breaking of the shell of classicism which has enveloped Islam for the last four or five centuries. On the constructive side it involves the setting in motion of several forces which include—besides nationalism—modernization, secularization and liberalization. The secularizing movement attained its most violent expression among the Kamālist Turks, the first in the history of Islam to separate Church from State. In an apt phrase Halide Edib calls them "the Protestant Moslems of the world."[19] Turkey's antipode is conservative Yemen and puritanical Nejd-Hejaz. Outside of these two Arabian territories Moslems in independent states are more liberal in religious and social matters than in states under European control. But whether liberal or conservative, in public life all defend

[19] *Turkey Faces West* (New Haven, 1930), p. 209.

Islam as a symbol of group solidarity. Travelers like Palgrave and statesmen like Cromer who maintained that Islam is stationary, does not change, and if it does change is no more Islam, will find no counterparts in our days.

Coupled with the movement toward secularization is the attempt at integrating and ameliorating the economic and social forces inside of the community. Throughout these lands a vast experiment is now going on in cultural synthesis, in reinterpretation of national history, in the revaluation of modern experiences and in the scrutiny of Western systems with a view to adopting and adapting whatever is considered appropriate. Unlike the Turk the Arab is accepting elements of European culture with mental and moral reservation, seeking a compromise which will allow him to participate in the politico-economic system of the West without losing his soul. But his soul is not as different from that of the Westerner as it looks. As heir of the Judaeo-Christian tradition and of the Greco-Hellenistic scientific and philosophic lore, the Arab-Moslem has stood throughout the ages with his face toward Europe, feet on Africa and back toward Asia. Thus is the Arab progressively consolidating not only his political but his intellectual and spiritual forces as well, an achievement of the utmost importance to himself and to the world at large.

CONSIDERATIONS FAVORING AMERICA

Certain immediate considerations make the United States a favored center for Oriental studies, Arabic and Islamic included, pending the full development of such centers in the Orient itself. The present turmoil in Europe and the widespread anti-Semitic movement tend to deflect the current of Asiatic and African students America-ward. For years after the present war, even if it were to cease tomorrow, European libraries, universities and museums will be too impoverished from the standpoint of personnel and finance to cope with the normal demands from local students and students from abroad. It may not be too much to assume that for our generation Europe seems finished culturally. Asia is coming into its own, not only culturally, but economically and politically. From our point of vantage here we can view and teach Islam more objectively and detachedly. We have no imperial designs on any part of the world. Our universities have no government connections as is the case with the European universities. Near Easterners, especially since the First World War, have come to trust and respect Americans as they do no other Westerners. American colleges in Istanbul, Cairo, Beirut and other places provide valuable points of cultural contact as do the hundreds of thousands of Arabic-speaking immigrants scattered throughout the United States. The recent establishment in Princeton of a scholarship for Oriental studies by the Syrian and Lebanese American Federation of the Eastern States points to hitherto undiscovered avenues of cooperation. Our aim should be so to develop our centers of Arabic-Islamic studies and so to promote their implementation that should the present cataclysm destroy or render impotent intellectual centers in the Old World we would be in a position to carry on in the New.*

* This essay was inspired by Mr. Mortimer Graves, administrative secretary of the American Council of Learned Societies, who was also the first to suggest the organization of the Summer Seminar in Arabic and Islamic Studies. The part relating to the future of these studies was presented in a modified form in leading a discussion at the centenary celebration of the American Oriental Society, held at Boston, April 9, 1942.

PRE-ISLAMIC ARABIA

GIORGIO LEVI DELLA VIDA

ARABIAN ORIGINS

The statement, "Arabia is the Cradle of Islam" is commonplace. It may mean nothing at all, or may bear a profound meaning, which we ought to enucleate through careful and wide investigation. Should we succeed, we may be pretty sure to have set a sound foundation for the discussion of the historical development of Islam.

It lies outside the writer's task to investigate in its entirety what Islam is. It is necessary, however, to stress the distinction between Islam as it was preached and practiced by Muhammad and the very complex and heterogeneous type of civilization, both religious and cultural, which developed after the conquests and the rise of the Islamic Empire. This later and wider Islam, although the Arabians were the leading element in it, is by no means Arabian, or at least it is not Arabian only. The essential character of Islam has been a favorite subject for discussion in recent times, especially after C. H. Becker about thirty years ago pointed out that Islamic civilization, far from being the antithesis of Classic civilization, was an offspring of it and had continued, in its own way, the trend which had started in the Near East with the conquest of Alexander the Great. Stimulating and substantially correct as I think it is, this theory of Becker's should be accepted only with a cautious reserve, and ought to be supplemented with other elements. It is dangerous to restrict the multiformity of history to a narrow dogmatic formula. History as actual life itself, be it the life of individuals or of nations, is always manifold in its issues. Each feature of history, as each feature of an individual's life, cannot be traced back to a single cause; nothing which is happening in history is the plain reproduction of what had happened before. Similarity of cause and circumstances does not mean identity, and each historical event, exactly as each individual life, is something absolutely original and unique, although its components are not.

Nevertheless, to understand an historical occurrence without realizing the elements of which it is the result is an impossibility. In the development of Islamic civilization, a very important part has been taken by the ancient Near East, and not only by Hellenism: it would be incorrect to overemphasize the second above the first. Another factor, too, should be considered in the formation of Islam, besides Hellenism and the ancient Near East, namely Arabia. The function which that country took in the shaping of the permanent aspect of Islam should not be underestimated; since the Prophet of Islam, the first generation of believers, and the men who conquered and set up the Islamic Empire, were all of pure Arabian stock and the surroundings in which they had grown up were entirely Arabian. This is, of course, a truism, but we often forget it is one. But do we know exactly what Arabia *was*? If the history of pre-Islamic Arabia were perfectly clear to us, the problem of setting apart the Arabian elements in Islam from the non-Arabian ones would be comparatively simple and the measure in which Arabian tradition affected the development of Islam would be easy to estimate. Unfortunately, our knowledge of ancient Arabia is scanty and incomplete. What we know about it is just enough to let us understand how much we don't know.

In the following pages we will try to point out the gaps in our information about ancient Arabia rather than to summarize a long and monotonous sequence of items, most of which, if not all, are certainly well known to the reader. The history of Arabia, from the little we actually know of it, has proved to be tremendously complicated, and the numerous dark spots in it have encouraged many scholars to try to fill them up with attractive theories of their own. Because they are theories and because they are attractive, we should be on our guard against them. Let us hope that the results of our inquiry, even if they may be negative, will prove useful. At least, we shall see how wide and complicated the subject is, and how much work is still to be done before we attain the two goals we would reach: first, to understand, as well as we can, how far Arabian civilization had developed at the time when Muhammad started his religious movement; second, to see how much of that civilization was still alive at Muhammad's time and in which way it influenced his religious and political ideas.

The historians of the Islamic age, in spite of their lack of correct information and method, were not unaware of the great antiquity of Arabian history. They knew how to tell about the descent of the Arabian tribes from Ishmael and other biblical heroes; they were able to report the fabulous peoples of 'Ād, Jurhum and Jadīs, who had settled in the Peninsula before the later Arabians had spread on it and were responsible for the ancient buildings, the ruins of which were scattered all over Arabia. We think we know a little better than the Moslem historians that the origins of Arabian history lie far behind the time of the biblical patriarchs, a time they thought was the highest chronological limit of historical recollection. However, we must honestly acknowledge that we know almost nothing of that millenary history. For many capital items, evidence is practically non-existent; where it exists, its interpretation is difficult and ambiguous. Some evidence is supplied by literary sources; but the foreign ones, Hebrew, Latin and Greek, are scanty and fragmentary, and the native are late and desperately tainted with legend.

Our most valuable help in the attempt to attain an understanding of pre-Islamic Arabia is epigraphical evidence, but by its very nature it is one-sided and obscure. Archaeological evidence is missing entirely, since regular excavations have never taken place in any part of Arabia.

Things being as they are, we must frankly admit that none of the theories which have been offered so far can stand the test of accurate criticism. Nevertheless, theories are necessary. But we should never forget that they are nothing more than hypotheses, and that any new discovery is likely to demolish them. Before they may be accepted, even as a provisional solution, the amount of sound evidence which they contain should be accurately tested, and we should set apart what we *know* from what we may legitimately *guess* and from what we *don't know.*

Starting from the very beginning, there is at least one thing which we know beyond any doubt: Arabia is quite a large country. Its area is as wide as one-third of the territory of the United States. On such an area, there is room enough for more than one center of civilization. On the other hand, Arabia is an exceedingly barren country. With the exception of a narrow strip of land on the southern coast and some oases scattered along its wadies, there is very little, in Arabia, which may supply the conditions for a permanent settlement of numerous human beings. The first question which arises from this statement is the following: has Arabia always been a desert, or are the present conditions comparatively young, and was there a time when Arabia was able to support a more dense population? The assumption of an original fertility and a progressive desiccation of Arabia has been taken as a basis for a theory about the Semitic race, about the migrations of the Semitic peoples, and finally for an explanation of the conquests of the Arabians and the expansion of Islam, "the last Semitic migration." This "Winckler-Caetani theory" (so called after the first and most authoritative sponsors) is comprehensive and attractive, but how far does it tally with well ascertained facts? Undoubtedly, the present barrenness of Arabia has been preceded by a phase of fertility. Although the geological survey of Arabia is only in its beginnings, the presence of the wadies, which are dried-up river beds, supplies an unmistakable evidence of a process similar to that which took place in the Sahara, in the great desert of Central Asia and in the southwest of the United States. In all these territories, the period of desiccation began after the appearance of man, since prehistorical settlements have been found in the now desert areas. The desiccation of Arabia, too, may be later than the first appearance of man. But, unfortunately, we have no evidence either on the date of desiccation or on the date of the oldest human settlements in Arabia. Some neolithic implements have been found by Doughty in the most northern part of Arabia, and some others by Bertram Thomas in the south. These findings prove that man is ancient in Arabia, but they say nothing about the age in which he appeared there, or about the size of the inhabited area during the Stone Age, and they are silent about the kind of civilization which this proto-Arabian man may have possessed.

Our information about the racial aspect of the first inhabitants of Arabia is by no means better. Were they Semites, or did the Semites supersede a more ancient layer of inhabitants? Anthropological evidence seems to point to the presence of a non-Semitic type among some of the Arabs of today. But is "non-Semitic" the same as "pre-Semitic"? We don't know.

Furthermore, who were the Semites who settled in Arabia and where did they come from? The theory that Arabia is the original seat of all Semites is appealing indeed, but is far from being generally accepted and is objectionable from more than one side. The Semites must have entered Arabia from somewhere, since it is highly improbable that they sprang from the earth. Did they come from Africa, as the unquestionable affinity of the Semitic and Hamitic languages would make it likely? Did they come from the north, since the linguistic type of Hamito-Semitic (which, incidentally, is far from having been reconstructed) seems to be cognate with other linguistic groups—Indo-European, Ural-Altaic and others—which could hardly be supposed to be of African origin? Let us not forget that the only unmistakable evidence which we possess about a Semitic-speaking people in a very remote period—the beginning of the third millennium B.C.—comes from Mesopotamia. Had the Semites come there from the north or from the south? Nobody can tell. Therefore, the problem of the early inhabitants of Arabia is so far unsolved. It will be solved one day, but not before Arabia has been opened to archaeological exploration and comparative linguistics becomes so advanced as to be able to establish, beyond any doubt, the relationship between some major groups of languages.

We are in the dark about the *prehistorical* problems of Arabia. But the *historical* problem is not much clearer. There is an unexplained phenomenon in the early history of Arabia. In its southern part we find a highly developed civilization, about the origin of which we know absolutely nothing. From the imposing ruins of several cities, from thousands of inscriptions written in a peculiar alphabet and in the so-called South Arabic language, and from a few passages of Greek and Roman historians and geographers, we know that South Arabia was organized under four main kingdoms—of Sabaeans, Minaeans, Hadramautians and Qatabanians—and some other minor states. The ruins, unfortunately, are incompletely known, since excavations have never been permitted and very few travelers, most of them untrained for archaeological research, have been allowed to see them. The inscriptions have been deciphered: their script is undoubtedly connected with the Phoenician script, although we do not know whether it is derived from it or is an independent development from a common prototype. Though we are able to understand the language of the South Arabic inscriptions, which is very close to classical Arabic and Ethiopic, many words and constructions are still obscure. We can get an idea of the political and social organization of the South Arabians and know something about their religion. The later history of the South Arabian kingdoms is pretty well known, at least in its main features. What remains a mystery is the origin of South Arabian civilization. We would be glad to assume that it arose under the influence of Mesopotamia, and actually such great scholars as Winckler and Hommel, and more recently Dougherty, have asserted that trade relations were established between the Sumerians and the southern part of Arabia since the very beginning of Mesopotamian civilization. This may be possible, although there is no direct evidence of it. Some elements in South Arabian art, chiefly in decoration and seals, are unquestionably of Mesopotamian origin.

But the bulk of South Arabian civilization is not of Mesopotamian origin. If it were, why would cuneiform writing be unknown in South Arabia? Why would architecture be so entirely different from the Mesopotamian pattern? Why, finally, would all that we know about religion and political organization in South Arabia bear a character which by no means is Mesopotamian? The main deity of the South Arabians is the Sun (Shams), but it is a goddess, not a god as the Accadian Shamash. On the other hand, the great female deity of all Northern Semites, 'Ashtart, is masculine in South Arabia (under the form of 'Athtar). A certain similarity may be found between the priest-kings of the ancient Sabaean period, the *Mukarribs*, and the priest-kings of the Sumerians; but the South Arabic word for king is "*malk*" (or "*malik*"), as in all West Semitic languages, as against the Accadian "*sharru.*" This difference in vocabulary points toward an independent development of monarchic government in South Arabia and Mesopotamia. The Southern Arabians seem to have parted from the other Semites before they attained a higher degree of civilization.

How old South Arabian civilization is, is another unsolved problem. According to Glaser (followed by Winckler, Hommel, Grimme, and others), the Minaean kingdom preceded the Sabaean, and since the latter goes back to the eighth century B.C., the beginning of the Minaean kingdom should be put as early as the fifteenth century B.C., or even earlier. This theory lacks any serious foundation: a Minaean inscription, which Glaser believes capable of proving the correctness of his chronology, cannot be earlier than B.C. 525, since it mentions the Persian conquest of Egypt, which took place in that year.

Surely, the South Arabian civilization goes back to an age much older than the sixth century B.C., since at that time we find it entirely developed. But, before that age, we know practically nothing about it. The Bible and Assyrian annals constantly refer to the North Arabians, and only occasionally mention the South Arabians. The famous story of King Solomon and the Queen of Sheba would be a precious document, if her personality were less obscure. The Sabaean inscriptions, which mention several kings, never mention a queen; and monarchy, as we saw, began in Saba many centuries after the alleged age of the Queen of Sheba. On the other hand, we know from the Assyrian annals that, among the North Arabians, queens were eventually rulers of a state. Therefore, we become suspicious about the actual location of the kingdom of the beautiful friend of the King of Israel.

What lies beyond any doubt is that the political power of South Arabia spread towards the north. We know about Minaean colonies in North Arabia. The most important of them was Dedan, a place which is often mentioned in the Bible and the location of which has been archaeologically identified. It corresponds to the modern al-'Ula, in Northern Hejaz, and several hundreds of Minaean inscriptions have been found there.

The main topics of South Arabic inscriptions are religious dedications or building records. The names of many kings of the four main kingdoms and of the minor states are often mentioned. Through a comparison of these names, it has been possible to establish a certain amount of synchronisms and to get a general outline of the development of South Arabian history. The epigraphic evidence may be supplemented with some information drawn from Greek sources. Unfortunately, they are scanty and often distorted. The spelling of the names is often incorrectly reproduced, identifications are made difficult by homonymy. What we can ascertain is that the development of the South Arabian states was bound to their economic function. The South Arabians were the producers and conveyors of frankincense and spices to the whole ancient world. Their caravans carried the national and foreign products across the Arabian Peninsula to the ports of South Syria. (Gaza was one of their favorite staples.) They had commercial agents in the Eastern Mediterranean and in Egypt, as is proved by the finding of a Minaean dedicatory inscription at Delos in the Aegean Sea and of a burial inscription on a coffin found near Cairo (both are comparatively late, from the third or second century B.C.).

The political organization of the South Arabian kingdoms is comparatively well known. Besides the king, there was a strong aristocracy which restrained the king's power. The state had an almost feudal aspect. The standing of religion was prominent. We have hundreds of names of gods, most of which are not found in any other Semitic religion, but their true character is not very clear. An attempt which has been made to reduce them all to an astral triad, Sun, Moon and Venus, cannot be accepted in its entirety, in spite of the admitted ingenuity of the Danish scholar Nielsen who is chiefly responsible for it.

What we know about South Arabia is not much. But our information about North Arabia before the Hellenistic period is even poorer. It seems to have been under the economic control of South Arabia, but how far this control was accompanied by political supremacy and cultural influence is still obscure. It is likely that in ancient days North Arabia was essentially a country of nomads, as it has been ever since. In a series of Assyrian reliefs, which graphically reproduce the campaign of Ashurbanipal (seventh century B.C.) against the land of Aribi, the Arabians appear with typical Bedouin features, living in tents and riding camels, as they ever did—at least since the domestication of the camel, which does not seem to have taken place before the end of the second millennium B.C. Climatic conditions were certainly the same as they are now. The meagerness of the grazing places, especially during periods of drought, urged the Bedouins to migrate northwards, where they hoped to find an easier life. The continuous flood of nomadic Arabians towards Mesopotamia and Syria was favored by the geographical shape of the country. The desert penetrates like a wedge into the Fertile Crescent, and the nomads of Central Arabia, who pushed towards the north, found themselves on the very border of the cultivated land without leaving their desert. This was the line which was followed perhaps by the Amurru, who entered Mesopotamia at the end of the third millennium, and, a half millennium later, by that other "wave" of Semites who occupied Syria: Moabites, Ammonites, Israelites, Edomites and Aramaeans. All those peoples came from Arabia, but we scarcely would be justified in calling them "Arabians." It would be dangerous, indeed, to stress their ethnic, linguistic and religious connections with the historical Arabians and to ascribe an Arabian origin to the civilization and religion of the Israelites, as D. S. Margoliouth has done in a book which is full of stimulating remarks but whose main thesis should be considered as not proven.

The earliest North Arabians who really deserve this name are those against whom the Assyrian kings, from Sargon II to Ashurbanipal, intermittently fought for almost one century, and who paid tribute to them. We do not know exactly where they were located, although some of the geographical names mentioned in the Assyrian records point towards the great Syrian Desert, i.e. outside Arabia proper. We can assume that these Arabians were following the ordinary trend of the nomads and were about to expand towards the Fertile Crescent. They were barred by the presence of a strong power which was able to keep them aloof from the cultivated land. Among the petty rulers who were subdued by the Assyrians, we find some who bore authentic North Arabic names, as Gindibu (Jundub). Some tribes appear to have been governed by queens, a feature which has not yet been satisfactorily explained: anyhow, it should not be interpreted as a sign of actual matriarchy among those Arabians. The mention of Iti'amar of Saba among those petty kings is rather hard to explain; his identification with a king of the same name mentioned in Sabaean inscriptions is far from being ascertained. The mention of Saba proves only that South Arabian influence was present in North Arabia in the seventh century B.C., a fact which was already known from other sources; but it gives no proof of an actual connection between Assyria and the South Arabian kingdoms.

After the Assyrian records, the only evidence about the North Arabians which we possess up to the Hellenistic age consists of a few lines by Herodotus and a short passage in the Book of Nehemiah. Both go back to the fifth century B.C. Where, exactly, the Arabians of Herodotus were located is another of the many points we do not know. Probably they were settled in Southern Palestine, near the seacoast. The Arabian chief who camped in the outskirts of Jerusalem at Nehemiah's time and bore the good North Arabic name of Geshem (Jusham) probably was not very distant from the Arabians of Herodotus.

Let us sum up the results of what has been so far said. All that we know about Arabia before the Hellenistic age is a little about South Arabian history and civilization and almost nothing about those of the North Arabians. The latter appear as a nomadic people, with some centers of sedentary life which had arisen as colonies from South Arabia, impelled by a tendency to move from the desert of Central Arabia towards the cultivated lands of Syria and Mesopotamia. Yet, despite the scantiness of our information, we are in a position to realize that South Arabia was an important center of economic life, of political power, and of high culture.

The Macedonian conquest of the Near East and the collapse of the Persian Empire brought a tremendous shift in the whole political and economic set-up of both North and South Arabia. Some of the old features, of course, remained untouched: no conquest or revolution is able to abolish entirely the legacy of the past. Yet as a result of both conquest and collapse, the ties between East and West grew tighter, and the influence of the successors of Alexander, the Ptolemies and the Seleucids, became decisive for the future of Arabia.

During the third century B.C., perhaps as early as the fourth, we notice the rising of the first North Arabian state which attained international significance. The Nabataeans—

about whose origin and position among the Arabian tribes we are entirely in the dark—became the successors of the Edomites in the region between the Dead Sea and the Gulf of 'Aqabah and of the Moabites and Ammonites in Transjordan, where they occupied such important cities at Petra, Bostra, Gerash, and even Damascus, for a while. Their territory, however, stretched far to the south, where their original home had undoubtedly been in the past. We know more about the Nabataeans than about any other Arabian people before the rise of Islam. However, they do not appear to us as pure Arabians but rather as sedentarized Bedouins, who, through a shift in many of their old habits, had fallen under the influence of Aramaic civilization. The inscriptions through which they still speak to us are in Aramaic, although their everyday language was Arabic. Their religion, about which we are pretty well informed, shows the coexistence of Arabian and Aramaic features. We can follow the history of the Nabataean kingdom with a certain degree of certainty through the evidence supplied by Greek authors, though the Greeks are more concerned with the political and commercial relations of the Nabataeans with Syria, Palestine and the Mediterranean than with the events which took place in Central Arabia. Nevertheless, the action of the Nabataeans in that country must have been important. The archaeological exploration of Transjordan has yielded a great amount of evidence about the Nabataean civilization, and the campaigns led by Dr. Nelson Glueck of the American School of Oriental Research at Jerusalem have succeeded in throwing an entirely new light on it. The Nabataeans appear now to us as a nation much more advanced than the camel drivers they were supposed to have been who carried the goods of South Arabia to the ports of the Mediterranean. In addition, they developed an agricultural life and built, or rebuilt, several important cities; briefly, they arose to a level of civilization which may stand comparison with any other of the states in the Near East in ancient times.

The taking over of the South Arabian trade by the Nabataeans was the consequence, and at the same time the cause, of the decay of the South Arabian kingdoms. Of course, those states did not disappear suddenly, but gradually their power weakened. The Sabaeans, who had held the supremacy among them, were superseded at the end of the second century B.C. by a new people, the Himyarites. These are the only South Arabians whose memory has survived as late as the Islamic age. The Himyarites carried over the ancient trade, but they had to share the profit with the Nabataeans and eventually lost their position in Central Arabia. From then on, the Nabataeans were the leading power there. However, Central Arabia succeeded in developing an independent political life. In the oasis of Dedan (al-ʿUla), beside the old Minaean inscriptions we find many other inscriptions written in an alphabet which is connected with that used in South Arabia, but whose language is North Arabic, closely allied to classical Arabic. The authors of those inscriptions belonged to the kingdom of Liḥyān, a name which was still alive in the sixth century A.D. and later, as the name of a nomadic tribe which settled in almost the same locality.

It is highly probable, in the present writer's opinion, that the Liḥyānite kingdom arose after the decay of the South Arabian states, was for a long time under the supremacy of the Nabataeans and enjoyed a new period of prosperity after the fall of the Nabataean kingdom. An entirely opposite view, which assigns the Liḥyānites a high antiquity, has been taken by D. H. Mueller, who first attempted to decipher their inscriptions. It was taken up again five years ago by F. V. Winnett. This scholar, however, who improved the correct understanding of the inscriptions more than anyone else in recent years, has withdrawn his chronological theory in later writings.

The so-called Thamudic inscriptions, quite similar to the Liḥyānite in script and language, have been found at the same place and certainly belong to a people who developed after the Liḥyānites. The Thamud are mentioned at a very early date, in the Assyrian records, and later by Greek and

Roman authors. They must have had a rather important position in the history of Central Arabia, since their memory survived in later times, while that of the Nabataeans vanished entirely. In the Koran, the Thamud are mentioned as an example of the wicked people of the past who disobeyed God's law and were punished by total destruction. In the fancy of the Arabs the ruins in al-Ḥijr and al-'Ula were the places of their ancient city. As a matter of fact, the center of the Thamudian state must have been in Midian, where the Czech scholar Musil discovered the remnants of a temple and a bilingual Greek and Nabataean inscription in which the Thamud are mentioned. It is clear that they must have been under the supremacy of the Nabataeans, and later have become independent. However, their identification with the authors of the inscriptions in al-'Ula is purely hypothetical.

Other inscriptions and graffiti, which have been found in the region of Safa in the Hauran, are written in South Arabic script but in a North Arabic dialect, like the Liḥyānite and Thamudic inscriptions. Later and poorer as they are, they bear witness of the vitality of South Arabic influence in North Arabia.

In the first century B.C., the Hellenistic states of Egypt and Syria fell under the dominion of Rome. Through the Romans, Arabia began to appear in world history. The impact of Rome on the development of ancient Arabia was decisive. At the beginning the Nabataeans were Rome's allies, and the Romans hoped, through their help, to reach South Arabia and get control of the Indian trade. A Roman army crossed the desert in B.C. 25, but either through lack of proper organization or by treachery of the Nabataeans, it perished in the wilderness, and the Romans never again dared to penetrate Central Arabia.

During the Roman period, the Nabataean merchants went far into the west. Nabataean inscriptions, which they dedicated to their gods, have been found in the Aegean area and in Italy. The influence of Greek and Roman civilization was very strong on Nabataean art, as may be seen from the ruins in Petra and Transjordan, where architecture and sculpture show a curious mixture of Greek and Oriental style. In a way, the Nabataean civilization looks almost like the forerunner of what Islam achieved on a much larger scale, i.e. a merging of Arabian, Near Eastern, and Greek elements in a unitarian civilization. But the Nabataeans not only lacked the tremendous religious enthusiasm of Islam; they also lacked the military impetus of the Arabian conquerors, and confronted the Roman Empire at the peak of its power. They were nothing else than a pawn in the policy of the Romans, and fell as a victim of the centralization of the Roman Empire. In A.D. 106, Trajan destroyed the Nabataean kingdom and created a "Provincia Arabia." In Central Arabia, out of reach of the Romans, the Nabataean state and civilization went on living for a while and then vanished. About the beginning of the fourth Christian century, Arabic drove out Nabataean speech as a literary language.

Several other Arabian tribes, besides the Nabataeans, left the desert and entered Syria and Mesopotamia during the Hellenistic age. They became the founders of dynasties, as in Emesa (Ḥimṣ), where the royal house gave two emperors to Rome, and in Edessa (al-Ruhā'), the city which had the privilege of introducing Christianity into Northern Mesopotamia and becoming the mother of the Syrian Church. Other dynasties of Arabian origin arose in Characene and Iturea. All those kingdoms, however, were Aramaean in their civilization and population; only the upper class was of Arabian descent.

The Arabian element seems to have been stronger in Palmyra, that amazing city which grew up around a spring in the middle of the Syrian Desert and became the rival and successor of the Nabataean commercial enterprises. The old site of Tadmur was already known to the Assyrians; but it expanded into a state during the Hellenistic age and, through its emporium at Dura on the Euphrates, it controlled another road of the Indian trade. This road (which from the Persian Gulf went up the Euphrates, then crossed the desert up to the coast of Syria) became particularly important after the fall of the Nabataean kingdom and the interruption of the road of Arabia. In the second and third Christian centuries, the Palmyrenes, under the protectorate of Rome, attained an extraordinary degree of prosperity and their merchants and soldiers spread all over the Roman world. It is well known that they nourished the dream of disrupting the power of Rome in the East and that their king Odenathus and his wife Zenobia almost succeeded in their attempt. The Palmyrenes, indeed, were Arabians, but Aramaized and Hellenized Arabians of a higher degree, it would seem, than the Nabataeans. Their inscriptions are in Aramaic; their religion is strongly under the influence of Aramaic and Mesopotamian ideas and traditions. Only their personal names and their tribal organization betray their Arabian origin.

The Arabian world was dependent on another mighty state which was growing in the East. After the fall of the ancient Persian Empire, the Parthians had slowly grown independent, during the Seleucid period, and they proved able to match the Roman Empire in the East. Their successors, the Sassanians, succeeded in unifying all Persia in the third Christian century and proved strong enough to challenge the Romans with even greater energy. The fight between the two world powers was waged for four centuries and Arabia became one of the many objects of their rivalry.

On the opposite coast of South Arabia, in East Africa, colonies of South Arabians had been settled from a very remote time—we do not know when or under what circumstances. Some leading groups of Semites subdued the Hamitic population of the country which is now Ethiopia and brought in their own civilization, language and religion. We are entirely in the dark about the origin of a kingdom which appeared there at the beginning of our era and reached the peak of its power in the fourth Christian century. Axum, in modern Tigre, was the capital of that kingdom and some imposing ruins, still imperfectly explored, bear witness to its greatness, while several royal inscriptions throw some light on its history. During the fourth Christian century the kings of Axum became Christian; they had already entered the orbit of Roman policy and seconded it in attacking and conquering the Himyarite kingdom in South Arabia, which was bound to Persian policy. Their conquest, however, was a temporary one: they were obliged to withdraw and the Himyarite kingdom was again independent. But its old days were over. The ruin of the trade and loss of political power, coupled with domestic discord, upset South Arabian civilization. Where civil life had once attained a high level, nomadism and anarchy steadily gained ground. Arabia entered its medieval age.

During the following centuries, the Bedouins of Central Arabia went on widening the area of their anti-economic way of life. Most of the towns were either abandoned or impoverished, and the standard of life was lowered. From the fourth to the seventh centuries Arabia was much more isolated than it had been for several centuries. Yet, during that Dark Age, the seeds of a revival were ripening until they produced a fruit of unexpected maturity, Islam.

THE DARK AGE OF ARABIA

When we attempt to survey the Middle Ages of Arabia, we face the same problem which we met in our study of ancient Arabia. What we know is not much, compared to what we do not know, and the field of unconfirmed hypothesis is wide.

However, the reasons for the lack of certitude in dealing with the history of that period are of an entirely different kind. The sources for the history of Arabia during the centuries immediately preceding the rise of Islam are chiefly literary and not, as they are for the history of ancient Arabia, epigraphic. They are copious, perhaps even too copious; we suffer from an overabundance rather than from a scarcity. But, alas, quality does not match quantity. The tremendous amount of information they impart comes not from firsthand documents; in a way, it is similar to the sources with which we are familiar in Greek, Roman and Hebrew history. Most of the Arabic sources consist of records gathered and set up by scholars of the Islamic age. Direct evidence is supplied by poetry, which has come down to us through the selection and editorial work of other Islamic scholars. Historical evidence, being indirect, cannot be admitted as reliable unless it has been submitted to criticism.

As usually happens, the results of criticism are discordant. A group of contemporary scholars feel radically skeptical towards Arabic tradition; according to them most of it is spurious and represents a tendency which developed in the second and third centuries of Islam, when the faithful recollection of pre-Islamic history had been entirely lost and the philologists and antiquaries tried to fill the gaps by forging or embellishing what they did not find in authentic documents. Arabic historical literature, therefore, would be little better than historical novels, and most of the poetry forged. Neither the one nor the other would supply a safe foundation for a correct understanding of what took place in Arabia during the Dark Age.

In the present writer's opinion, this skeptical attitude is exaggerated. The historical tradition about the Middle Ages of Arabia is neither better nor worse than any other tradition about a period of history for which direct evidence is no longer available. It is not worse than, say, Livy is for the first five centuries of Roman history, or Saxo Grammaticus for the older age of Denmark. In a way, it is better, though it is not free from gaps and mistakes. We do not possess everything which was written about pre-Islamic Arabia in the second and third centuries after the Hijrah, since many works have been entirely lost, and others survive only in abstracts and fragments. In spite of the diligent work of scores of Western scholars, some texts are still unpublished and the scattered fragments have not yet been systematically collected. A good deal of work is still to be done by future scholars. Above all, most of the tradition is one-sided. Instead of aiming at an exhaustive record of the past, traditional historiography had three particular purposes: to supply a faithful interpretation of certain allusions contained in some passages of the Koran; to explain the historical contents of the old poems; and, finally, to serve the national pride and claims of the Arabian aristocracy, giving extensive genealogies of the most prominent families and relating the exploits of the tribes.

An example may show the consequences of the method in which tradition has grown up. Among the innumerable tribal feuds which were the main feature of the history of the Bedouins, we know those referring to the Tamīm, a large tribe in East Arabia, far better than those of any other tribe. The only reason for this is that our evidence about the wars of the Tamīm goes back, almost entirely, to an extensive commentary which abu-'Ubaydah, a scholar of the end of the second Moslem century, wrote on the poems of Jarīr and al-Farazdaq, two famous poets of the Umayyad age and members of the Tamīm tribe who continually referred in their verses to the glorious deeds of their ancestors. Had we a similar commentary on poems belonging to a different tribe, our knowledge of the history of that tribe would be as complete as it is for the Tamīm.

Since the Islamic historians were chiefly interested in the Koran, in poetry and in genealogy, they have described two main features in pre-Islamic history: the first, the city of Mecca and its sacred shrine, the Ka'bah; the second, the life of the nomads with the scenery of the desert as its background, and with the monotonous repetition of minor raids and fights for the possession of a well or the revenge of a murdered kinsman. Undoubtedly, Mecca was an important center in Arabia, and Bedouin life was the most characteristic feature of the pre-Islamic age. However, they are far from filling up the whole history of Arabia. Other features have been entirely neglected by historical tradition. We should, therefore, try to find minor sources, in which those neglected features are emphasized.

There is no doubt that what characterizes the Middle Ages of Arabia is the transition from city life to nomadic life. This phenomenon is exactly parallel to what happened in Europe during the Middle Ages there, when the disruption of the Roman Empire caused a shift from urban to country life. International trade which had brought into Central Arabia a higher level of civilization was almost paralyzed. The Nabataean and South Arabian kingdoms, the two main centers of sedentary life in Arabia, had collapsed. Nomadism always had been characteristic of Arabia, but from now on it became much more widespread, and the desert overlapped cultivated land. This phenomenon may be observed both in North Arabia and South Arabia. South Arabian civilization had not entirely disappeared. The Himyarite kingdom which had succeeded, as we have seen, the four kingdoms of South Arabia, preserved its power from the fourth to the sixth centuries, between two Abyssinian conquests. A number of important changes took place. Not only did its economic background grow worse, the authority of the kings weaken and the independence of the feudal families increase, but the old national religion began to be shaken by the two new religious movements which had spread in the East: Christianity and Judaism. The Abyssinian kingdom had become Christian in the fourth century, and its conversion had tightened its connection with the Christian Roman Empire. South Arabia, too, had partially responded to the appeal of the new faith. The other religion, Judaism, had also found many proselytes in South Arabia: it would seem (although the tradition on this point is rather confused) that the last king of the Himyarites had officially adopted it as the state religion. He is the famous dhu-Nuwās of Islamic tradition, who was killed fighting against the second Abyssinian invasion in the first half of the sixth Christian century. His death put an end to the Himyarite kingdom. The memory of one of the Abyssinian governors of South Arabia, Abraham or Abrahah, has survived in the Koran, where his unsuccessful expedition against Mecca is mentioned: an event which legend has amplified and embellished. Through an inscription, one of the longest and at the same time most recent products of South Arabic epigraphy, the name of this Abrahah has come down to us in an authentic record.

The supremacy of the Abyssinians was not long. After less than fifty years, they were expelled by a national revolution supported by the Persians, who were of course opposed to the Abyssinians, the allies of the Romans. However, the Himyarite kingdom was not restored, and South Arabia was practically divided among scores of local rulers under the lax supervision of a Persian governor. Economy was ruined, since direct connection with the Roman Empire was cut off. Agriculture, which flourished chiefly by irrigation, had been neglected for a long time and the desert gained ground. This long process of decay is graphically summed up in the legend of "the break of the dam of Ma'rib." As a consequence of this catastrophe, many tribes of South Arabian origin are said to have migrated into North Arabia. Of course, this is not literally true: the movement towards the north, originally a consequence of the commercial policy of the South Arabian states, had lasted for centuries. Later on, however, what had previously been a settlement of colonists became a wholesale migration of nomadic tribes. Linguistic evidence, besides genealogical tradition, shows that some of the most important tribes which in the centuries immediately preceding Islam were settled in the Syrian Desert—the Ṭayyi', the Kalb, and so forth—were of southern origin. But there is a striking difference between the early colonization of North Arabia and the later migration. The first carried South Arabian civilization into North Arabia; during the second, South Arabian tribes underwent the influence of North Arabian civilization. In the history of writing we have good evidence for this new trend. The South Arabic scripts which we noticed in North Arabia—Liḥyānite, Thamudic and Safaitic—disappeared, and the Nabataean script, of Aramaic origin, took their place. Slightly modified, it produced the alphabet of classical Arabic. One of the most precious documents of that age, an inscription found at al-Namārah in Transjordan, is the oldest known example of classical

Arabic: it is in Nabataean script, but in Arabic language, and mentions the burial place and the year of the death of Imru'-al-Qays, "King of all Arabs," who died in 328. The two inscriptions of Zabad and Harran are two centuries younger. The first is trilingual (Arabic-Greek-Syriac) and the second bilingual (Arabic-Greek), and both bear witness to the spread of Christianity and Greek-Aramaic culture in North Arabia.

The Byzantine territory, as well as the Persian, appealed strongly to the nomadic Arabians, who were grazing their cattle on their borders. The wish to settle as sedentaries, to live in towns instead of camping under tents and to enjoy the comfort of civilization was often stronger than the love for nomadic freedom. The Romans and Persians, on their side, were eager to have their borders guarded against the raids of other Bedouins and used the sedentarized tribes against the wildlings of the desert. The same phenomenon took place on the northern and southern borders of the Empire, where Germanic and Numidian tribes formed regular garrisons against their kinsfolk.

The movement which had begun in the Hellenistic age, namely the development of the Nabataean kingdom and of the other states of Arabian origin, was reproduced five or six centuries later by a second wave of Arabians. Two states arose, at Damascus under the Ghassanian dynasty, and in al-Ḥīrah on the Euphrates under the Lakhmite dynasty. The former were under Byzantine supremacy and the latter under Sassanian, but both were fundamentally identical. They were former Bedouins who, having settled as sedentaries, had attained a higher political and cultural level. Both had adopted Christianity, the Ghassanians according to the Monophysite rite and the Lakhmites according to the Nestorian, since the former was dominant in Syrian territory and the latter in Persian. On behalf of their mighty protectors, they were fighting each other. Their rulers were granted high titles, as "patricios" and "king," and were allowed to wear the crown as the symbol of their rank.

Ghassanian and Lakhmite chiefs were by no means the

only Arabians who endeavored to develop into absolute rulers. The Imru'-al-Qays of the Namārah inscription, who was labeled as "King of all Arabs," has been assumed by different scholars to have belonged either to the Ghassanian or to the Lakhmite dynasty. Possibly, he was the ruler of another state, the memory of which may have been lost. His claim of actual supremacy over all Arabs should not be taken literally.

We possess a great deal of information about another Arabian state, two centuries later than that of Imru'-al-Qays of al-Namārah: the kingdom of the banu-Ākil al-Murār from the tribe of Kindah, another of the South Arabian tribes which had settled in North Arabia.

However, our knowledge of the history of those Arabian kingdoms is not very extensive. What Arabic tradition is able to report about them is chiefly connected with their fights with the Bedouin tribes, which leagued against them on many occasions and eventually beat them or were beaten by them. If Byzantine and Syriac sources did not help us in arranging the succession and chronology of the kings of Damascus and al-Ḥīrah, we would hardly be able to understand their history correctly. We would, in particular, entirely misunderstand their connections with the Byzantine and Sassanian Empires.

The main reason for such lack of correct information is that Arabic tradition considers history from the standpoint of the nomadic tribes of Central Arabia and is not concerned with general subjects. The records which were collected by the Islamic scholars refer only to the narrow horizon of certain tribes. They ignore wider implications and have no chronology of their own. They offer even less than tribal chronicles; their stories cluster around some outstanding personalities or follow the outbreak and episodes of some tribal wars and neglect all the rest. Only through a painstaking comparison of the personal names which appear in different stories and through an accurate checking of genealogical items may we succeed in bringing together that scattered material to gain a wider outlook of the history of North Arabia.

We have already pointed out that contemporary poetry is another source of our knowledge of Arabia during what we have called the Arabian Middle Ages. But, is poetry in itself a reliable source? The problem has been discussed by many scholars and is a difficult and delicate one. The problem of authenticity has been overemphasized. Even if some of the poems be forgeries, the bulk of poetical tradition is certainly authentic. Yet, poetry fails to give us a complete and faithful picture of Arabia. The Arabian poets did not reproduce the actual and total experiences of nomadic life but rather the idealization of some of its aspects. The ideal which they admired and praised in their verses was something quite similar, *mutatis mutandis*, to the ideal of the Homeric poems and the French *chansons de geste*. It is the ideal of chivalry. Neither the Homeric poems nor the *chansons de geste* may be accused of purposely altering the historical environment of the Mycenean or Carolingian ages, but both reproduce only one aspect. So does the ancient Arabian poetry. The heroic side of life is pushed into the foreground, while other aspects, not less important, are entirely overlooked.

One of those neglected aspects is religion. It has often been assumed that the nomadic Arabians lacked any religious feeling. This opinion seemed to be corroborated by the reproaches addressed by the Koran to the rude and faithless Bedouins. In later times, the period preceding the rise of Islam was termed "Jāhilīyah," after a word used by Muhammad which means "ignorance" or "barbarism." This term, however, has only a meaning when opposed to the age of Knowledge (of God) and (religious) civilization, which is supposed to have begun with Islam. It stresses the ignorance of "true religion," not the absence of any religion. On the other hand, from the Safaitic inscriptions and from some scattered evidence from Greek and Roman writers, we get quite a different picture about the religious attitude of the Arabians. The *Book of Idols* by Hishām ibn-al-Kalbi, one of the outstanding scholars of the oldest period of Arabic literature who died in 204 or 206 after the Hijrah, we find some information about the gods of pre-Islamic Arabia. But ibn-al-Kalbi's book (incidentally, only a short pamphlet) is rather disappointing. The main interest of its author lies in the attempt to bring in further information on those Arabian deities which are mentioned by the Koran, i.e. the gods worshiped at Mecca. Besides them, other gods are mentioned, but only in a short and perfunctory way. Furthermore, we miss many items which we would expect to find there. Practically nothing is said in the *Book of Idols* about astral worship, whereas we know from Greek, Latin and Syriac sources, that it was one of the main features of the religion of the nomads. Unfortunately, the Greek and Roman sources are scanty and refer only to those nomadic tribes who settled in the neighborhood of Roman territory, the so-called Saracens. Syriac sources are more comprehensive but far from exhaustive.

The most prominent feature of Bedouin life is aversion to change. The tribal organization represents a very primitive type of social and political set-up, and it scarcely altered through millennia. Of course, this immobility is a relative one, and is subject to turn into an amazingly quick dynamism, as soon as the nomads are severed from their surroundings. However, as long as they stay in their desert, they adhere faithfully to the manners and customs of their fathers. The vitality of certain tribes is astonishing: in our own time, some Arabian tribes still preserve the names which they bore in the sixth Christian century, or even earlier. On the other hand, some tribes split very quickly. They changed their names, or even completely disappeared, leaving no trace behind. In spite of these mutations, the tribal organization preserved most of its original features through centuries: the modern nomadic tribes of Arabia, notwithstanding the tremendous shift produced by Islam and the Western technical achievements, do not differ substantially from the pre-Islamic tribes in the aspect in which they appear to us today and in the social feeling of their members.

Another characteristic feature of the nomadic tribe is its isolationist, hyper-individualist attitude. A tribe is a unity in itself and forms no part of any higher social or political unity. Yet, federations of tribes were often heard of, and even the largest tribes realized their common origin from a more ancient group. The genealogical system, built up by the Islamic historians, which goes back to mythical ancestors connected with biblical and South Arabian traditions, is undoubtedly artificial; but the feeling of belonging to a common stock was very strong among the Arabians. To call it nationalism would be an illegitimate intrusion of a foreign concept; still this term would define a feeling which was not unknown to the Arabians. Nevertheless, as a social and political unity, the Arabian tribe is autonomous. Inside it, its members realize the tie of solidarity and are bound to follow the unwritten customary law. But they all stand on the same footing. A hierarchic organization does not exist, and the chief of the tribe himself has a moral authority rather than an absolute power.

The hatred of tyrants is commonplace among pre-Islamic Arabians. One of the most itemized boasts of their ancient poets is that their tribes "fought the kings" and refused to submit to any of them. As a matter of fact, besides the Ghassanians, the Lakhmites and the kings of Kindah, we hear of several other attempts to establish a monarchic power in Arabia. Certain chiefs of tribes endeavored to attain an effective authority over their own tribe or to subjugate other weaker tribes. Sometimes they succeeded in their aim; but their triumph was generally short-lived. The nomadic Arabians were so jealous of their freedom (or, if we like it better, were so deep-rooted in their anarchy), that they regularly ousted or killed the would-be monarchs. Their attitude towards the two great world powers established on their borders, the Caesars and the Chosroes (as the Arabians called them), was not very different: it was a mixture of fear and hatred. Byzantium and Persia never endeavored seriously to conquer Arabia; they were satisfied with the keeping of a police force on their borders, poised against the raids of the nomads. The Sassanian kingdom, already on the verge of disintegration, made the great mistake of destroying the dynasty of the Lakhmites at the end of the sixth century. With the fall of that buffer state, the door was opened to the Arabians for invasion, and at the beginning of the seventh century a coalition of Arabian tribes succeeded in defeating the Persian troops at dhu-Qār on the Euphrates. That unusual victory was praised in numerous poems as a wonderful achievement, though in reality it was little more than a skirmish. Nevertheless, it showed the Arabians that it was not impossible to defeat the Great King, and a generation later a much larger coalition of Arabian tribes, now animated by transcendent and all-conquering belief, the faith of Islam, eventually destroyed the Sassanian kingdom.

Notwithstanding the lack of regular political units in Central Arabia, and the steady spread of nomadic life, a few city centers still remained; some of them the old towns of South Arabia, now deprived of most of their ancient splendor; others situated on the coasts of the Persian Gulf and the Indian Ocean, and on the old caravan road which led into Syria through the highland of Hejaz. Some cities were ruled by petty dynasties (e.g., the banu-Jalandah in Oman), others had a half republican form of government. They all were more or less under pressure from the Bedouins who encamped around and about them, never strong enough to conquer them and expel their rulers, but sufficiently strong to compel them to pay tribute for their security. An example of a city which after a period of independence was obliged to yield to the nomads is afforded by Yathrib (the later Medina), a rich oasis in Hejaz where some Jewish tribes had settled, only later to fall under the control of two Bedouin tribes which occupied the town and reduced the old inhabitants to the condition of tributaries. Something similar took place in another Jewish settlement, Khaybar, further north on the way to Syria.

Very few cities were strong enough to cope with the threat

of the Bedouins and keep fully independent. The most important and the best known of them was Mecca. Located in a barren valley among the volcanic rocks of Hejaz, Mecca, like Palmyra, owed its origin to a spring. Near the spring a sacred shrine arose. The tribe which was the owner of the shrine developed sedentary life. Since Mecca was a caravan center and partially took over the trade with Syria which had been in the hands of the South Arabians and Nabataeans, it grew wealthy and developed a more advanced social and political system. Some families of the aristocracy (probably the early organizers of the worship of the shrine) held the privilege of leading the trade caravans and governed the city as an oligarchy. The tribal set-up was still preserved, as in Palmyra, but nomadism had been given up.

Since our information about the worship at Mecca is much more copious than about any other shrine in pre-Islamic Arabia, it may help us to get a correct idea of the Arabian religion. As we have seen, the Greek, Roman and Syriac sources concerning the religion of the nomadic Saracens emphasize its astral aspect, and especially the worship of the Sun and Venus. It is difficult to decide whether that worship was a survival of the early Semitic religion or was due to the impact of South Arabian religion on the nomadic Arabians. Strangely enough, the astral moment seems to be absent from the Meccan worship, or, at least, not to be prominent. The Meccan shrine was a square building, the Ka'bah, also known as "the House of Allah." What kind of deity the Arabian Allah was is another dark spot in our knowledge of the ancient Arabian religion. The opinion of modern scholars diverges on this point: some assume that Allah was the direct continuator of the common Semitic deity El, the general word for "god" or "the divine," whereas another opinion, which has recently been renovated by Winnett, maintains that Allah was nothing else than an imported name and idea, namely the Aramaic "Allāhā," the Jewish and Christian name for the universal God. This latter opinion, in spite of Winnett's ingenuity, cannot be correct, since Allah is found as a component in Nabataean personal names at a time when Jewish influence cannot be admitted. Whether Allah was a general Arabian deity or a local god whose worship expanded is not yet clear. Be that as it may, the Ka'bah was the house where Allah was worshiped together with his three daughters, al-Lāt, al-'Uzza and Manāt. Each of these well known female deities was worshiped elsewhere, independently of Allah, so that there is no doubt that the set-up of the Meccan worship was the result of a syncretistic development. The tradition according to which Allah would have superseded an older worship of Hubal has not yet been explained thoroughly, but since, according to other traditions, there were hundreds of idols in the precinct of the Ka'bah, it is easy to see that the worship was a complicated one. The so-called Black Stone, which is still immured in one of the walls of the Ka'bah, was certainly a very ancient object of cult, and other sacred spots in the city itself and in its surroundings undoubtedly referred to a great number of other deities.

The ceremonies of the great feast at Mecca were embodied by Muhammad into Islam and therefore an old heathen pre-Islamic ritual has been preserved up to our days, almost unchanged. Many of its features are similar to what we find in the Nabataean religion and since, according to tradition, the Ka'bah worship was reorganized by a man called Quṣayy who came from Syria, we may well assume that Nabataean religion influenced the religion of Central Arabia. But the religion of the Nabataeans was nothing else than the ancient Arabian religion transformed under the influence of the Aramaeans. Therefore, it is extremely difficult to distinguish exactly, in pre-Islamic Arabian religion, what may be a survival of very ancient times, possibly reproducing the proto-Semitic attitude towards the gods, from what may be due to the Nabataeans. Anyhow, certain features of the nomadic religion are extremely old, such as the animistic belief in the jinn, the impersonal and anonymous spirits acting in nature, and the office of the *kāhin*, the magician and soothsayer, who represents in a very crude form the original aspect of the

Hebrew prophets. I must frankly say here that I cannot admit the opinion recently expressed by Professor Albright with his customary brilliancy, according to which both jinn and *kāhin* would be later innovations in Arabian religion and would go back to Aramaic models.

We know little about other Arabic shrines outside Mecca, although the names of many of them have been preserved. We may judge from our scanty knowledge that the worship, as practiced there, represented a merging of Nabataean elements and of very crude animistic practices. There is no doubt that Nabataean influence was stronger in the cities than in the desert and that the Bedouins, who seldom took part in the city worship, were comparatively indifferent towards it. That might explain why they gave it up so easily when Islam appeared.

The spread of Judaism and Christianity in pre-Islamic Arabia and their impact on the formation of Islam will be dealt with thoroughly in the next article. What may be pointed out here is that, strong as the penetration of Judaism and Christianity in Arabia certainly was, we know very little about its real efficiency, except in the regions which were on the northern and southern borders. The way in which they penetrated and affected Central Arabia is still obscure. Therefore, we should be skeptical towards any attempt to establish too precisely their influence upon Muhammad's religious attitude. We of today do not know how new his references to Jewish and Christian tradition may have sounded to his auditors.

From what has been said so far, we can see that in spite of our incomplete information it is still possible to get a general idea of what Arabia looked like in the time immediately preceding the rise of Islam. A millenary civilization, which had attained a very high level, had spread from the south to the north and had deeply affected the city life of the whole Peninsula. Another civilization, which crystallized later but which originated in old Mesopotamian and Aramaic tradition, had developed in the north, and from there had expanded towards Central Arabia, especially after the decay of the South Arabians. However, at the age which we are now considering, both civilizations had been entirely disrupted and nomadic barbarism had spread all over the Peninsula, except in a few city centers where some traces of the ancient civilizations survived.

Therefore, the main feature of Arabia from the fourth to the end of the sixth century is nomadism. Nomadism has often been assumed to reproduce, without any important change, the pattern of life of the primitive Semites. This assumption should be accepted with caution. Even primitive ways of life undergo some changes in the course of many centuries, especially when surrounded by a superior civilization. No doubt, even the most remote and wildest Bedouins of Arabia had learned something from the Southern Arabians and the Nabataeans. Nevertheless, what the Bedouins had preserved from the old Semitic pattern was perhaps more essential than what they had lost or modified. In their social organization, in their language, in their spiritual attitude, they had remained faithful to the ways and traditions of the past. This may explain why they reacted in a fresh and spontaneous way to the tremendous upheaval which Muhammad's preaching and church organization brought into Arabia.

At the very beginning, however, the reaction was a negative one. Muhammad was a sedentary; his spiritual horizon was entirely different from the Bedouins'. The influences and experiences which he had undergone were foreign to them. It has been maintained, especially by such scholars as Grimme and Nielsen, that Muhammad's religious trend was a revival of certain religious ideas from South Arabia. In the present writer's opinion, this view is incorrect: Muhammad drew his main inspiration from the north. Anyhow, it was foreign to the Bedouin Arabians. In a way, the Islamization of Arabia was directed against the nomadic pattern of life. All that was characteristic in it and dear to the Bedouin's heart was bitterly assailed in Muhammad's preaching: the tribal organization, the individualistic freedom, and the coolness towards regular worship.

Muhammad succeeded in binding the Bedouins to Islam. How that could have happened cannot be explained in the frame of the present discussion: that topic belongs to the history of Islam and not to that of pre-Islamic Arabia. In the course of our own discussion, we have reached the conclusion that the ancient history of Arabia is a very complex one and most of it is still obscure, but that, in spite of the wide zone of darkness, certain main lines in its development may be ascertained. It belongs to the future of our studies to throw some light into this darkness. A deeper investigation of the literary texts and of the epigraphical evidence will lead to more knowledge. But, as in many other fields of ancient history, the key for a deeper and wider understanding of the history of ancient Arabia can only be supplied by archaeology. Arabia is still archaeologically untouched. Let us hope that after this present war it will soon be opened to scientific investigation. Before that may happen, however, two things are necessary: first, that the present rulers of Arabia become so broad-minded as to understand the legitimacy and the advantage of having their country investigated by Western scholars; and, second, that the prestige of Western scholarship, which is tied up with the prestige of the whole Western civilization, may not perish in a new "Dark Age."

BIBLIOGRAPHY

F. W. Albright. "Islam and the Religions of Ancient Orient," *Journal of the American Oriental Society*. 60 (1940), 283-301.

A. P. Caussin de Perceval. *Essai sur l'Histoire des Arabes avant l'Islamisme*. Paris, 1847-48.

G. L. Della Vida. *Les Sémites et leur rôle dans l'histoire religieuse*. Paris, 1938.

———. "Ḳuṣaiy" and "Liḥyān," *Encyclopaedia of Islam*.

R. Dussaud. *Les Arabes en Syrie avant l'Islam*. Paris, 1907.

Nelson Glueck. *The Other Side of the Jordan*. New Haven, 1940.

A. Grohmann. "Minaioi," Ed. Pauly-Wissowa-Kroll, *Reallexikon der klassischen Altertumswissenschaft, Suppl.* VI (1935), 461-88.

———. "Nabataioi," Ed. Pauly-Wissowa-Kroll. XVI (1935), 1453-68.

I. Guidi. *L'Arabie antéislamique.* Paris, 1921.

M. Hartmann. "Die arabische Frage," *Der islamische Orient II.* Berlin, 1909.

P. K. Hitti. *A History of the Arabs.* 2nd ed. (London, 1940), pp. 1-108.

H. Lammens. *Le Berceau de l'Islam.* Rome, 1914.

———. *L'Arabie occidentale à la veille de L'Hégire.* Beirut, 1928.

E. Littmann. "Thamūd und Ṣafā," *Abhandlungen zur Kunde des Morgenlandes.* XXV. 1 (1940).

D. S. Margoliouth. *The Relations between Arabs and Israelites Prior to the Rise of Islam.* London, 1924.

J. A. Montgomery. *Arabia and the Bible.* Philadelphia, 1934.

B. Moritz. *Arabien.* Hanover, 1923.

———. "Die Nationalitaet der Arumu—Staemme in Suedost-Babylonien," *Oriental Studies in Commemoration of . . . Paul Haupt . . .* (Baltimore-Leipzig, 1926), pp. 184-211.

A. Musil. *Northern Ḥejâz.* (New York, 1926), pp. 243-321.

———. *Arabia Deserta.* (New York, 1927), pp. 477-516, 531-2.

D. Nielsen and others. *Handbuch der arabischen Altertumskunde.* Kopenhagen, 1927.

Th. Nöldeke. "Die Ghassânischen Fuersten aus dem Hause Gafna," *Abhandlungen der preussischen Akad. der Wissenschaften.* 1887.

G. Olinder. "The Kings of Kinda of the family of Ākil al-Murār," *Lunds Universitets Arsskrift.* N.F., avd. 1, Vol. XXIII, no. 6 (1927).

T. W. Rosmarin. "Aribi und Arabien in den Babylonisch-Assyrischen Quellen," *Journal of the Society of Oriental Research.* XVI (1932), 1-37.

M. Rostovzeff. *Caravan Cities.* Oxford, 1932.

G. Rothstein. *Die Dynastie der Lahmiden in al-Ḥīra.* Berlin, 1899.

Tkač, "Saba," Ed. Pauly-Wissowa-Kroll. 2.I (1920), 1299-1515.

———. "Saba'," *Encyclopaedia of Islam.*

J. Wellhausen. *Reste arabischen Heidentums.* 2nd ed. (Berlin, 1897.)

F. V. Winnett. *A study of the Lihyanite and Thamudic Inscriptions.* Toronto, 1937.

———. "The Daughters of Allah," *The Moslem World.* XXX (1940), 113-30.

ISLAMIC ORIGINS: A STUDY IN BACKGROUND AND FOUNDATION

JULIAN OBERMANN

Background

The Situation in General

Islam is the youngest of three Semitic religions that are marked off from the common type of religious organization in antiquity by a number of striking characteristics. Each of them had a definite, dated beginning; each of them evolved from a single personality; and each of them spread beyond its native home over an area of world-wide dimensions—to mention only the most obvious of those characteristics. In addition, all of them originated in the same general vicinity of Western Asia. Of the two older religions one is a direct offspring, a specific form of continuity, of the other. Are we therefore justified in seeing in the rise of Islam a form of evolution or repercussion from the two older members of the triad? If due allowance be made for the factor of the prophetic personality of Muhammad—a factor which is by no means inconsiderable—the above question will have to be answered in the affirmative.

Even upon superficial examination, we come in Islam upon well defined tenets, trends and institutions closely parallel to those present in Judaism, in Christianity, or in both. In themselves, these parallels need not necessarily presuppose a historical nexus of any kind; rather, they might represent analogous effects brought about by analogous conditions and bespeak a problem of inner development rather than one of outside influence. As such, the parallels in question would properly fall within the province of the comparative study of religion. They would become the object of historical-philological research only to the extent to which it could be demonstrated that they had been effected by actual contact, whatever the nature of the contact might have been: direct or indirect, personal or literary, accidental or deliberate. In point of fact, numerous elements in Islam can be so demonstrated. That is, they can be shown to represent results of unmistakable borrowing, of faithful imitation, often indeed of explicit and solemn adherence to, and endorsement of, "what had been revealed before."

And yet it is not at all easy to ascertain in which branch of primitive Islam the legacy of "what had been revealed before" makes itself felt the most; or to determine the precise manner in which the bearers of this legacy exerted its force and impact. What can be said, offhand, is that the germinating forces of the two older religions are apparent in every phase and mode of the manifestation of the new religion. Whether we consider the literary make-up of its authority as a whole or the individual branches in detail; whether we examine the principal articles of its creed or the manner in which they are worded and expounded; whether we study its figures of speech and terminology or the ethical, eschatological, ritual, and legal minutae to which they refer —invariably we are led to Judaism and Christianity as the two vital spheres of influence, the two regenerating factors, in the preparation and making of Islam.

Many scholars have indeed felt inclined to assign to Judaism a greater share and weight, and accordingly a greater measure of responsibility, than to Christianity. Such, it is true, is the impression we receive from the volume of materials, the frequency of reference, the proximity of correspondence. However, what with the vast overlapping of Jewish and Christian lore, especially in the period and area involved, such an impression may be illusory or at least inexact, unless it be borne out by detailed evidence for each element under discussion. Obviously, Old Testament and even rabbinical materials might have been transmitted to Arabia by Christian channels; while seemingly New Testament matter might easily have been derived from rabbinical homilies. Indeed, the situation is of a kind that in a considerable number of instances we can go only as far as to demonstrate a given element in Islam as of Judeo-Christian origin, but not further.

We should hasten to add, however, that this difficulty of a clear definition of the forces involved in the making of Islam is conditioned not by scarcity of evidence but, on the contrary, by too much evidence, too great a variety of contact, too confusing a diversity of sources. The plain truth is that the genetic history of Islam anteceded its pragmatic history by many generations. Well known is the statement of ibn-Qutaybah how, in pre-Islamic times, Judaism and Christianity had prevailed among some of the most prominent tribes of both northern and southern Arabia and how, specifically through the mediation of al-Ḥīrah, the Quraysh had even come under the sway of the *Zandaqah*, which term we may safely take to denote a doctrine of Christianized Gnosticism, in all probability that of the Mandaeans. The barest outline of the conditions epitomized in the statement of ibn-Qutaybah should suffice to make us realize how thoroughly the mission of Muhammad had been prepared by that of the People of the Book, to whom he so persistently refers.

Variety of Contact

Long before the time of Muhammad, the Arabians had been witnessing an ever-growing encroachment—political and social as well as cultural—of the two monotheistic religions upon their pagan world. Great numbers of their kin had been converted; whole tribes and districts of their domain, especially in its outposts, had come under the sway of the Church, of the Synagogue, or of the one as well as the other. Eventually, the tide was to reach Arabia proper. In the period immediately preceding the rise of Islam, inhabitants of the main caravan cities of the Hejaz, particularly of Mecca and Medina, had more than ample opportunity to absorb Jewish-Christian ideas; in fact, the opportunity was overwhelming. The career of Muhammad himself can be best understood as that of a proselyte so truly stirred by the idea of one God of the world, so deeply merged in the teachings and expositions that led him to conversion, that he would have been well fitted to convert others even if the prophetic call had never reached him.

As early as the third century, the pagan Arabs of Palmyra employ, in their Aramaic inscriptions, certain terms and phrases that are remarkable for their Jewish-Christian coloring. In the following centuries we find Christianity firmly entrenched in the two Arab kingdoms that bordered the Peninsula on the east and the north, respectively; the kingdom of the Lakhmids in al-Ḥīrah, which held allegiance to Persia and whose strong Christian community, termed significantly *al-'Ibād*, was in the main of the Nestorian creed; and the kingdom of the Ghassanians in Syria, who allied themselves with Byzantium and of whose princes some were zealous Monophysites. In the south of the Peninsula, on the other hand, we find Judaism represented by the renowned Jewish communities of Yemen, which must have settled there as early as the second century, if not much earlier, but which continued to maintain close contact with the centers of Jewish authority, especially, it would seem, with those in Babylonia. So vigorous was the Jewish mission in Yemen that it succeeded in making converts even among members of the royal house of the Himyarites—a counterpart to the Christian mission among the Lakhmids in Iraq and the Ghassanians in Syria and, in Yemen itself, among the people of Najrān. Undoubtedly, the massacre of the Christians of Najrān by the Jewish convert dhu-Nuwās, the last Himyarite ruler of the indigenous Tubba' dynasty, was precipitated not only by the proverbial zest of the neophyte but also, if not primarily, by his hatred of the Abyssinians, who at that time (ca. A.D. 523) had occupied parts of Yemen, taking the Christian population under their particular protection. A stronghold of Christianity since early in the third century, it was no doubt Abyssinia rather than Syria whence the Christian mission had first come to South Arabia.

In North Arabia itself, we find Judaism prospering in several centers. In particular, Moslem historians agree in appraising the preponderance, social, political, and economic, of the Jewish community of Medina—the city that was destined to become the home of Muhammad's first triumphs. The very change of its old name Yathrib to that of Medina would seem to have been brought about by its Jewish inhabitants, *mᵉdīnā* being the common word for "town," "city" in Aramaic; except that to the Moslems it was to become *the City* (*al-Madīnah*). Indeed, at one time in its pre-Islamic history, Medina was on the way toward consolidating into a kind of Jewish commonwealth, with the Synagogue as its state-church.

Professor Charles C. Torrey has shown that, in all probability, we have here to do with a very old colony of Jewish settlers from Palestine; and he would undoubtedly agree that, in all probability, too, the original settlers had undergone gradual fusion with very large numbers of converts from the indigenous population. In point of fact, one of the two principal Jewish tribes of Medina, the banu-Naḍīr, are said to have originally belonged to the banu-Judhām, the latter, first cousins of the Lakhmids, having occupied the vast territory north of Medina that had formerly been held by the Nabataeans. While not differing appreciably from their pagan neighbors either in their speech and proper names or in their dress and occupation, the Jews of Medina appear to have retained their religious lore on a rather high level. The great biographer of Muhammad, ibn-Isḥāq, compiled a list of the rabbis (*aḥbār*) of the Jews of Medina who had refused to acknowledge him as a prophet. Concerning one of these rabbis, 'Abdullāh ibn-Ṣūrah, we are informed that none in the Hejaz exceeded him in the mastery of the Torah; an equally high rank of Jewish learning, we are told, was held by the renowned 'Abdullāh ibn-Salām. In keeping with this is contemporary testimony to the great scholastic proficiency among the Jews of Medina, contained in a poem of Sammāk (*al-Yahūdi*), a member of the banu-Naḍīr themselves.

We may well assume that the cultivation of their religious

lore by the Jews of Medina was facilitated by contact with, and influx from, Jewish communities of Palestine and, especially, of Yemen. Well known, at any rate, is the case of the Yemenite Rabbi Ka‘b ibn-Matī‘ (*al-Aḥbār*), who after his conversion to Islam became a source of religious instruction for the first generation of Moslems in Medina. Muhammad himself is said to have visited a "house of learning" of the Medinan Jews, an institution which is referred to in Arabic by close adaptation of the corresponding rabbinical term (*bêt ham-midrāš* > *bayt al-madāris*). The same is also related of the first two caliphs, abu-Bakr and ‘Umar, while the latter is said to have stated that he was frequenting the Jewish house of learning in order to gain a better understanding of the teachings of Muhammad.

Because of the relative proximity and kinship of the two cities, the situation in Medina was bound to be reflected in Mecca, the native home of the Prophet. This is neatly illustrated by the tradition according to which Muhammad, when five years of age, was taken by his mother to Medina, where she visited with her kinsfolk and that following her death there he was brought back to Mecca by his nurse umm-Ayman. While the tradition as such may well be tendentious, it clearly points to universal recollections of a rather vivid intercourse between the two cities in pre-Islamic times. Direct historical information about Jews and Christians in Mecca is very meager indeed; but the indirect testimony in our possession, above all that supplied by Muhammad himself, is as lucid and eloquent as could be desired. In al-Ṭā'if, less than a hundred miles to the southeast of Mecca and a favorite resort of the Quraysh, the poet Umayyah ibn-abi-al-Ṣalt is said to have confessed monotheism prior to the appearance of Muhammad. If only some of the pertinent fragments attributed to him are genuine—and this we have no reason to doubt—it was unquestionably a Jewish-Christian monotheism with its characteristic stress on eschatology. In Mecca itself, Zayd ibn-‘Amr ibn-Nufayl, a member of the Quraysh, is said to have been persecuted by his family for forsaking their pagan cult; having penetrated to the belief in a single God, he is said to have considered himself a follower of the religion of Abraham and even to have predicted the coming of Muhammad. Offhand, too, we should have to recognize that Mecca had been even more exposed than Medina to influence from the various centers of Judaism and Christianity, which we have seen to have extended all around the Hejaz during the last pre-Islamic centuries. In the hands of the wealthy and enterprising Quraysh, Mecca was the capital of a vast commercial empire before it became the holy city of Islam. The meeting point of far-flung caravan and trade routes from Babylonia, Syria and Palestine to South Arabia, and from the shores of the Mediterranean to those of the Indian Ocean and the Red Sea, Mecca maintained commercial agreements with the Negus of Abyssinia, the Qayls of Yemen, the Phylarchs of the Lakhmids and Ghassanians. In the year of Muhammad's birth (570 or 571), the Abyssinian viceroy of Yemen, Abrahah, led a military expedition against Mecca that amounted to something like a Christian crusade, the avowed purpose of the campaign having been to destroy the temple of Mecca, the Ka'bah, which under the resourceful administration of the Quraysh was on the way to becoming the central sanctuary of pagan Arabia.

Forty years later, when Muhammad first embarked upon his mission, Jewish-Christian ideas had become so familiar to the Meccans that he apparently had no difficulties in converting the common people to the creed of one God of the world, meeting opposition only from the nobility of the Quraysh, whose vested interests militated in favor of the status quo against so sweeping a change of creed. And when, in an often quoted tradition, he relates his experience on Mount Ḥirā' to the aged cousin of his wife Khadījah, Waraqah ibn-Nawfal, the latter breaks forth in the solemn exclamation, "*Quddūs quddūs*" ("Holy, Holy")—an Old Testament doxology (Is. 6:5) that had become an integral part of the liturgy of the Jewish Synagogue as well as of the Christian Church. Again, in a conversation which the theologically minded Heraclius (575-642) is said to have held in Jerusalem with abu-Sufyān, a powerful leader of the Quraysh, the Christian emperor undertakes to enlighten the pagan Arabian about the symptoms of a true prophet. Whether or not the conversation, or even the encounter, had a basis in fact, it does typify the kind of influence to which the merchants of Mecca were exposed while traveling abroad with their caravans. Indeed, Moslem tradition makes Muhammad himself the subject of an encounter of this kind during a caravan journey to Syria prior to his appearance as the messenger of Allah.

Writing and Literacy

Quite apart from the all-important contribution of their lore and ideology as such to the foundation of Islam, the impact of the two older religions was essentially enhanced by what they contributed, directly and indirectly, to the spread of writing and literacy in the generation and the environment of Muhammad. It would be impossible to overestimate the importance of this purely technical-cultural contribution for the success of his mission; it is fair to say that it was the *sine qua non* of that success. To be sure, the art of writing itself had reached the Arabian world many centuries before. But it had been used in the main, if not indeed exclusively, for epigraphic purposes, and this for inscriptions written as a rule either in South Arabic (Sabaean, Minaean, Liḥyānite, Thamudic, Safaitic) or, in younger times, in Aramaic (Nabataean, Sinaitic, Palmyrene, Syriac). Of the great mass of inscriptions produced by the Arabians in pre-Islamic times only three are thus far known in which the language employed was North Arabic: the Namārah inscription of Imru'-al-Qays and the two votive records from Zabad and Harran, respectively. Whether Arabic writing, or indeed any writing, was used in pre-Islamic Hejaz for commercial purposes, we have no way of knowing. At any rate, the very considerable literature of the Arabs in pagan times—poetry, proverbs, folklore—was neither collected nor committed to writing, certainly not as a rule, until after the full development of Islam, and then only by the pious endeavors of Moslem grammarians, lexicographers, historians. The plain truth is that the first Arabic book, the first known literary product intended as a written composition, was the Koran. Within a single generation the Arabic language—not the stereotyped legends of inscriptions, the crude pattern of business records or the formalized technique of verse, but the whole breadth of living speech—was molded into written form. And by the deed of a single man the Arabian world came to be focused on a written document, on a text recorded "between the two covers of the Book."

This is a phenomenon hardly less epochal, in itself and its consequences, than the rise of Islam as such. There would be nothing to account for this phenomenon unless it should be understood as a result of conscious emulation of the two older religions; and we shall see later that, by the overwhelming testimony of Muhammad himself, it must actually be so understood. At the moment it will be well to remember that nearly all epigraphic and literary evidence bearing on the beginning of North Arabic writing and on the spread of literacy in the Hejaz points to Jewish and Christian influence. Thus, of the three North Arabic inscriptions of pre-Islamic origin, two are Christian. In both of them, moreover, the Arabic text is paralleled by one in Syriac, the holy language of the Oriental Church; and, in the inscription from Zabad, also by one in Greek, the holy language of the Byzantine Church. As far as one can see, the only pre-Islamic poet praised for his proficiency in the art of writing in Arabic is the celebrated Christian poet of al-Ḥīrah, 'Adi ibn-Zayd. Of two other poets, Ṭarafah and al-Mutalammis, we are told that the former died a violent death and the latter came close to meeting with the same fate, because being illiterate they were unable to read the treacherous letter in which 'Amr ibn-Hind, king of al-Ḥīrah (ca. 554-70), ordered his governor in Bahrain to do away with the two poets—presumably because they had incited his displeasure. The last king of al-Ḥīrah, al-Nuʻmān ibn-al-Mundhir (ca. 580-602), who was brought up and educated by the family of ʻAdi ibn-Zayd, is even said to have owned a *dīwān*, which later, we are told, came into the possession of the Umayyad caliphs; if so, the only known case of Arabic poems put into writing and collected in pre-Islamic times would have occurred at the Christian court of al-Ḥīrah.

Both al-Ḥīrah and al-Anbār, the two Christianized cities of the Lakhmids, figure prominently in the Moslem accounts about the beginnings of writing in the Hejaz as well. We hear, for example, that the Christian Bishr ibn-ʻAbd-al-Malik, having acquired the art of writing Arabic in al-Ḥīrah, taught it in Mecca to Sufyān ibn-Umayyah and abu-Qays ibn-ʻAbd-Manāf. Apparently, however, the art spread rather slowly, so that when "Islam came," we are told, there were only seventeen men among the Quraysh who knew how to write. In the list of these men as given by al-Balādhuri—which contains such outstanding figures of primitive Islam as ʻUmar, ʻAli, ʻUthmān, Ṭalḥah, abu-Sufyān, Muʻāwiyah—no mention is made of Waraqah ibn-Nawfal; presumably, because he was not considered a Moslem, having died before "Islam came" to Mecca. What tradition does relate of him is that "he had been converted to Christianity and had read the Books," and that he had received instruction from (*samiʻa min*) Jews and Christians. It is also said of him that "he wrote from the Gospel in Hebrew," which may well be taken to mean that he copied an Arabic translation of the Gospel that had been written in Hebrew characters—a counterpart of the Arabic inscription of Imru'-al-Qays that was written in Aramaic (Nabataean) characters.

Writing in "Hebrew" characters, not only of Hebrew and Aramaic texts but no doubt of Arabic texts as well, was apparently a sight not unfamiliar in the cities of the Hejaz. Muhammad knows of books and scrolls and folios (*kutub*, *qarāṭīs*, *ṣuḥuf*) in the hands of the Jews, obviously referring to copies of their sacred literature. The Hebrew script of a rabbi or scribe (*ḥabr*) of Taymā' is used as a simile by the poet al-Shammākh, a contemporary of Muhammad. The Jews of Medina are said to have taught the art of writing Arabic; so that the youth there had acquired it in the days before Islam. This, however, merely means that the Jews taught the Medinans how to put Arabic into alphabetic writing, but it does not indicate which particular brand of alphabetic characters they had used. In point of fact, the Medinan Zayd ibn-Thābit, the celebrated secretary of the Prophet, is said to have been able to write both Arabic and Hebrew, and to have acquired the latter art of writing in less than half a month—which obviously means that he could write in the customary Aramaic characters that had come to be used for Arabic as well as in square Hebrew characters. Indeed, the Jews of Medina seem to have employed Hebrew script even in their unquestionably Arabic correspondence with Muhammad; and the clear implication is that it was this circumstance that made it necessary for Zayd ibn-Thābit to learn from them the use of this script (*kitāb yahūd*) as well as the more common type of Arabic writing.

Diversity of Sources

From what has been said it will be apparent that Jewish and Christian elements could have drifted into the Hejaz through a great variety of channels, and for a very long period of time, prior to the appearance of Muhammad. He would thus have found the ground well prepared and many of his pagan countrymen sufficiently susceptible to a message, the basic trend of which would have become familiar to them long since. Even his opponents among the Quraysh, although rejecting the message, do not appear to have denied his claim that it is a message in "clear Arabic"—a claim on which he lays great stress. In reality, however, his message was packed with foreignisms; with words, phrases, technical terms and proper names non-Arabic in origin but used more or less widely in the vocabulary of Judaism, of Christianity, or both. Yet his listeners had not only no difficulty in understanding the mass of foreign elements in Muhammad's message, but they did not even suspect them to be foreign. This would clearly indicate that many, if not indeed all, of the Jewish and Christian ideas that penetrated into the Hejaz in pre-Islamic times continued to bear the names and terms that had been applied to them in their former environment; and that at the time of Muhammad these names and terms had been so completely absorbed by and adjusted to the language of their new environment that they were commonly understood, by his followers and opponents alike, in Mecca as well as Medina.

It is obvious, however, that the general channels of contact—such as those brought about by trade, travel, political and ethnic affiliation—could not possibly have precipitated the full volume and weight of Jewish and Christian influence that comes into display with the appearance of Muhammad. Effective as these channels must be assumed to have been in preparing the ground upon which Islam was to be founded, they do not suffice to account for much once we behold the foundation itself. In considering Muhammad's message not for its basic trend but rather for the wealth of minutiae it entails, we are made to realize that it could only have been conceived and composed under the intimate, systematic, missionary effectiveness of Jews and Christians in the Prophet's immediate environment. The inference is of such a kind that it would have been unanswerable even if we had nothing else to go by. In truth, however, it is Moslem tradition itself that bears witness to the aggressive, proselytizing impact of the two older religions on the birth of Islam: the tradition of how Waraqah received instruction from Jews and Christians and how, upon learning of Muhammad's prophetic experience, broke forth into the doxology "Holy, Holy"; the tradition of how 'Abdullāh ibn-Salām, who is said to have been one of the foremost scholars among the Jews of Medina, interrogated Muhammad in a number of esoteric questions and then acknowledged him as the Messiah; the tradition of how the first caliphs used to visit a synagogue-school in Medina;

the tradition of how 'Umar received a copy of the Torah from the Rabbi Ka'b and promised to read it "by day and by night"; the tradition of how the Jews would read Scripture in Hebrew and explain it in Arabic to the first generation of Moslems, and many similar traditions.

It goes without saying that the Jews and Christians of the Hejaz spoke Arabic and that their vernacular could hardly have differed from that of their pagan neighbors; at any rate, not to an extent that would have impeded the flow of conversation between members of the different groups. This is also presupposed by all accounts and traditions of the kind just quoted. At the same time, it is just as clear—and borne out by numerous analogies in times both older and younger than the period under discussion—that when referring to tenets and institutions of their religion, the Arabian Jews and Christians would naturally use the corresponding terms established, for a given tenet or institution, in the sacred language of the Synagogue and the Church, respectively. In particular, they would be bound to do this in their congregational gatherings, when performing service and sacred rites, when holding forth their discourses, homilies and sermons. Thus the Jews would be well-nigh certain to refer to their lore as Torah, and to those engaged in its dispensation as rabbis; the Christians, whether Nestorians or Monophysites, would just as certainly speak of their Scripture as the Evangel; while both Jews and Christians would refer to their day of rest and worship as Sabbath. In point of fact, these and a great many other non-Arabic words do occur, some with very considerable frequency, in the teachings of Muhammad and the vocabulary of Islam in general; the Torah is *al-Tawrāh*, the rabbis are *al-rabbānīyūn*, the Evangel is *al-Injīl*, and Sabbath is *al-Sabt*. The same type of non-Arabic words are used by the poet Sammāk mentioned above, who thus furnishes us with explicit, if inadvertent, testimony as to one source of supply for borrowings of this kind.

The great diversity of sources upon which Muhammad might have drawn for the materials of his message is apt to obliterate the exact identity of a given element. Thus the ever-present problem in the study of the vocabulary of primitive Islam is not so much to identify the large number of its Jewish and Christian components, which is simple enough, as rather to determine which of these components had reached the Arabians by the general channels extant in pre-Islamic times and which of them were absorbed by Muhammad himself through the missionary work of Jews and Christians in his immediate environment. Nor does the problem end here. The difficulty of exact identification is often enhanced by the linguistic affinity of the sources, notwithstanding their great diversity. Quite apart from the overlapping of Jewish and Christian materials, the languages of the Synagogue and of the Oriental Church, excepting only that of Byzantium, are related to one another as well as to Arabic. Hence, a given religious term in Islam, whether legitimately Arabic or not, is frequently of such a kind that it might have been transmitted equally well from Abyssinia, Yemen, Mesopotamia, Syria, or Palestine; e.g., the highly important Islamic terms "Day of Judgment," *Yawm al-Dīn*, "Hell-fire," *Jahannam*, "Satan," *Shayṭān*, "sacrifice," *qurbān*, and many others. Only by minute linguistic analysis is it sometimes possible to identify the immediate antecedent of a term of this kind as peculiarly Hebrew, Aramaic, Syriac or Ethiopic. Even this, however, is not necessarily conclusive. Syriac was used not only both by Nestorians and Monophysites but it was virtually identical with the Mesopotamian dialects of the Jews and the Mandaeans; while Aramaic—more specifically West Aramaic—was used in Palestine and Syria by Jews, Samaritans, Monophysites and Melkites alike.

We are confronted with a very similar situation in the study of the ideological and literary components of primitive Islam, with which components we shall find ourselves dealing in the main during the following discussion. The contributions of the two older religions, and particularly of Judaism, are obvious and indeed omnipresent. But it is often daring and hazardous to determine the exact source that is ultimately reflected in a given thesis, tenet or homily current in the teachings of Muhammad. And it is even more hazardous to define not only the ultimate but the direct and immediate source that supplied Muhammad with the ideological or literary element in question. Yet, precisely this is the prime task in our study of the making of Islam.

Inner Foundation

A. Theory of Revelation

The Book = The Torah

We have seen already that reading and writing was a thing virtually unknown among the Arabians, notwithstanding their highly developed literature, especially in the field of poetry. Except for the efforts made in their behalf by Moslem posterity, the very considerable literary products of pre-Islamic Arabia would have remained unrecorded. Such a situation, in which literature is as yet wholly unrelated to the mechanism of written documentation, is by no means exceptional among the ancient Semites. The poem (*shiʿr*, literally "knowledge") of the pagan Arabian, just as the oracle (*tôrâ*) of the Israelitish priest and the vision (*ḥāzôn*) of the Hebrew prophet, was an inner process objectified only by the spoken word; it was memorable for its form or binding by its contents, but it had no independent existence other than in memory and no manner of recording except by recital.

In this respect the pagan Arabians found themselves in sharp contrast to the Jewish and Christian communities in their midst, to whom literacy had long since become a common, and indeed indispensable, institution. By a development which need not concern us here, the Synagogue and no less the Church had their most sacred possession in a literature objectified by written records. Here revelation and Scripture had become coextensive as well as coexistent. To the Jews, Torah is not merely the contents of God's words and commandments as revealed to Moses but also the documentation of these words and commandments, their written manifestation in a scroll or a book. Ever since prophecy, oracle, revelation had been reduced to and indeed replaced by Scripture, the cultivation of the latter—conservation and copying of it, and above all diligent reading and study of it—was bound to become the foremost function of the Synagogue. In the language of the rabbis, "It is written in the Torah" or merely "It is written" (*kāṯûb*, *kᵉṯīb*) means as much as "It is God's demand of man." Hence, in the New Testament *hē graphē* is often synonymous with *ho nomos*; and utterances like that of the jot and the tittle (Matt. 5:18) or "They believed the Scripture" merely reflects a well established manner of referring to things divine in terms of their written documentation.

That the Jews of the Hejaz shared in the development just described we might assume beforehand as a matter of course. But we need not depend on assumption. It is rendered superfluous by the overwhelming, if incidental, testimony of Muhammad. In fact, if we had no information on the subject from indigenous Jewish sources, we could arrive at an accurate and detailed understanding of the concept of revelation in Judaism by means of the pertinent utterances of Muhammad alone. Inadvertently, he epitomizes this basic feature of Judaism by his standard reference to the Jews as the "People of the Book" or, less frequently, "those who were given the Book"; and he leaves no doubt that he uses the word *al-Kitāb* in the sense in which *hak-kāṯûb* is used by the rabbis, and *hē graphē* in the New Testament. He makes God say, "We gave Moses the Book" (2:81 and often); "We gave Moses the Guidance and made the Israelites inherit the Book" (40:56); "We sent down the Torah" (5:48); "We gave Moses the Book and established it as a Guidance for the Israelites" (17:2); "We decreed for the Israelites in the Book" (17:4). Here "the Book," "the Guidance," "the Torah" are used interchangeably; at other occasions "the Book" is coupled with, rather than paralleled to, quasi-synonymous words of the same kind. In the "covenant of the prophets," by which Muhammad means a law concerning prophecy (and which obviously reflects Deut. 18:15), he makes God say to the Israelites, "Whatever Book and Wisdom I have given you" (3:75); or he makes God say of Abraham, "And We established among his offspring the Prophethood and the Book" (29:26; cf. 57:26). Similar coupling we meet in God's words, "We have given Moses the Book and the Salvation" (2:50), or, "We have given the Israelites the Book, and the Law, and the Prophethood" (45:15; cf. 6:89).

The Mother of the Book

If *al-Kitāb* is thus clearly employed by Muhammad to denote the contents of God's revelation to Moses, he uses the vocable just as clearly in its concrete signification: the Book embodying that contents, the written record of its volume and wording. In truth, *al-Kitāb* means just as much the one thing as the other; and its rendering by some such hendiadys as "the Book and the Wisdom" or "the Book and the Guidance" is always implied and, as we have just seen, often expressed. Accordingly, each of the two significations may be found referred to in terms of the other, with no sharp line of demarcation between the divine realm of the Book and its human realm. Many of his pertinent utterances clearly reflect the rabbinical idea that the Torah had existed with God prior to its revelation and even prior to the creation of heavens and earth, and that it had indeed served as a sort of blueprint for creation. This primeval Torah, to which Muhammad sometimes refers as the "Mother of the Book," would naturally have been written by God Himself. In fact, he makes God say, "We have written for the Israelites that . . ." (5:35); "We have written for them therein . . ." (5:49); "We have written in the Psalter" (21:105); "We have written for him [for Moses] in the Tablets" (7:142); reflecting a rabbinical interpretation of Gen. 1:14, Muhammad says that the twelve months were established "in the

Book of God on the day He created heavens and earth" (9:36).

It would seem, too, that the "Mother of the Book" came to be connected in Muhammad's mind—or better no doubt in the mind of the Jews or Christians of his milieu—with two other kinds of heavenly books; namely, the divine tablets that were believed to contain all future happenings of the universe and the race, and the divine register recording the destiny and deeds of the individual soul. "For every event there is [mention in] a Book; God deletes what He wills or confirms; with Him is the Mother of the Book" (13:38 f.). It is, indeed, as if God Himself drew, for His omniscience, upon this total record: "There is not a hidden thing in heavens or earth but it is in a clear Book" (27:77); "He knows the unseen; there does not escape Him as much as the weight of an atom in heavens or earth; there is naught smaller or bigger than that except it is in a clear Book" (34:3). Consult also 35:12; 23:64; 6:59 (cf. 10:62; 11:8); 20:54; 6:38.

Undoubtedly, it is with this idea in mind, the idea of an all-inclusive heavenly Book, that Muhammad often applies to God the verb "to write" in the sense of "to establish, to order, to prescribe, to promise, to decree, to impose" and the like, whereby the verb may refer not only to the past but to the present and the future as well, and may even be found employed in supplication. Thus Moses is made to say to the Israelites, "Enter the Holy Land which God has written down for you" (5:24); in an utterance strongly reminiscent of a rabbinical sentiment, Muhammad says of God, "He has written mercy upon Himself" (6:12, 54). To Moses' prayer, "Write Thou down for us good in this world and the Hereafter," God replies, "I shall write it down" (7:155); similarly, the Disciples pray, "Write Thou us down among the witnesses" (3:46). Noteworthy also are utterances like "Nothing will befall us save what God has written down upon us" (9:51; cf. 58:21); "God writes down what they conceal" (4:83); "We shall write down what they said" (3:177; cf. 19:82; also 36:11).

For the group as well as the individual—but specifically, it would seem, for the latter—the heavenly Book signifies also the balance sheet to be applied on the eschatological day of reckoning. On that day "the Book shall be put up" (18:47; 39:69); "the sheets [of the Book] shall be spread out" (81:10); "each group shall be called to its Book. . . . 'This is Our Book which speaks about you the truth' " (45:27 f.); "and every man. . . . We shall bring forth to him on the day of resurrection a Book which he will find spread open" (17:14; cf. 17:73; 69:19, 25). As is well known, these notions of celestial planning and eschatological bookkeeping with their Babylonian and Persian coloring have become an integral and popular part of the beliefs held in rabbinical Judaism, where the Tablets of Destiny are occasionally confused with the preexistent heavenly Torah; and there is no reason to doubt that they were less popular and, for that matter, less confused among the Jews of the Hejaz. The Synagogue has lent these notions a prominent place in the liturgy of New Year's and the Day of Atonement. Indeed, such formulas occurring in this liturgy as "Write Thou us down in the Book of Life," "And write Thou down to good life all the children of Thine covenant," "Thou wilt open the Book of records," "And Thou wilt write down their decrees," might well have been directly responsible for some of the utterances of Muhammad which we have quoted.

The Book and the Rabbis

What Muhammad has to say about the Jews of his environment amounts to a further demonstration, if such were needed, that it was in their midst, in prolonged and close association with them, that he acquired the intimate familiarity with the Jewish concept of revelation which we have found him to display. Some of his references to the Jews have a direct bearing on that concept and are therefore of special interest in our present connection. Unfortunately, most of the relevant statements date from the time when, because of their opposition to him as a prophet, his attitude towards them had changed from friendliness and admiration to distrust and eventually to downright hostility. But this does not lessen the historical value of his observations, however polemical and caustic the point he intends to bring out often is. The decisive thing is that the Jews of his environment, we are told, adhere to the Book as their highest possession, holding it up as their source of divine revelation, reading it and copying it, reciting, studying and expounding it. No wonder that he, with a genius for coining a phrase, had come to refer to them as "the people of the Book."

This picture remains intact even in his moods of anger and reproach. "Do ye preach piety [to others]," he once addresses them, "but forget your souls, yet ye yourselves recite the Book?" (2:81). On another occasion, he makes Gabriel ask him, "How shall they make thee their judge, seeing that in their hands is the Torah containing the Judgment of God?" (5:47). And in the same rhetorical vein: "Who did send down the Book which Moses brought as a light and guidance to the people [and] which ye copy into scrolls?" (6:91). Referring no doubt to an extracanonical code in their possession, he states, "They write the Book with their hands and then proclaim: This is from God!" (2:73); further, "They twist their tongues about the Book, so that ye should think it to be of the Book; but it is not of the Book! And they say 'It is from God,' but it is not from God" (3:72). This utterance of Muhammad would betray a very fine and true appraisal of the attitude of the rabbis toward postcanonical law, if the last clause had been intended by him as part of their statement; namely, "And they say: It is from God and yet it is not from God," which is syntactically quite possible and would well account for his branding the statement as a twisting of tongues.

An even more intimate observation about the make-up of authority in Judaism is his utterance that the prophets gave judgment to the Jews by the guidance and light of the Torah, while the "Rabbis and the Doctors" do so "by that which they [alone] have been entrusted to guard of the Book of God, and to which they [alone] have been witnesses" (5:48). He even comes close to giving us a definition of the duties of the rabbis as he had known them. In an exhortation obviously addressed to the leaders of the Jewish community in Medina and intended to allay their suspicions, he says: "Remain ye Rabbis by virtue of your having taught the Book and by virtue of your having expounded it" (3:73).

The Book = The Evangel

The epithet "People of the Book" Muhammad also applies to the Christians (cf. 4:164); occasionally he refers to them as the "People of the Evangel" (5:51). This is closely in keeping with his idea of the Christian revelation and of Jesus as its human exponent. Essentially, it is the idea that the revelation of Jesus is that of a prophet sent by God to "confirm" or "verify" the revelation of Moses. I think it highly probable that this idea was conveyed to Muhammad by Christians with reference to the many New Testament passages where an utterance or an act of Jesus, or an event bearing on His life, is said to have occurred so that a word of Scripture "might be fulfilled" (Matt. 1:22; 2:15, 23; and elsewhere). Semantically the Arabic word used by Muhammad for "confirming" or "verifying" comes so close to the "fulfilled" of the New Testament, that the former might very well represent a bona fide rendering of the latter. Except that, psychologically, the idea appealed so much to the personal and religious temper of Muhammad that he saw in it the very essence of Jesus' mission. It is conceivable, however, that even in this he was merely guided by a particular brand of Christianity extant in his immediate environment.

The fact is that in the mind of Muhammad the revelation of Jesus is essentially a repetition of that of Moses, for the sole purpose that the teachings of the Torah might be "confirmed"—it is very tempting to say "might be fulfilled"—by those of the Gospel. Apart from this specific feature, then, we find Muhammad applying the very same phraseology to the legacy of Christianity which we have seen him use so fittingly with regard to the legacy of Judaism. He makes God Himself say, "We gave Moses the Book . . . and We gave Jesus, son of Mary, the Evidences" (2:81); "We gave him the Evangel" (57:27); while Jesus is made to say of God, "He has given me the Book and has made me a prophet" (19:31).

Speaking to Jesus God says, "I taught thee the Book and the Wisdom and the Torah and the Evangel" (5:110), and in reference to him: "We have given him the Evangel, containing Guidance and Light, and confirming what there was before him of the Torah" (5:50); in the message to Mary: "He will teach him the Book and the Wisdom and the Torah and the Evangel and [make him] a messenger to the Israelites" (3:43); in turn Jesus is made to say to the Jews: "I have come to you with a sign from your Lord . . . to confirm what there was before me of the Torah" (3:43-44). In a narration that seems to reflect that of Luke 1, Muhammad makes God say even to John, "Take thou the Book with power" (19:13; cf. Lk. 1:76 ff.); of Mary he says, "She believed in the word of her Lord and His Books" (66:12); and he voices disapproval of Jews and Christians denouncing one another, seeing that "they both recite the Book" (2:107). By these and similar utterances Muhammad clearly implies that, since both Moses and Jesus were given the Book, the Torah and the Evangel are each in itself only a part of the heavenly Book.

Evidential and Binding Force of the Book

Muhammad gives emphatic expression to his awareness that it is possible, and highly desirable, to reach monotheism without the aid of revelation. He dwells with particular relish on the instance of Abraham, who had arrived at the idea of a single God of the world by his own power of reasoning, independent of guidance from the Book (6:67-79). Well known are rabbinical utterances to the same effect, such as the statement of the Mishnah (Qidd. 4:14) that the patriarch performed all the precepts of the Torah before the latter "was given." Altogether, the greatness of Abraham and the high perfection of his religious genius constitute an ever-popular topic in the apocryphal and agadic literature, which can be shown to have lent color and substance to the picture drawn by Muhammad. This would clearly indicate that the piety of Abraham was also a frequent topic of instruction and edification among the Jews of Muhammad's intercourse, who would naturally draw on that literature. But the peculiar fascination with which he follows the career of the patriarch makes it apparent that he saw in it an analogy to his own career. Hence the epithet *ḥanīf* which he pointedly, and no doubt deliberately, applies to Abraham. *Ḥanīf*, in fact, is the standard attribute of the patriarch in the utterances of Muhammad, often coupled, antithetically, with the phrase "yet not an idolator."

An all but identical word is employed in the Targum (*ḥanēpā*) and in Syriac (*ḥanpā*) in the sense of "a pagan, a heathen, a Gentile," and since in pre-Islamic times there naturally existed no Arabic equivalent, it is highly probable that Arabian Jews and Christians had come to borrow this word for their vernacular; very possibly Muhammad had heard them apply it to himself. We may even go a step further and recognize that eventually *ḥanīf* came to be employed, in particular, to denote a "heathen" who had been converted, and thus it could serve as an Arabic equivalent for "proselyte" as well. In the mouths of native Jews and Christians the word would naturally have been used with a measure of snobbery and derision; and this is perhaps why later on Muhammad preferred to designate his own converts as *muslimūn* rather than *ḥunafā'*. It is well to bear in mind that in the Agada Abraham is sometimes called a "proselyte" (*gêr*), and that in the language of the rabbis, too, this epithet of honor is often used with more than a grain of caustic salt.

There can be little doubt, at any rate, that in his own utterances Muhammad employs the word *ḥanīf* to describe persons who, although not belonging to the "People of the

Book," and therefore properly classed as "heathens," have penetrated to the belief in one God of the world. To him, such a person par excellence was Abraham. On one occasion Muhammad is ordered to say concerning himself: "As for me, my Lord has guided me to a straight path, a lasting religion, the confession of Abraham [who was] a heathen yet was not among the idolators" (6:162); and in a word from God to Muhammad: "Thereupon We inspired thee: Follow thou the confession of Abraham [who was] a heathen, yet was not among the idolators" (16:124); and in another utterance: "They [the People of the Book] maintain: Ye must be Jews or Christians, [so] ye will be guided. Say thou: Nay, [what about] the confession of Abraham [who was] a heathen, yet was not among the idolators!" (2:129). Once he exclaims: "Who is more beautiful in religion than one who surrenders himself to God, in sincerity, and follows the confession of Abraham as a heathen!" (4:124). In an utterance addressed to the People of the Book, he says "Why do ye argue about Abraham, although neither the Torah nor the Evangel were sent down except after his time?" (3:58). And consistently: "Abraham was not a Jew, nor was he a Christian; rather he was a heathen (*ḥanīfan*), surrendering himself to God (*musliman*) and not one of the idolators" (3:60).

If nevertheless God did "send down the Book" to some of His messengers, such as Moses and Jesus, it is because of its force as "a light and guidance," as an unanswerable evidence (*bayyinah*) of the divine truth, as a tangible manifestation, "a sign" (*āyah*), of His will. It is noteworthy that in this connection Muhammad often uses the word "for the people" (*lil-nās*), as if implying that, whereas outstanding individuals may obtain salvation out of their own resources, this may not be expected of the multitude, who need the guidance of "signs" and the demonstration of "evidences." Only by such a demonstration do the people to whom it was sent down become subject to the truth, and does its disregard become an offense, an act of disobedience and unbelief. Muhammad makes God say: "We sent Our messengers with the Evidences and We sent down with them the Book and the Balance, that the people should prevail in equity" (57:25). The Book was given to Moses as "a light and a guidance for the people" (6:91); "as demonstrations for the people, as a guidance, and as an [act of] mercy" (28:43); "as a specification for everything, as a guidance, and as an [act of] mercy" (6:155). In keeping with the terminology of Judaism, where the Torah and indeed each of its precepts have the weight of a *bẹrīt*, Muhammad refers to the Book as a "covenant," a treaty by which alone the parties that enter it become responsible to one another. "Has there not been laid upon them the covenant of the Book?" (7:168). "When God took the covenant of those who were given the Book [He said]: Surely, ye shall make it manifest to the people and shall not conceal it" (3:184).

The rabbis, indeed, take the position that, while a heathen may become the equal of a High Priest by volunteering to study the Torah, his merit would have been greater had he been under obligation to do so (*mẹṣuwwāh wẹ-'ôśāh*); contrarily, the heathens, since they have not received the Torah, are neither subject to its fulfillment nor punishable for its neglect; they even have a just grievance that the Torah should have been imposed exclusively upon Israel (B. 'Ab Zara 2b-3a). Muhammad clearly follows this attitude, which he could not possibly have failed to observe in the theory and practice of the Jews of his environment. He makes Moses admonish the people to "remember the grace of God towards you when He appointed prophets among you . . . and gave you what He had not given anyone else" (5:23). And he often points to the dire consequences of "those who conceal the evidences and the guidance which We have sent down, after We have made this manifest to the people in the Book" (2:154; cf. 2:86, 207; 4:163). But most remarkable, for its bluntness and all but halachic precision, is his utterance: "Those of the People of the Book who disbelieved and the pagans did not become deceders [from the truth] until there had come to them the Evidence: a messenger from God reciting purified sheets that comprise Books everlasting. Nor did those who have been given the Book separate [into believers and disbelievers] except after there had come to them the Evidence" (98:1-3).

The Book = The Koran

Next to his ineffable experience on Mt. Ḥirā', no single factor may be said to have played more decisive a part in the shaping of Muhammad's career, and hence in the making of Islam, than the theory of revelation as it had crystallized in Judaism long before his time. We have seen how deeply it had impressed itself on his mind, how thoroughly he had familiarized himself with its various phases and implications, and how accurately he described its pragmatic functioning among both the Jews and the Christians within his observation. Without the truly astonishing susceptibility that enabled him to appropriate that theory, his own revelation on Mt. Ḥirā', if it had at all materialized, would most likely have remained an episode of no practical consequences. *With* it, the path before him was determined in its essential course and direction. If God's voice and word, the *qawl Allāh*, did come down to him it could only have come down in the manner he knew so well from the People of the Book: in the manner the word of God had descended to His prophets and messengers "before." And if what had come down to him was to become a "light and guidance" to others, for this, too, precedents had been firmly established "before"; it was initiated in the instance of Moses and it was "verified" in that of Jesus. To become a light and guidance for the multitude, God's word must reach them by the same clear "signs" and indisputable "evidences" by which it had reached the Jews and Christians "before." Thus the Book was bound to become the central theme of Muhammad's own message to "all the world."

He never tires of playing upon it, by repetition, expansion, variation. God Himself describes the revelation to Muhammad as "a blessed Book which We have sent down to thee that they may contemplate its signs" (38:28); "It is signs [and] evidences" (29:48); "Recite thou what has been revealed to thee of the Book of thy Lord" (18:26); "We have sent down upon thee the Book as a clarification of everything, as a guidance and [an act of] mercy" (16:91; cf. 7:50). Consult also 29:46; 39:2; 4:106; 4:113; 42:52; 28:86; 29:47.

While in these and similar utterances "the Book" is clearly what has come down from God to Muhammad, in other utterances it is what Muhammad is in turn to deal out to the people. Hence in many instances it figures in the superscriptions and the opening formulas of the individual Chapters or Sūrahs: "This is the Book" (2:1); "These are the signs of the Book" (13:1); "These are the signs of the wise Book" (10:1; 31:1); "These are the signs of the clear Book" (12:1; 26:1; 28:1); and with omission of the pronominal subject: "[This is] a Book that has been sent down to thee" (7:1). See also 11:1; 39:1; 40:1; 45:1; 46:1; cf. 32:1; 42:1. Once the Book is even replaced by Chapter: "[This is] a Sūrah which We have sent down and sanctioned, and We have sent down in it signs [and] evidences" (24:1). In three of the Sūrahs that open with an adjuration formula the Book serves as the object: "By the Book that makes clear!" (43:1; 44:1); "By the Mount! By the Book inscribed on parchment unrolled!" (52:1-3), the latter adjuration apparently referring to the Book in terms of the Sacred Scroll of the Synagogue, hence no doubt the association with the Mount, *al-ṭūr*, which term is employed by Muhammad for Mt. Sinai as the locale of the Mosaic revelation. On one of the occasions where Muhammad tells the stories of the messengers of "before," he is bid by Gabriel to enter each story in the Book: "Relate thou in the Book [the story of] Mary" (19:16); "And relate thou in the Book [the story of] Abraham" (19:42), and so forth.

Insofar as the revelation was sent down to him "from God," Muhammad conceives of it as identical in origin and function with "what had been sent down before." In this sense, he employs "the Book" as a general term which he applies indiscriminately to the revelation of Moses, to that of Jesus, and to his own revelation as well. Accordingly, the Book sent down to him had its origin in the heavenly archetype, the Mother of the Book; it was sent as a light and guidance for the people; and it was designed to share the particular function of the revelation of Jesus in that it "verified" the truth of its former manifestations. Indeed, his own revelation is not only "verifying" that truth, but it is also "vouching for it" (*muhayminan 'alayhi*)—an Aramaic term prominently employed in the religious literature of the Jews and the Christians.

Insofar, however, as his revelation was to assume human proportions and to be cast into concrete "signs" and tangible "evidences," Muhammad is aware of course that it differed from its two predecessors as the latter differed from one another. The three messages from God were manifestations of the same Book, to be sure, but they were not the same manifestations as well. The Book brought to the Israelites by Moses was the Torah, the Book of Jesus to the Christians was the Evangel, while the Book as proclaimed and recited by himself was the Koran. It is quite possible, and indeed probable, that in "Koran" (*Qur'ān*) we have an attempt on the part of the Jews of the Hejaz to form an Arabicized equivalent of *miqrâ* (< *miqrā'*), "reading, reciting," which latter came to be used in rabbinical Hebrew as a term for Scripture, thus representing a synonym of Torah. It thus lent itself well as an appellation for the particular manifestation of the Book to Muhammad, since in contrast to "Torah" and "Evangel" it sounded like a word in "clear Arabic." The important thing is that he is aware that with its appearance the religious status of the Jews and Christians has undergone a profound change. They are no longer "those who were given the Book" plain and simple, but rather "those who were given the Book before." By its new manifestation—its last installment, as it were—the Jews and Christians have been reduced to owners of *part* of the Book and, unless they accept the added signs and evidences of the Koran, they no longer adhere to all of the Book. And a further point of distinction is that the new manifestation of the Book has been in Arabic. But this did not alter its equality in essence with the Torah and the Evangel; on the contrary: his proclamation of the Koran in clear, lucid Arabic, rather than in the foreign language of those who were given the Book before, was the surest kind of proof of its direct descendence from God (cf. 16:105).

The fact of the matter is that Muhammad emulates the Jewish-Christian theory of revelation even when stressing the distinction of his own message. Indeed, one gains the definite impression that, in his effort to make converts for his Book, he employs the very same arguments which in the past he had heard the Jews and Christians use when endeavoring to convert him and others to *their* Book; so that his pleading with them has the force of an *argumentum ad concesso*: "Oh, ye to whom the Book has been given, believe ye in what We have [now] sent down to confirm what ye possess" (4:50); "This Koran is not such as to have been invented [by anyone] apart from God; but it is a confirmation of what preceded it and a specification of the Book" (10:38). See also 3:2; 10:94; 35:28 f.; 3:22; 2:95.

Precisely this is the quintessence of his challenge: that the Arabic Koran is nothing but a manifestation of the Book on a par with its previous manifestations, and those who accept or reject the one must of necessity accept or reject the other. He is never more solemn than when emphasizing the identity of the Koran as the Book. He makes God say: "Behold We have made it [the Book] an Arabic Koran . . . and behold it was in the Mother of the Book with Us" (43:2-3); "Verily, it is a Koran noble, in a Book treasured" (56:76 f.); "Preceding it was the Book of Moses, a model and [an act of] mercy; and this is but a verifying Book in Arabic speech" (46:11). Consult also 39:29; 41:2; 12:2; 22:112; 13:37; 42:5; 36:1; 15:1; 27:1; 18:1.

A New People of the Book

Throughout the vicissitudes of his career, Muhammad upheld uppermost the idea not only of a single God of the world but also—and in this he belonged to a large class of religious dreamers and reformers before and after him—of mankind as a single community united in the belief of such a God. In the past, so he had learned, individual heroes and prophets had made strides towards the realization of this idea, but Moses was the first to initiate monotheism as a binding force; and he did so by the evidence and covenant of the Torah, a revelation and manifestation of God's own Book sent down to him by God Himself; thus he succeeded in uniting the Israelites in the belief of a single God of the world. Subsequently, when because of differences and disagreements among the Israelites a need arose to reinforce the work of Moses, to rededicate the people to their inheritance, this was done by a further manifestation of God's Book: by the Evangel sent down to Jesus that he might reunite the people in God, "my Lord and your Lord"; that he might serve as an "example to the children of Israel," verify the revelation in their possession, and solve the differences among them; but his message, too, like that of Moses was only partly successful (3:44; 5:48 ff.; 43:5-9; 61:6, 14).

Thus a new reinforcement was needed; and it was effected by a still further manifestation of God's Book and he, Muhammad, was chosen as the messenger. "It was sent down upon him from God with the truth to verify, and to vouch for, whatever manifestation of the Book had previously been sent down" (5:52). He was made a messenger of the one God of the world to all of the human race (34:27; 7:157 f.), and there can be no doubt that he firmly believed that he would succeed in bringing to full realization the work begun by Moses and continued by Jesus. He was equipped with powerful evidence and impregnable premises to win over the People of the Book: their own evidence, the premises of their own logic. They could not possibly accept one manifestation of God's Book and reject another or believe some of His messengers and disbelieve others (4:149). To win over the pagans, he was equipped with the wonder of God's revelation having now come down as an Arabic Koran. He was even equipped to convert the Jinn; having listened to a recitation of the Koran, they went back to their kinsfolk and said: "We have heard a Book which has been sent down after Moses, verifying what preceded it, guiding to the Truth" (46:29; cf. 72:1). Yet, it was precisely in his message to the People of the Book, to whom it merely verified their own truth and was only sent to clarify their disagreements among themselves (16:66), that he too failed. To be sure, they did not weaken the force of his argument. He had challenged them to admit that their revelation and his were at one, "that we shall serve naught but God" (3:55, 57). Over against the mutual denunciations of Jews and Christians (2:107), he had called upon them to unite in their own belief of a single God by accepting "the Torah and the Evangel and what has [now] been set down from your Lord." But far from having this effect, his revelation only strengthened them in their arrogance and unbelief (5:72). And consistent with the logic of his plea is the comfort which God accorded him in his disappointment over its failure: "If they reject thee, messengers have surely been rejected before thy time who had come with the evidences and the Psalms and the light-giving Book" (3:181; cf. 6:34; 22:43; 35:4, 23).

He did succeed in converting his own people to the belief in a single God of the world and in His Book. This was the beginning of Islam, to remain for all time its basis: that the belief in God and the belief in the Book are tantamount to each other. In the formal wording of this tenet *There is no god but Allah* (the God)—*Muhammad is the messenger of Allah*, whereby *messenger* merely means the bringer of Allah's message (*risālah*), the human transmitter of the Book (5:71; 6:124, and elsewhere). In Himself God is "the Lord of heavens and earth," "the creator of all things," but in relation to the worshiper "Allah is my protector who has sent down the Book" (7:195). Therein lay for Muhammad the crucial test of his mission, the sole criterion of his triumph. The transference was complete, thoroughgoing and astonishingly consistent. All the synonyms of the Book in the hands of the Jews and Christians, all the adjectives and attributes which we have seen him use of the Torah and the Evangel, he has been led to apply to his own manifestation of God's Book: it is or it offers light, guidance, wisdom, salvation, prophethood, signs, evidences. The Book is at once the premise, the demonstration, and the object of his teaching to the Arabians whom he had already won over and of his pleadings with those still to be converted.

To the Jews and Christians Muhammad demonstrated the binding force of his message by its being but a new manifestation of their own Book. To the Arabians, on the other hand, he demonstrates his message as no less binding, seeing that their pagan lore has no Book and no evidence to stand on. Whatever counterarguments were offered by the latter he holds to be just as gratuitous as those advanced by the former. Some of the Arabians had maintained that in refusing to follow his message from Allah they merely obeyed the legacy of their fathers and their gods. But how can anyone "argue about Allah without knowledge or guidance or a light-giving Book?" (22:8; 39:19); "Do ye own a Book in which ye study?" (68:37); see also 43:20; 35:38; cf. 46:3; 34:43. Others had maintained that his message did not involve them, since it verified a Book that was sent down for two other parties, the Jews and the Christians. But this was no longer true now that the new evidence had come with its new guidance and mercy (6:157 f.). "We have sent among you a messenger, one of your own, to recite to you our signs, to purify you, to teach you the Book and the Wisdom, and to teach you what ye did not know before" (2:146; cf. 3:158; 62:2). Through him they have now become a People of the Book no less than the Jews and the Christians. And while he has failed to unite the latter under the new manifestation, he admonishes his followers to unite in the "belief in all of the

Book" (3:115), not merely in one particular manifestation of it.

Muhammad's formulation of the basic tenet of Islam that may well be older than the one quoted above is: "Say ye: We believe in Allah and what has been sent down to us, and what has been sent down to Abraham and Ishmael and Isaac and Jacob and the Patriarchs, and what has been given to Moses and Jesus, and what has been given to the Prophets from their Lord; we make no distinction between any of them; it is to Him that we are submissive" (2:130; 3:78). In a variant of the same formula a phrase is added that obviously reflects Israel's reply to Moses in Deuteronomy 5:27. Here Muhammad and his followers "believe in Allah and His angels and His Books and His messengers . . . and they say: We shall hear and obey" (2:285).

In arguing with Jews and Christians, Muhammad's followers are to stress this universalistic scope of their basic tenet: "Say ye: We believe in what has been sent down to us and [also in what] has been sent down to you; our God and your God are one and it is to Him that we are submissive (29:45; 42:14). First and above all, however, they are to believe in Allah's messenger from among themselves and his manifestation of the Book in their own clear Arabic language (4:135; cf. 26:193 ff.), to follow it (6:156), to read it and to recite it (73:20; 35:26; 2:115), to study it (cf. 68:37), to cleave to it (7:169). Muhammad has even given his followers the exact date in which "the Koran was sent down as a guidance to men and as evidences of the guidance and salvation": in the month of Ramaḍān, in the Night of al-Qadr (2:181; 97:1; cf. 44:1 f.), which month and night were to assume great religious significance for his followers. "Fasting [of Ramaḍān] was prescribed for you as it was ordered to those before you" (2:179). The rabbis, too, it will be remembered, had established the date of the giving of the Torah; it was the sixth day of Sīwān, the date of the Feast of Weeks; and it is entirely possible that already the Jews of Medina knew of the great mystical significance of the *Night of Šābû-*

'ôt. To Muhammad the Night of al-Qadr is better than a thousand months; "in it the angels and the spirit came down by permission of their Lord" (97:4). The Midrash speaks of thousands of angels that ascended with God upon Sinai to witness the revelation of the Torah (Exod. R. 29:2).

Thus Islam was founded on a ready-made theory of revelation that had resulted from the gradual development of the religious history of Judaism: the theory of revelation as a Holy Script, a heavenly emanated Book. It was in consequence of this theory that Jews and Christians had been the universal disseminators of the art of writing and, as we have seen, had greatly contributed to the spread of literacy in the Hejaz. And it was by Muhammad's forthright, thoroughgoing, persistent emulation of this theory—including the peculiarly Christian phase of Jesus' having come to fulfill the revelation of Moses—that Islam emerged as the religion of a newly revealed Book, the Prophet reciting an Arabic Book of God to the community of his followers. Having adapted the Torah and the Evangel as the combined model of his Koran, he also found the technical means by which to record it in writing: they had been made available thanks to the very People of the Book who provided him with that model. We have seen that Muhammad's secretary, Zayd ibn-Thābit, who in Moslem tradition is prominently associated with recording and editing the Koran, acquired the art of writing "in Hebrew" from the Jews of Medina: undoubtedly it was also from them, directly or indirectly, that he had learned to write "in Arabic" as well.

Muhammad was once given the remarkable assurance from Allah that, if those who had been given the Book—namely, the Jews and the Christians—should fail to accept his message, the Book would then be entrusted to the custody of another people; that is, to the custody of the people who did accept his message (6:89). In its positive aspect, this prediction was to come true to the fullest extent. In accepting Muhammad's message of a single God of the world, the Arabians had *ipso facto* become a People of the Book, and this more literally so than had ever been the case either of the Jews or the Christians. What in Judaism and Christianity had been the result of a long and gradual development, an outgrowth of evolution under a great variety of political constellations, cultural changes and religious personalities, came to the Arabians with revolutionary swiftness; it was accomplished by the deed of a single man and was completed in a single generation. Within a few decades after its conception and proclamation, the world of the Arabians became centered for all time on the Arabic documentation of the word and will of God. And with the sweeping spread of Islam, an ever wider multitude of communities became engrossed in a book, reading and reciting it, studying and expounding it, copying and recopying it.

When, during the assembly of al-Jābiyah, where he was to be elected to the caliphate, Marwān ibn-al-Ḥakam was called on by a visitor, the latter found this seasoned statesman and general sitting "in a tent, his armor by his side, his spear stuck into the ground nearby, his horse tied to the side of the tent, and the Book in front of him; he was reading the Koran." The assembly at al-Jābiyah took place about the year 65 after the Flight. This picture of a noble Arab from the Hejaz had been the same for many centuries. But since the Flight something had been added to the habitude of the roaming and raiding Sheikh; a new item of equipment: a copy of the Koran; and a new mode of occupation: reading. The illiteracy of the Jāhilīyah had been replaced by a documented monotheism. In taking as a model the Torah of Moses and the Evangel of Jesus, Muhammad furnished his people with a Book that inaugurated one of the greatest periods of recorded literature: the written literature of the Arabs.

B. SUBSTANCE OF REVELATION

Manner of Acquisition

By the design of its human transmitter as well as by its actual function, the Koran is a document of the same class, of the same religious-historical category, as the canonical writings of Judaism and Christianity. To Moslems, the Book of Muhammad is what he intended it to be: a counterpart of what the Torah is to Jews and Scripture is to Christians. Indeed, in one important aspect the Moslem concept of the Koran as a literal transcript of Allah's revelation to Muhammad is even more pragmatical, more realistic, than the corresponding Jewish-Christian concept of the Bible. We have already referred to the long evolution by which the scope and theory of revelation had been crystallized in the two older religions, in contrast to the deliberate, emulative process under which the Koran was produced. It might be said that Muhammad was his own Ezra, or that the Koran was its own Deuteronomy. The simple truth is that, for once, we have here the entire canon of a revealed religion made articulate by its ultimate human transmitter. There is no fusion of sources here; no synopsis of different ages, schools and strata; no posterior compilation of trusting hearsay and pious fable. From the beginning to the end, the Koran is the genuine pronouncement by Muhammad of what he believed to be God's revelation to him, the authentic record of his teachings as the messenger of Allah.

He himself would thus suggest a literal equation between Koran and Scripture rather than an equation of function or category. In fact, he wants his followers to believe, and no doubt he firmly believes himself, that the very substance of Scripture has been recast for him from Heaven, for the purpose of making it part of the Koran. We recall how he is told to relate "in the Book" the story of Mary, of Moses, of Abraham; in the opening of his story of Joseph in Egypt he is told: "These are the signs of the clarifying Book. Surely, We have sent it down as an Arabic Koran, perchance ye might understand. We Ourselves shall recount to thee the best of narrations in revealing to thee this Koran" (12:1-3). At first sight, a reader versed in Scripture would find this to be true in the sense that a very considerable bulk of biblical matter appears to be actually "recounted" in solemn Arabic style throughout the koranic revelation: narratives and episodes, admonitions and maxims, rules of religious practice and regulations of pious conduct, to say nothing of incidental allusions and references of one kind or another. And, offhand, such a reader would naturally take this to indicate direct dependence of the Koran on the Torah of Moses and the Evangel of Jesus, both of which it aims to reinforce and reaffirm. In reality, however, nothing could be more gratuitous than such an inference.

We come here upon one of the most vital contributions of modern research to the understanding of the genesis of Islam. With virtually no dissent, Western scholars have been led to the recognition that Muhammad cannot possibly have had direct, firsthand acquaintance with Scripture—notwithstanding his constant appeal to matters and persons of biblical history and the bona fide implications that his familiarity with things biblical were of the most intimate kind. "Not only the Hebrew original but any sort of a translation would surely have precluded the gross discrepancies, inaccuracies and delusions he exhibits, almost invariably, when his revelation involves data from the Old Testament or, for that matter, from the New Testament." The decisive thing, however, is that in a great many instances where a biblical element appears misrepresented or distorted in the revelation of Muhammad, the very same misrepresentation and distortion can be shown to recur in postbiblical sources as homiletical or expository embellishments characteristic of the treatment of Scripture both in the Jewish Synagogue and in the Christian Church. Indeed, his "recounting" of biblical materials, while entirely out of keeping with their corresponding Scriptural prototypes, agrees with the exposition of the same materials in noncanonical literature so often and so closely that his knowledge of this literature, especially of rabbinical Agada, would seem to be astonishingly wide, solid and versatile. Yet, it is altogether out of the question that Muhammad had direct access to the written works of the Agada or any other branch of postbiblical literature, either rabbinical or patristic. If, for all his glowing "recounting" and incessant references, the actual documents of the Torah and the Evangel were inaccessible to him, how much more must this have been the case of the highly technical rabbinical writings, which he never proposes to "recount," to which he never refers as a source, of which he does not mention a single specific title, school or authority.

The situation becomes clear once we recognize that Muhammad had acquired his entire store of knowledge about Scripture, and about Judaism and Christianity in general, through oral channels and personal observation during a long period of association with the People of the Book. His was the case of a pagan converted to monotheism, who absorbed its theory and practice by attending services and pious assemblies of worshipers, by listening at the feet of popular preachers and missionaries, but who never read a line of Scripture, of a breviary, or even of a hymnbook. He was engrossed in the discourses telling about revelations of the one God of the world in times bygone, about the Book of God given to chosen messengers as a light and guidance for the children of Israel; he was fascinated by observances "written" by God "upon" the worshipers, such as prayer, fast, almsgiving. How was he to distinguish between the biblical nucleus and the homiletic embellishment, or to realize that various passages from the Book had been woven together into a single sermon or liturgy, or to discern the true nature of a given observance? To be sure, this proved a most favorable circumstance when, following his prophetic call, he began to draw on the store of knowledge he had absorbed. Had he acquired it from books, it is hardly conceivable that he would have ever come to make prophetic use of it: that he would have experienced the "recounting" from heaven of matter made hard and fast in a text before him. As it was, he merely heard now from Gabriel what he had heard before in worshipful assemblies and pious recitals, in various applications and connections—except that now he heard it in the lofty, solemn recital of lucid and pure Arabic instead of the "barbaric" vernacular of the Jewish and Christian discourses with their inevitable admixture of Hebrew-Aramaic and Syriac-Greek, respectively.

Hence we may specify the matter of equation as follows: (1) By the emulative design of its author and its actual historical function, the Koran occupies in Islam the position which in Judaism and Christianity is held by the canonical writings. (2) To the extent, however, to which it "recounts" biblical material and embodies a mass of Jewish and Christian lore, the ultimate sources of its substance must be looked for not in Scripture itself but rather in the postcanonical periphery of Scripture: in the Agada, the Targum, the Midrash of the Jews, and the apocryphal, patristic, homiletical and liturgical literature of the Christians. (3) But the actual, immediate sources from which Muhammad had drawn his knowledge of that material and that lore were oral and personal rather than written and literary: divine services such as held daily in the Synagogue and the Church, especially on Sabbath, Sunday, holidays; sermons and discourses by Jewish and Christian preachers; probably also disputes between learned Jews, Christians, and pagans, such as had been universal in the Near East ever since the beginning of the Christian, if not indeed the Hellenistic, period; last, not least, private conversations with devout individuals, Jewish and Christian, perhaps also Gnostic, missionaries eager to make a good proselyte out of the impressionable pagan.

On evidence from the substance of the Koran in the sense just described, the largest contribution to this substance would have come from Judaism. The volume and nature of Jewish lore appropriated by Muhammad would thus indicate that his association with Jews had continued for a long period of time and had been of the closest thinkable kind. That this did not hinder him from absorbing a very considerable amount of Christian lore as well, thus maintaining correspondingly close contact with Christians, is not at all surprising. In themselves, we may assume, the Jews and Christians of the Hejaz exhibited much more strongly the elements they had in common than those in which they differed. A more or less Judaized Christianity may be said to have been the rule in the Orient during the period in question. To Muhammad, a recent and ardent convert to monotheism, the mutual segregation and denunciation of Jews and Christians must have appeared inexplicable. Later he finds for this particularism of the People of the Book words of stern rebuke; and, as we have seen, he warns his followers to make no distinction between any of God's prophets. Apparently, he had also associated with more than one brand of Christians. His emphatic rejection of the doctrine of Sonship combined with his "recounting" of Mary's immaculate conception and of Jesus' having been "empowered" by the Holy Spirit, especially his reference to the disagreement of "the sects" (*al-aḥzāb*) with regard to the question of Sonship, would seem to point that the Christians of his personal contact included both Nestorians and Monophysites (cf. 19:36-38; 43:64 ff.). Such utterances of Muhammad as "He [God] did not beget, nor was He begotten"; "He [Jesus] was only a servant upon whom We bestowed grace," only "a messenger of Allah" (112:3; 43:59; 4:169), may well reflect a radical school of monophysitism, such as those termed *Phthartolotrae* among the followers of Severus of Antioch.

In receiving instruction in their divine lore from both Jews and Christians, or even different sects of Christians, and in making this eclectic instruction part of the Koran, Muhammad merely manifests the one feature in the religious make-up of his personality which, as we have noted above, remains predominant throughout his career as a prophet. We recall how he relishes the stories of Abraham who "was a heathen yet not one of the idolators"; how he pleads with the People of the Book to unite into one community of the one God of the world; and how, even after his break with the Jews and Christians, he admonishes his followers to stress the more comprehensive scope of their creed: their belief in all of God's Books, all messengers, all prophets. He virtually implies that the very eclecticism in the substance of the Koran is a mark of the advance of its monotheism as compared with that of the Books "that have been revealed before" (cf. 48:28). In all his polemics against the Jews and Christians the underlying premise is that because of their particularistic discriminations they fall short of being good enough monotheists. Since in his own words he and his followers are to "make no distinction between any of God's prophets" even after he had received the Book in clear Arabic, how much less was he to make such a distinction while still in need of light and guidance himself.

Perhaps the clearest postulation of what might be termed Muhammad's interconfessionalism is his utterance to the effect that salvation is not confined to this or that group or sect but may be secured by anyone upon fulfillment of certain basic conditions regardless of his particular ecclesiastic affiliation: by "those who have believed [in his own message], and those who have been Jews, and the Christians, and the Ṣābians, anyone who believes in God, and the Last Day, and acts uprightly" (2:59; cf. 5:73). Just who the Ṣābians were, Mandaeans or some other Gnostics, whether they too had contributed to Muhammad's religious education and, hence, perhaps also to the substance of the Koran, is a question that cannot at present be answered with certainty. Very possibly, Muhammad knew of them, as well as of the Magians, only by name; as groups who, although neither Jews, nor Christians, nor Moslems, nevertheless believed in God and the Hereafter and thus fulfilled the primary conditions of salvation. If so, his "Ṣābians" or "the Ṣābians . . . and the Magians" (22:17) would have a connotation not unlike that of the "publicans and sinners" of the New Testament.

Muhammad's Early Message

In discussing the *theory* of revelation followed by Muhammad in his conception and composition of the Koran, we have referred to his utterances without regard to the age or period of the individual Sūrahs in which those utterances occur. For a proper understanding of the *substance* of his revelation, however, the criterion of age and period is highly important and often indeed decisive. Yet, within the limited scope of the present discussion, it must suffice to survey only those of his utterances that represent the earliest stage of his teaching: the Sūrahs that have been recognized, by Moslem tradition as well as modern investigation, as having been composed during the first period of his mission in Mecca. Beforehand we would expect these Sūrahs to differ from those of the later Meccan periods, and more so from those of the Medinan period, in accordance with the far-reaching changes which his status—social, political and above all psychological—was to undergo during the twenty-odd years of his activity as a messenger of God. The difference is one of style and form no less than of scope and content. In the early Sūrahs we have to do with oracle-like pronouncements of a prophet and visionary: brief, tense, compact, impassioned, struggling for expression, cryptic in word and phrase, breathless and overwhelmed with his ineffable object. Eventually his style was to become more calm and fluent and, at the same time, more profuse and more vindicative, until in the end his discourses assumed the polish and eloquence of a self-assured lawgiver, of a cunning statesman, or of a long-winded yet popular preacher. In contents, his early message is of extreme simplicity; it is marked by complete absence of either ritual or legal elements of any kind. What it offers is an outline, the barest rudiments, of monotheistic theology. God is One, He has no equal; He is the creator of the universe and His care provides bountiful sustenance for man and beast (argument from creation); in the past He had punished peoples for their wrongdoing (argument from history); in the future He will judge man according to his deeds; rewarding obedience with the delights of Paradise and requiting disobedience with the scourge of Hellfire; the coming of this eschatological Judgment will be preceded by a universal cataclysm: the heavens will be rent, the earth will quake, the stars will be scattered, the seas will boil up, the mountains will soften and move, and so forth.

We see at a glance that what Muhammad proclaims in the

earliest period of his mission is a set of beliefs that had long been the common property of the two older monotheistic religions—beliefs variously formulated and incessantly alluded to in the writings, the prayers, the everyday practice of the People of the Book. This and the fact of the very general character, the often vague context, and the always exalted wording of Muhammad's formulations make it impossible to determine their ultimate, literary sources with any degree of certainty—at least as far as his principal theses are concerned. For each of these theses of his early message—oneness, creation, judgment-cataclysm—Jewish and Christian writings offer so great a variety of parallels as to preclude identification in particular. Nevertheless, we find even here, in the earliest Sūrahs of the Koran, all the evidence that could be desired as to the general nature of Muhammad's immediate, oral sources. By way of illustration a few out of the great mass of pertinent details may be mentioned here.

Muhammad refers to God very often as *rabb*, "lord," sometimes as *rabb al-'ālamīn*, "lord of the worlds" (56:79; 82:29; 83:6); occasionally he speaks of God as *al-raḥmān*, "the Merciful" (55:1; 78:3 f.); the latter two manners of reference represent an exact counterpart of the *ribbôn hâ-'ôlāmîm* and *hâ-raḥmân* frequently used in Jewish liturgy as well as in the Agada—as has been noted by scholars.

The standard formula of the Moslem credo to which we have referred above does not occur in the early Sūrahs. Instead, we find God's oneness here expressed by Muhammad in the phrase *Allāh aḥad* (112:1) "God is one," in striking agreement with the final phrase of the *Shema* formula (Deut. 6:4): *Yahweh 'äḥād*. The Talmud recommends that the word *'äḥād* be dwelt on ("lengthened") in recital, and this became the actual practice. Muhammad could thus have heard the very phrase *Allāh aḥad* recited daily with great emphasis both by individual Jews and by a Jewish congregation.

Negatively God's oneness is expressed by Muhammad in the admonition "and do ye not set beside Allah another god"

(51:51), the last two words (*ilāhan ākhar*) exhibiting a literal rendering of the corresponding two words (*ălôhîm 'aḥērîm*) in the First Commandment (Exod. 20:3; Deut. 5:7).

Commenting on Genesis 2:2, the Midrash states that God's creation of the world was "without toil or fatigue." This or a similar homily is clearly reflected in the early koranic utterance: "We have created the heavens and the earth and what is between them in six days, and no fatigue affected Us" (50:37). Along with the biblical "six days," Muhammad's teaching of creation includes also the purely agadic notion of "seven heavens" (78:12 and frequently in younger Sūrahs).

The utterance "He created man from clay like pottery" (55:13) might be taken to paraphrase the biblical simile of the "clay in the hands of the potter" (Jer. 18:6) or its parallels in younger scripture (especially Sirach 33:13; Romans 9:21); more likely we have here a reflection of the liturgical use of the biblical simile among the People of the Book. To this day the order for the Day of Atonement includes a liturgical poem based on that simile.

In his argument from creation Muhammad often points to man's lowly origin: he was created "from a drop" (80:18 and frequently elsewhere), "from water dripping" (86:6) and more specifically "a drop of semen emitted in desire" (75:37). In the early Sūrahs this is connected with man's death and his ultimate Judgment. Puzzling as the connection would seem at first, it becomes admirably clear when Muhammad's utterances in question are compared with a homily found in the Mishnah, where the same three phenomena are recommended as objects of contemplation: "Consider three things and thou wilt not come into the realm of sin. . . . (1) Whence thou comest—from a drop fetid. (2) Whither thou goest—to a place of dust, worms and maggots. (3) And before whom thou art to give answer and account—before the King of the kings of kings, the Holy One, Blessed be He." One of Muhammad's homilies begins very much in the same manner: "Let man consider—from what was he created? He was created from water dripping. . . . Verily He has power to bring him back, on the day when the secrets will be tried" (86:5-9). Another homily reads: "From what kind of thing did He create him? From a drop! . . . Then He makes him die and buries him. Then when He wills, He makes him rise again" (80:17-22). Note that the word for "drop" used by Muhammad (*nuṭfah*) is a true equivalent of the Mishnaic word (*ṭippâ*) and that the same is true of the word for "consider" (*histakkēl-falyanẓur*); also, that the particular Mishnah tract, because of its edifying and ethical character, enjoyed wide and quasi-liturgical popularity. It is all but impossible to escape the impression that what Muhammad offers here he had very often heard, in substance and to some extent even in wording, from the mouth of Jewish preachers discoursing upon the above Mishnah (*Aboth* 3:1) before an Arabic-speaking congregation.

Muhammad seems to lay great stress on the dichotomal principle of creation. Not only was man created "in pairs, male and female" (51:49; cf. 75:39; 78:8), but God says, "Of everything We have created pairs" (51:49), even of every fruit in Paradise and indeed of Paradise itself (55:46-52). The Midrash (Deut. R. 2:22) too makes God say that all creation was "in pairs," heaven and earth, sun and moon, man and woman, this world and the hereafter; and, again, the word used by Muhammad (*zawj*) is identical with that of the Midrash (*zūḡ*), which here is especially remarkable, perhaps, since it is a Greek loan-word (*zeugos*). It is conceivable, however, that Muhammad reflects here impressions he had received from conversations with Gnostics.

The absoluteness of God's power, especially in relation to the fate of man, is frequently dwelt on by Muhammad throughout the Koran. In an early Sūrah we come upon the utterance: "It is He who causes to laugh, and causes to weep. And it is He who causes to die and causes to live" (53:44 f.). At once we are reminded of the biblical words "I cause to die, and I cause to live; I wound, and I heal" (Deut. 32:39), and this connection accounts well for the peculiar order to die-to live in the koranic passage. The same order in the biblical passage is taken by the Talmud to hint at the doctrine of resurrection, which latter forms a most favorite topic of the Agada. When a preacher is called upon to deliver a homily in praise of God, he winds up with the benediction: "Praised art Thou, O Lord, who restores the dead to life" (B. Ket. 8 b; Sanh. 91b). An all but identical phrase is used by Muhammad in discoursing upon God's power over man: "Is not That One capable of restoring the dead to life?" (75:39). If Muhammad was in the habit of visiting synagogues, he could not have failed to hear this very benediction chanted in the daily service.

Still another eschatological benediction of the daily prayer of the Synagogue would seem to be reflected in Muhammad's early message. He describes the time of Judgment as "the day when the trumpet shall be blown and ye shall come in crowds" (78:18); "When on the trumpet shall be blown a single blast" (69:13); "A blast shall be blown on the trumpet [to announce]: This is the day of threat" (50:19); and in a younger Sūrah: "The trumpet shall be blown and We shall gather them together" (18:99). The particular benediction of the synagogue service begins with the words: "Blow on the great trumpet for our redemption" and ends with the formula: "Praised be Thou, O Lord, gatherer of the dispersed of His people Israel." Of course, both Jews and Christians could have told him of the role of the great trumpet at the "end of days" and quote witnesses from the Book (such as Is. 27:13; Joel 2:1; Matt. 24:31) and many, and much more outspoken, witnesses from postcanonical writings.

In the eschatology of the Koran—as similarly in that of Judaism and Christianity—universal cataclysm, resurrection, and judgment form one great complex of the things to come. Muhammad refers to this complex in terms of the vivid imagery characteristic of his early utterances: "the Event" (56:1), "the Portending" (53:8), "the Crack" (80:33), "the Striking" (101:1). But already in his early message he employs the terminology deeply rooted in the language of the two older religions: "the Day of Judgment" (82:17 f.; 83:11), "the Day of Resurrection" (68:19), "the Day of Separation" (77:13 f.; 78:17), "the Hour" (54:1), "the Hereafter" in contrast to "this world" (53:28-30), "Gardens of Delight" or even—with direct reference to the Hebrew word for paradise—"Gardens of 'Adn" (68:34; 98:7), "Gehenna" or even "the fire of Gehenna" (85:10; 89:24; 98:5).

Concerning the events to come, Muhammad cites an age-old query: "When is the Day of Judgment?" (51:12); "When is the Day of Resurrection?" (75:6); "They will ask you about the Hour: When is its arrival?" (79:42). Beginning with Daniel (12:6), we find this question recurring in Old Testament apocryphal, rabbinical, and Christian writings: "When shall these things come to pass?" "When is the Messiah to come?" "When shall these things be?" Already in Daniel these "things are closed up and sealed" (12:9), and in later times speculation about the *end* was so widespread as to lead to the stern censorship of a query which, in God's design, was to remain unknown to man. Typical of the many rabbinical utterances is one based on the verse: "The day of vengeance is in mine heart" (Is. 63:4). In the interpretation of a rabbi: "To mine heart I revealed it, but not [even] to the ministering angels did I reveal it" (B. Sanh. 99 a). And in agreement with this attitude of the Agada are the words of Jesus: "Of that day and hour knows no one, no, not [even] the angels in heaven, but my Father" (Matt. 24:31). Muhammad's own reply to the query about the Hour is: "Unto thy Lord is [the knowledge of] its coming" (79:44); and in a younger Sūrah: "The knowledge of it is with my Lord only; no one will reveal it as to its time but He" (7:186). There can be little doubt that Muhammad had heard this agonizing subject discoursed upon a great many times by Jews or Christians, most likely by them both.

From what we have seen, Muhammad's early message culminates in describing the destiny of man in future life.

"When the souls shall be paired [with their bodies] . . . when the pages shall be spread open" (81:7, 10), "on that day the people shall come forth separately that they may be shown their works: he who has done a particle's weight of good, shall see it; and he who has done a particle's weight of evil, shall see it" (99:6-8); "As for him whose balances are heavy, he shall be in a life pleasing; but as for him whose balances are light, his mother shall be . . . a raging fire" (101:5-8); for, as Muhammad says in a younger Sūrah, "the balance that day will be the verdict" (7:7). Every one of these features re-echoes numerous apocryphal and agadic notions: the reuniting of the soul with its body, the opening of the heavenly Books in which man's deeds are recorded, the minute balancing of merit and guilt on the scale of justice, the exact proportion of merit and reward, of guilt and punishment.

One specific feature is particularly noteworthy. The Agada, following a widespread notion of folklore which occasionally finds expression in Scripture (e.g., Qoh. 10:2), identifies good and evil with the right hand and left hand, respectively. Thus Paradise is to the right, while Hell is to the left, of God; of the angels that assist God in the Day of Judgment, some give their verdict to the right, others to the left, according to whether the verdict is one of merit or of guilt; the two basic instincts of man, the good one (*yēṣär ṭôb*) and the evil one (*yēṣär ra'*), are placed on his right side and his left side, respectively; and in the classical separation of the sheep from the goats, the former are "on His right," and the latter "on His left" (Matt. 25:33; Cant. R. 1:45; Numb. R. 22:8). We thus understand why Muhammad refers to the two classes of man in the Hereafter as "fellows of the right" and "fellows of the left," respectively (90:17 f.); why, in describing the fate of man in the Hereafter, Muhammad says that he who will be given his book (i.e. the heavenly record of his earthly works) into his right hand shall enter Paradise, whereas he who will be given his book into his left hand shall be condemned to Hellfire (69:19, 25; cf. 84:

7 ff.); and that is what Muhammad has in mind when hinting, vaguely, at two forces that "meet" in man, "[one] on the right and [one] on the left" (50:16)—utterances that would remain extremely enigmatic unless they were formulated in an environment intimately familiar with the agadic ideology to which we have just referred.

Muhammad, however, knows also of another division of men on the Day of Judgment: a division not into two but rather into three classes. He speaks of the triple division only once (Sūrah 56), but here at considerable length, and he is apparently at great pains to impress the lesson upon his listeners. "When the earth is greatly shaken, and the mountains are mightily pounded, and become scattered dust, ye shall be three groups: (a) The fellows of the right—what are the fellows of the right? (b) The fellows of the left—what are the fellows of the left? And (c) the preceding ones, the preceding ones" (4-10). No interrogative phrase is attached to the mention of the third class; instead, Muhammad offers the following amplification: "the preceding ones" are "those that are brought near in gardens of delight [and consist of] a company from former times and a few from later times" (11-14). As he proceeds to describe their respective fates, it appears that (c) is given the highest station in Paradise, while (a) is given a somewhat lower station, and (b) is condemned to Hellfire. All of this becomes clear only upon the realization that—apart from the common old division into "righteous" and "wicked"—rabbinical Judaism developed the dogma of a triple division into "very righteous," "very wicked," and "intermediate." This applies to the annual as well as the final Judgment. Accordingly, we learn, on the one hand, that "Three groups there are [to be] on the Day of Judgment" and, on the other, that "Three books are being opened [in Heaven] on New Year's Day" (Bab. R. H. 16 b). In explaining the "intermediate" class, Rabba once said that they are people "like ourselves," the assumption being that only the great saints of the past may be classed as "very righteous" (B. Bev. 61 b). Quite obviously, then, we have in the Sūrah just quoted a homily in which an attempt is made to reconcile the double division into "right" and "left" with the triple division into "very righteous," "very wicked" and "intermediate," whereby the "fellows of the right" are made to correspond to the rabbinical "intermediate" class. Hence Muhammad makes them consist of "a company from former times and a company from later times," whereas his "preceding ones"—corresponding to the rabbinical "very righteous"—includes, as we have seen, only "a few from later times." Very possibly, the reconciliation of the two divisions is not of Muhammad's own making but reflects the type of sermons and discourses which he had long since appropriated and which he now merely "recounts."

The earthly conduct by which man earns reward or punishment in future life is described in the early Sūrahs in few and simple terms. They involve no ritual or legalistic elements; instead, they stress matters of caritative and devotional character only. Clearest perhaps is a description found in Sūrah 90: "[Those endeavoring] to set bondmen free; to feed on a day of famine an orphan of kin, or a destitute lowly; then, to be among those who have believed and who counsel one another in endurance and compassion—these are the fellows of the right hand" (13-18). Similarly: "They provide food, for His love's sake, for the poor, the orphan and the prisoner" (76:8). The scourge of fire shall avoid him "who gives of his property, acts charitably, though no one had done him a favor to be repaid, but only out of longing for the countenance of his Lord, the Most High" (92:18-20). Sometimes to the elements of charity and belief that of prayer is added—quite obviously in an as yet nonritual sense. "Surely, the God-fearing ones are amongst gardens and fountains [of Paradise]. . . . They were wont [in their earthly life] to slumber but little of the night and to pray for forgiveness [also] in the mornings; of their possessions [they gave] a due share to the beggar and the outcast" (51:15-19). Sometimes, too, the three elements are tersely combined into a triad: "Happy is [in the Hereafter] who had been charitable, mindful of the name of God, and given to prayer" (87:14 f.); "those who pray continually, and those in whose wealth there is a due share for the beggar and the destitute, and those who affirm the truth of the Day of Judgment" (70:23-26). Contrarily, the pangs of Hellfire are imposed upon the fellow of the left hand because "he used not to believe in God, the Mighty, nor did he urge the feeding of the poor" (69:33 f.); "he did not affirm [the truth of God] nor did he pray; but he belied [that truth] and turned away" (75:31 f.); "he was niggardly, tied up in his wealth" (92:8). Again combining the three elements: "Hast thou considered him who belies the Judgment, and he is one who repulses the orphan, and does not urge the feeding of the poor?" (cf. 107:1-5). And in self-confession of the fellows of the left: "We were not among those who prayed; nor did we feed the destitute . . . and we belied the Day of Judgment" (74:44-47). Addressing himself to this class, Muhammad says: "Ye do not honor the orphan, nor urge the feeding of the poor" (89:18 f.). And in a remarkable homily juxtaposing the care of God and the charity of man: "Did He not find thee an orphan and give [thee] shelter? Did He not find thee erring and guide [thee]? Did He not find thee destitute and make [thee] free from want? Therefore, as for the orphan do thou not oppress; and as for the beggar, do not scold" (93:6-10).

It would be tempting to see here a "recounting" or, at least, a re-echoing of Scripture. Justice to the poor, the orphan, the oppressed, is a standing topic in the teachings of the Law as well as in the sermons of the Hebrew prophets. Caritative compassion for the afflicted and destitute is no less outspoken a theme in the New Testament, where it is even prominently connected with the Day of Judgment and made a symptom of "them on His right hand" (Matt. 25:33 ff.). Nevertheless, the scriptural reminiscences here are only of psychological interest, significant merely as bearing on the mental disposition of Muhammad during the early period of his mission. For the actual, material source we have to look again to rabbinical Judaism, which in its theory and practice raised the imperative of charity to the position of "righteousness," *kat exochen*. Hence, the word for "righteousness," which in Law and Prophets, Psalms and Wisdom signifies the supreme virtue obtainable by men, came to serve as the term for charity in the language of the Synagogue (*ṣẹdāqâ*). Almost countless are the agadic sayings, exhortations, homilies, narratives, in highest praise of charity. It weighs as much as all precepts of the Torah taken together. It secures the utmost reward in the Hereafter and is a sure protection against the "Judgment of Hell" and the trials of the Last Day. God showed Moses the treasures of heaven in store for those who do works of charity, especially for those who provide for orphans. Just as sacrifice expiates the transgressions of Israel so charity expiates those of the gentiles. To neglect it is a sin as grave as heathenism. Although one has exercised it not for God's sake but for the reward it secures in the Hereafter, he is nevertheless a "perfect righteous." It renders man God-like; in fact, it makes him God's creditor; for such is the expressed word of Scripture: He that hath pity upon the poor, lendeth unto the Lord (Prov. 19:17; cf. B. Baba Bath. 10 a-b; Lev. R. 34:15; and elsewhere).

That it is this attitude of rabbinical Judaism toward charity which is reflected in Muhammad's early message would seem sufficiently clear from the respective utterances which we have cited above. But he has provided us with evidence more tangible even than those utterances. When, in the course of his mission, he posits almsgiving as a precept of Islam in the technical-legal sense of the word, one of the two terms he employs is the very word, in Arabicized pronunciation, which we have seen to have been adapted by the Synagogue as a term for the same precept (*ṣadaqah*). Again, in admonishing his listeners about the importance of charity, he often uses a figure of speech which beyond any doubt is a paraphrase of the biblical proverb which, we have just seen, the Agada emphasizes so much in the same connection: "Verily, those who give alms, men and women, they have lent God a good loan" (57:17; cf. 64:17; 73:20, etc.); unquestionably, it is purely accidental that Muhammad does not happen to use the phrase in the earlier Sūrahs. Lastly, the triad "belief-prayer-almsgiving" was to be retained by Muhammad and to be established as uppermost in the tenets of Islam. An all but identical triad, coined in the Agada, had become prominent in the liturgy of the Synagogue: "Repentance, prayer, and charity avert the harsh decree [of Heaven]."

Already in the earliest Sūrahs, Muhammad's argument from history aims at demonstrating not only how in the past God destroyed whole peoples for their iniquity but also how this might have been avoided if they had heeded the warnings and admonitions of messengers He had sent to them. Three of the instances frequently cited by Muhammad involve matter from Scripture: the story of the Flood, the destruction of Sodom and Gomorrah, and the disasters experienced by the Egyptians in the period of Exodus. Except for the element of God's visitation and the "messengers" connected, respectively, with the above incidents—Noah, Abraham and Lot, Moses—Muhammad's renderings are tantalizingly vague in themselves and altogether out of harmony with the biblical pattern of the three stories. Nor is it understandable why, out of the great store of scriptural narrations of unheeded warning followed by divine punishment, he should have chosen just these three and none other—although only one of the three stories, that of Pharaoh "warned" by Moses, actually proved his point. The situation, however, becomes wholly clear once we realize that neither the choice of material nor the oddities of his rendering are of Muhammad's own making.

As is well known, the biblical incidents in question occupy a prominent position in the homiletical, and indeed even the legal, literature of rabbinical Judaism. The generation of the Flood, we are told, and the people of Sodom were punished by the same "East Wind" by which the wicked are to be punished in Hellfire. When a case of breach of promise cannot be condemned on a point of law, the rabbis apply the formula: "He who punished the generation of the Flood is sure to punish him who does not keep his word." The Mishnah teaches that the generation of the Flood and the people of Sodom shall have "no portion in the world to come." In a Midrashic homily God is made to say to Israel: "I am a judge and I am [also] full of mercy; I am a judge to punish and I am [also] faithful in paying off reward. It is I who punished the generation of the Flood, the people of Sodom and the Egyptians; and I shall punish you as well, if ye do like their doings" (Yalq. Jer. 18:17; Mish. Ba. Meṣ. 4:2; Sanh. 10:3; Sifre Lev. 18:2).

It would thus seem that we have come here upon the ultimate, literary sphere that accounts for Muhammad's choice of biblical material for his argument from history. And nothing would be more natural than that he should have often heard the above homilies, or very similar ones, treated among the Jews of his association. Thus we also understand the nature of the oddities that mark his references to that material. They can be shown to be popular agadic embellishments of the same biblical incidents: that Noah preached repentance to his generation but preached in vain—"Before them [i.e., the Meccans] the people of Noah belied [his warning]; they belied Our servant and said: A madman" (54:9; cf. 71:1 ff.); that even Lot was something of a preacher—"The people of Lot belied the warning. . . . He did warn them of Our visitation, yet they cast out upon the warning" (54:33, 36); that the angels who on their way to Sodom visited Abraham never partook of his meal and that he surmised their true nature—"He said: Do you not eat? then he felt a dread of them" (51:27 f.; cf. 11:13); that Pharaoh claimed divinity for himself—"And he assembled [his people] and proclaimed and said: I am your Lord, Most High" (79:23 f.). It is noteworthy, too, that Muhammad uses here the word *ḥadīth*, obviously to indicate the nature of the material he is about to introduce in support of his argument. "Has there come to thee the Ḥadīth of Abraham's entertainment of the honored ones?" (51:24); "Has there come to thee the Ḥadīth of Moses?" (79:15); "Has there come to thee the Ḥadīth of the hosts, of Pharaoh and Thamud?" (85:17). I think it highly probable that the word was used by the Jews of the Hejaz to render their rabbinical *'aggādā* "an Agada, a sermon, a discourse, a pious, edifying narration." We shall have to return to the significance of this term later on.

As already indicated, the above examples do not by any means exhaust either the number or the variety of instances in which the early utterances of Muhammad manifest his material dependence on the lore of the two older religions, especially that of rabbinical Judaism. Methodically more important, however, is the evidence furnished by those utterances to the effect that, already in the initial period of his mission, Muhammad's concept of revelation and of himself as its bearer is completed in every essential particular—a concept that was to become the all-decisive contribution of Judaism and Christianity to the foundation of Islam, as we have seen. What is universally recognized as the very first Sūrah begins with the words "Recite in the name of thy Lord . . . who taught by the pen; taught man what he did not know" (96:1-4). And a Sūrah not much later in time begins with the words "The Merciful taught the Koran" (55:1). At a time when his message could not have comprised more than just a few utterances, he already refers to it, or even to the single homily he had just preached, in terms of the heavenly Book: "Nay, it is a Koran revered, in a Tablet preserved" (85:25 f.); "We Ourselves have revealed it in the Night of al-Qadr" (97:1); "Verily, it is a Koran noble, in a Book treasured . . . a revelation from the Lord of the worlds" (56:76-79); "Nay, it is an admonition . . . in pages honored, exalted, pure, by the hands of scribes noble, immaculate" (80:11-15). And just how the heavenly revelation did come down to him he describes in terms of stark realism that must have profoundly stirred his pagan listeners but which would have sounded very familiar indeed to People of the Book (81:19-24; 53:1-18).

From the beginning, his mission is "a reminder to mankind," "a warning to mankind," "an admonition to all the world" (74:34, 39; 81:27, etc.). God's commands to him are not only "Recite thou" (96:1), "Preach thou" (93:11), "Rise thou and warn" (74:2), "Admonish thou" (88:21), but also "Admonish thou by the Koran" (50:45), "Rise thou at night . . . and arrange the Koran" (73:2-4). Already now, he identifies his mission with those of the former messengers: "This is a warner, of [the species of] the warners of old" (53:37); "Surely, We have sent you a messenger, a witness over you, as We have sent a messenger to Pharaoh" (73:15); "Thus there has not come to those of before a messenger except that they said: A magician; or: A madman" (51:52). Hence he also employs interchangeably the terms that refer to the respective revelations of the "messengers." In one of his arguments from history, which includes the "warnings" of Noah, of Lot, and of Moses, he terminates the recital of each incident with the refrain, "We have facilitated the Koran to [serve as] the reminder" (54:17, 22, 32, 40). Conversely, when impressing upon the Meccans the weightiness of his own message, he once concludes with the words "Verily, this is in the ancient pages, the pages of Abraham, and of Moses" —precisely in the same sense as he often winds up a homily with phrases such as "Surely, it is an admonition," "Nay, it is a Koran," and so forth. Similarly, in pleading against one of his Meccan opponents, he exclaims, "Has he not been informed of what is in the pages of Moses, and of Abraham?" (53:37 f.).

And here we come again upon the word *ḥadīth*, to find it employed by Muhammad as one of the several interchangeable terms for the substance of his message. Thus he introduces a homily about the Day of Judgment with the words "Has there come to thee the Ḥadīth of the Enveloping?" (88:1); and in the finale of a similar homily: "So this Ḥadīth ye deem strange?" (53:59); and in an angry word of God: "So leave Me with those who belie this Ḥadīth!" (68:44). Having just reaffirmed the divine nature of his message, Muhammad exclaims: "And this Ḥadīth ye will hold light?"

(56:80); and once he challenges his opponents, "Let them produce a Ḥadīth like it, if they speak the truth!" (52:34). The latter instance is especially interesting in view of the same challenge occurring elsewhere in the Koran, with unmistakable clarity as to the object involved: "Produce ye, then, a Book from God that gives better guidance than these two [i.e., the Torah and the Koran] and I shall follow it" (28:49); and "Produce ye, then, a Sūrah like it . . . if ye speak the truth" (10:39; 2:71). It seems obvious that Muhammad would not possibly have used the term in this manner, unless it had already been charged with fitting religious significance. Precisely such a significance the word would have acquired, if, as we have suggested above, the Jews of Muhammad's association had come to use *Ḥadīth* as an Arabic equivalent of their own Agada. It is noteworthy that, eventually, Koran and Ḥadīth came to be used in Moslem lore in the sense in which the terms Torah and Talmud are used in Jewish lore: as terms for the inner and outer foundation of Islam, respectively.

Substance and Form

Despite their intense and searching style, most of the early Sūrahs tend to exhibit a rather rigid frame in structure and composition. Perhaps we should say that this is true of all Sūrahs of the first Meccan period that may be assumed to represent actual public utterances, rather than bits of private reflection and contemplation (e.g., 103; 108; 110; 113; 114). The tendency towards rigidity of pattern would have no doubt been more apparent, if all Sūrahs in question had remained free from later additions and interpolations, which is certainly not the case (cf. only 73:20). Quite clearly, Muhammad's public utterances during the period under discussion were confined to four major topics: (a) the coming of Judgment; (b) the divine nature of his message; (c) argument from creation; (d) argument from past history. Significantly enough, the oneness of God as such forms but rarely the subject matter of a Sūrah (e.g., 112) or even of part of a

Sūrah (e.g., 51:51, which, however, might have been intended as the conclusion of the "warning" of Noah); but it is clearly and unmistakably the underlying theme throughout his utterances. As a rule, a Sūrah begins with an introductory phrase, which mostly consists of one or more adjurations, and ends with a brief peroration, such as a eulogy, or a terse résumé. Often, too, the individual topics are kept quite distinct; sometimes, however, they flow into one another. To put it differently: a Sūrah may seem to be given entirely to a single topic, that of Judgment (99; 83; 70), of Creation (specifically of God's care: 93; 94), or of the Message (97); but more often two, three or even all four of the topics may be found combined into a single Sūrah. In three instances, Muhammad employs a refrain that marks off larger or smaller contextual units against one another. In one of these instances the refrain is confined to one section of the Sūrah, the section representing his argument from history (54:17, 22, 32, 40); in the two other instances the refrain is introduced early in the Sūrah and runs to the end, regardless of topics.

The substance of Muhammad's early utterances, which we have seen to be of so vastly derivative and eclectic a nature, would suggest a similar nature for their form. Is it therefore possible that in the frame and structure of the early Sūrahs we are confronted with more or less conscious emulations of the type of sermons that were in vogue among missionaries and preachers of the People of the Book at the time of Muhammad? At any rate, it would be hard to find a homily of the Fathers of the Church or of the Masters of the Agada that does not deal with one or all of the standing topics in Muhammad's early message. At the same time, the oneness of God, a constant theme of Jewish and Christian theologians in the Middle Ages, is rarely in the center, though always at the bottom of midrashic homilies. Again, might not the antiphonal arrangement so characteristic of Jewish and Christian liturgy have led Muhammad to his device of a refrain? In themselves, the adjurations represent no doubt a rhetorical device genuinely Arabic; but here we find Muhammad swearing by such objects as "the Koran" (50:1), "the [Sacred] Scroll" (52:2), "the Pen and what they write" (68:1), "Sinai" (95:2), and several times by the Day of Judgment (69:1;75:1;85:2).

In several instances a Sūrah of the early Meccan period concludes with a eulogistic formula: "So praise thou the name of the Lord" (69:52; 56:96); "Praise thou the glory of thy Lord . . . praise Him" (52:48 f.); "Blessed be the name of thy Lord" (55:78); once in our period, and more often in younger Sūrahs, a eulogy forms the introductory formula: "Praise thou the name of thy Lord" (87:1; cf. the Sūrahs 57; 59; 61; 64; 67). It is impossible to escape the suspicion that what we have here is an echo of the *Halleluyah* formula at the beginning and the end of certain psalms (146-150; cf. 111:118), which formula was to become so outstanding a feature in the service of both the Synagogue and the Church. Note especially the phrase "Praise ye the name of the Lord" in the opening of psalms (113; 135), and "Blessed be the Lord" at the beginning and the conclusion of many benedictions.

Occasionally the finale of a Sūrah offers a kind of summation, such as "This is naught but a reminder to the worlds" (81:27; 68:52). A similar phrase occurs twice again as the conclusion of a Sūrah: "Nay, it is an admonition, and he who wills be mindful of it" (74:54; cf. 81:11); "Lo, this is an admonition, and he who wills let him take a way to his Lord" (73:19). The phrase is peculiarly reminiscent of the "Who hath ears to hear, let him hear" which is used repeatedly in the Gospels as concluding an utterance of Jesus (Matt. 13:9; Mark 7:16; Luke 14:35, and elsewhere). Might it not have come to serve as a standard finale of Christian homilies current in the environment of Muhammad? In what now stands as the conclusion of a section (on Judgment), but may well have first formed the conclusion of the Sūrah, the phrase recurs in a form that would seem an even closer paraphrase of that of the Gospels: "Verily, in this is a reminder to whoever has a heart or lends his hearing" (50:36).

We have seen already how the tense and terse utterances of the prophet and missionary were to give way eventually to the ever more involved orations of the lawgiver, the statesman, the minister. As a result, we find the form of the early Meccan Sūrahs deteriorates more and more until, in the Medinan Sūrahs, nothing is left of their characteristic frame and structure. The basic topics of the early message remain in evidence, and continue to hold their prerogative; but they undergo new formulations and even inner modifications. And as in the course of his career Muhammad is faced with an ever larger realm of issues, the former topics are sometimes lost amidst the wider scope of new subjects: law, cult, ritual, affairs of state and of the Church, and on all but unending series of polemics. In proportion, the substance of his Jewish and Christian materials assumes ever wider dimensions, growing in volume and variety with nearly each new Sūrah. At the same time, the reference to these materials grows much bolder, becoming much more distinct and seemingly also more tangible than in the early Sūrahs. "We have written in the Psalms" (21:105); "We have sent down the Torah . . . and have written therein" (5:46); "those who follow the messenger [i.e. Muhammad] . . . whom they find mentioned in the Torah and the Evangel in their possession" (7:156); "and when Jesus son of Mary said: Oh, children of Israel, I am God's messenger to you . . . announcing the good tidings of a messenger who will come after me, bearing the name Aḥmad" (61:6); and many similar references which we have cited above. In point of fact, it is often far easier to identify the literary sources reflected in the younger Sūrahs than those that re-echo in the early ones which we have considered. Sometimes, indeed, it is possible to place a whole narration or homily in juxtaposition with the very text on which it can be shown to depend.

Only in one respect does the situation which we have encountered in Muhammad's early message remain unaltered throughout the Koran: in the nature of the Jewish and Christian materials which it incorporates. It would be truly phenomenal, but by no means inconceivable, if he had appropriated the immense store of these materials prior to his prophetic Call, and merely utilized it gradually during the following twenty years or so—according to need and occasion, above all according to the particular stage of personal piety, of political security, or of ecclesiastic consolidation, through which he was just passing. But there is nothing to preclude the assumption that he continued to widen his knowledge about things divine at the feet of learned Jews and Christians long after the Call, and even for some time after the Flight. What matters is that the character of his knowledge remains the same in all his utterances: Upon close scrutiny, they never offer evidence of his direct dependence, for the knowledge he had acquired, on written documents; but they always point clearly to acquisition by personal association and in immediate intercourse with the People of the Book.

In the interest of an exact appraisal of the Koran, each of the four groups of Sūrahs that represent, respectively, the four major periods of Muhammad's activity as a prophet—the early Meccan, the middle Meccan, the late Meccan, and the Medinan—should be subjected to an analysis of the kind which we have endeavored to exemplify here for the Sūrahs of the first of these periods. However, to serve its purpose, such an analysis would have to be much more minute and exhaustive than, owing to the exigency of space, could be undertaken on the present occasion.

The preceding discussion, at all events, is fragmentary and sporadic in yet another important aspect. The truth is that there is no justification whatsoever for limiting our inquiry to the revelation of the Koran, which forms indeed the inner foundation of primitive Islam, yet not its whole groundwork. The forces which we have found to dominate the mind of the Prophet cannot simply be assumed to have affected only his revealed thoughts and canonized utterances, or to have been arrested outside the sphere of his personal life and work. As conceived in the foregoing study, the problem of Islamic origins is that of the Jewish and Christian share in the making of Islam. A truly systematic solution of this problem thus involves the formation of the sacred lore of the Moslems as such, whether made sacred by the revelation of the Koran or by the extracanonical authority of the Ḥadīth. And the prerequisite of such a solution would therefore be an inquiry into the documented groundwork of primitive Islam in its entirety, in its outer no less than its inner foundation.

BIBLIOGRAPHY

Aboth-R. Travers Herford. *Pirkē Aboth.* New York, 1925.

Tor Andrae. *Die Person Muhammeds in Lehre und Glauben seiner Gemeinde.* Stockholm, 1918.

C. H. Becker. *Islamstudien.* Leipzig, 1924.

Richard Bell. *The Qur'ān.* Edinburgh, 1937-1939.

Abraham Geiger. *Was hat Mohammed aus dem Judenthume aufgenommen?* Leipzig, 1902.

Louis Ginzberg. *The Legends of the Jews.* Philadelphia, 1913-1938.

Ignaz Goldziher. *Muhammedanische Studien.* Zweiter Theil (Halle a.S., 1890).

———. *Die Richtungen der islamischen Koranauslegung.* Leiden, 1920.

———. *Vorlesungen über den Islam.* Heidelberg, 1910.

Hartwig Hirschfeld. *Beiträge zur Erklärung des Korân.* Leipzig, 1886.

Philip K. Hitti. *History of the Arabs.* 2nd ed. (London, 1940).

Joseph Horovitz. *Koranische Untersuchungen.* Berlin und Leipzig, 1926.

Arthur Jeffery. *The Foreign Vocabulary of the Qur'ān.* Baroda, 1938.

George Foot Moore. *Judaism in the First Centuries of the Christian Era.* Cambridge, 1927-1930.

A. Müller. *Der Islam im Morgen- und Abendland.* Berlin, 1885.

Reynold A. Nicholson. *A Literary History of the Arabs.* London, 1923.

Theodor Nöldeke-Friedrich Schwally. *Geschichte de Qorans.* Leipzig, 1909-1919.

Otto Pautz. *Muhammeds Lehre von der Offenbarung.* Leipzig, 1898.

Wilhelm Rudolph. *Die Abhängigkeit des Qorans von Judentum und Christentum.* Stuttgart, 1922.

Hermann L. Strack. *Einleitung in Talmud und Midraš.* München, 1921.

Charles Cutler Torrey. *The Jewish Foundation of Islam.* New York, 1933.

A. J. Wensinck. *Miftāḥ Kunūz al-Sunnah.* Cairo, 1933.

GROWTH AND STRUCTURE OF ARABIC POETRY, A.D. 500-1000

GUSTAVE E. VON GRUNEBAUM

Early Arabic poetry, as far as it is not a political instrument, is a lyrical art of descriptive character dealing with a conventionally restricted group of subjects. As Poetry is the Bedouin's only means of higher self-expression, it represents the integration of his spiritual life; therefore, the external world as well as his social relations are hardly ever introduced for their own sake but only to implement the poet's view of himself. Precise observation distinguishes his description of his mount, of an onager, of a terrifying desert which he traverses: the portraying of the object, however, is only a means to vaunt his own social status as the owner of such a remarkable mount, his skill in riding down the game, and his courage in braving the dangers of the journey. Consequently, although the poems rarely touch upon the intimate and passing feelings of the individual, the early poetry must be considered highly "subjective."

The origins of this amazingly developed poetry are beyond our reach. St. Nilus (d. about A.D. 430) when describing a Bedouin raid on the Sinai monastery in A.D. 410 tells of the well-songs with which these Saracens celebrate their arrival at a water-place. Numeri 21.17 f. preserves a Hebrew specimen of the same category and these artless songs continue to be improvised by the Arab nomads to this very day. There is, however, no connection between these and similar folk rhymes and the elaborate products of the purely artistic style. A closer resemblance to preserved semiliterary poems recalling tribal battles or, for instance, the triumphal Arabian victory over the Persians at dhu-Qār (A.D. 611), may possibly exist in those chants in which the memory of a Bedouin success against the Romans in 372 survived up to the days of Sozomenos who mentions them about 440 in his *History of the Church*.

The prosodical structure of such more or less popular documents is essentially identical with that of the "Kunstdichtung." Arabian prosody is quantitative as is Greek and Latin; hence word-accent and verse-accent do not, as a rule, coincide. With the exception of the *rajaz*, perhaps the oldest and certainly the simplest meter, the individual couplets are divided in hemistichs. From about A.D. 500 it increasingly becomes the fashion to have the hemistichs of the first couplet rhyme. The same rhyme is maintained from the beginning to the end of the poem and one might say that it is this identical rhyme rather than the contents that gives unity to a song.

The earliest remains of Arabic poetry exhibit great metrical variety and refinement in the handling of the language. It is obvious that a school tradition had been at work for some time. Different regions favored different meters, Persian influence being extremely probable in the elaborate technique of the early Mesopotamian poets. At least two, possibly even three, meters in which this group excels, the *ramal*, the *mutaqārib*, and perhaps the *khafīf*, seem to be adaptations to Arabic conditions of Persian (Pahlavi) meters.

The Syrians may have contributed to the first development of technical terms, such as the characteristic "*bayt*," originally "tent," "house" for "verse," but on the whole the theory of poetical technique was developed independently. Considerably later, al-Khalīl ibn-Aḥmad (d. 791) systematized Arabic prosody and his concepts have remained normative throughout the centuries. He recognized sixteen meters, thus tacitly weeding out some of the lesser varieties developed by the classical poets. Parallel to the system used by the grammarians to symbolize word-forms, he expressed the permissible prosodical units in derivatives of the root "*f'l*." Thus, the meter *ṭawīl* (the long one), which was the one most frequently used by the pre-Islamic poets, was presented in this formula (one hemistich only): *fa'ūlun mafā'īlun fa'ūlun mafā'īlun*. It is remarkable that his scheme even provides an appropriate place for some of the meters that were developed in his time.

During the approximately one hundred and fifty years (470-620) in which we can observe pre-Islamic poetry, a definite development is traceable: the unification of the "Hochsprache" in which the treasures of the individual schools or dialects are increasingly pooled is as good as completed about 600; the technique of prosody becomes stricter; new types of comparisons are introduced by one group and gradually accepted throughout; the range and therewith the dimension of the ode tends to expand. The analysis of this comparatively quick development, combined with the general impression of the early remains suggests that while it would be futile to assign a definite date to the beginnings of Arabic "Kunstdichtung," these beginnings probably do not go back very far beyond the earliest records.

This statement applies, of course, solely to the latest of the three strata of Arabic poetry which coexist in the classical period, but which clearly did not originate at the same time.

The belief in the magic power of the word gave rise to incantations and curses, originally composed in rhymed prose, *saj'*, later in "rhythmically disciplined *saj'*," the *rajaz*. This poetry of magical intent closely matches that produced by the Hebrew *môshelîm*, Numeri 21.27 ff., and the verses of Bileam, Numeri 22.5 ff. Gradually the range of this so-called *hijā'* poetry widened, other meters were admitted, the magic background, although not entirely obliterated, was less vividly felt and the *hijā'* came to be satire and polemics, expression of personal or tribal hostility, frequently incorporated in the literary ode. Thus transformed, the genre had a long development.

The position of the early "poet," which was that of a seer rather than that of an artist, is reflected in his Arabic designation, "*shā'ir*," the knower (of magic, of supernatural knowledge). And the belief in his connection with higher powers is shown by the many stories in which the poet is presented in his relation to his jinn, his "demon helper" who is supposed to inspire his verses.

The relation of the *marthiyah*, the elegy, to the primitive mourning-song, the *niyāḥah*, is similar to the relation of the later satire to the primitive incantation. Again a meter, the *hazaj*, was soon substituted for the original rhymed prose, and again an elaborate branch of poetry developed from very modest beginnings. Its origins in the improvisations of the wailing women made it a feminine domain and, while masculine poets such as Aws ibn-Ḥajar contributed some beautiful dirges, the *marthiyah* culminated in the work of al-Khansā', a poetess of the first half of the seventh century. The *marthiyah* developed a very definite style, characterized not only by certain formulae and a tendency to use identical beginnings in a number of successive verses, but also by formal peculiarities, such as a tendency toward a rudimentary strophic organization and toward having the hemistichs rhyme throughout the poem. And just as the *hijā'* has influenced the artistic standard poems, the *marthiyah* has contributed to the style of its erotic parts.

What is true of *hijā'* and *marthiyah* is particularly conspicuous in the youngest stratum of Arabic poetry, the *qaṣīdah*, or ode (literally: "purpose poem"; the exact explanation of the term is still wanting). The normative rules formulated in postclassical times by conservative critics have blinded most observers to the fact that the *qaṣīdah* underwent important changes during the pre-Islamic period. Its principal development is perhaps typical of many literary patterns: the *qaṣīdah* tends to lengthen.

Its gradual extension is, of course, accompanied by the widening range of its subject matter. With all this, the basic organization remains unaltered. The poet begins by telling of his longing for a lost love. He may complain to the forsaken homestead of his beloved, or he may call the attention of his friends to the caravan departing with her. In each case his experience is viewed in retrospect and his mind is clouded by melancholy. To tear himself away from his grief the poet concludes the *nasīb*, the amatory prelude, by setting out on a journey through the dangerous solitude of the desert. He describes his mount, sometimes at great length, and some of the animals of the steppe, occasionally inserting a vivid hunting scene. Tradition does not permit the poet to present any animal he may choose but limits him, in the main, to gazelle, wild ass, ostrich, and a few others. Finally, the journey is ended successfully and the poet arrives at the tents of an influential person. Here he either raises a political question or request, or he tries to stimulate the chieftain's liberality. For it must be borne in mind that the majority of the poets depended on the generosity of princes or tribal nobles. The pattern enables the poet to indulge freely in self-praise. Such passages combined with the *fakhr*, the panegyric, well depict the human ideal of the pagan period, the Jāhilīyah (probably: the time of ἄγνοια, in the sense of Acts 17:23 or Romans 11:25). Some poets allow their *qaṣīdahs* to end in apophthegms of occasionally rather shallow wisdom, *ḥikmah*.

The earliest *qaṣīdah* which has come down to us and can be considered complete, the tenth poem of 'Amr ibn-Qamī'ah (born *ca.* 480), does not yet fulfill all the requirements of the theorists. It contains in its nineteen verses, apart from the *nasīb*, nothing but the description of a rain cloud and the praise of one Imru'-al-Qays ibn-'Amrah. Only a short time later such a *qaṣīdah* would have been considered a very meager opus. Not only is the length doubled, or tripled, or even extended up to and beyond one hundred verses, but episodes are accumulated, until such masterpieces of composition are achieved as, for example, Poems 1 and 6 of al-A'sha (*ca.* 565-629), or the first ode of the *dīwān* of abu-Dhu'ayb al-Hudhali (d. *ca.* 650). This ode brings home in three impressive scenes the inescapable power of fate, which suddenly prostrates the fierce onager, the strong wild bull, and the armored warrior. Motivated by the death of the poet's sons, the poem masterfully combines features of both *marthiyah* and *qaṣīdah*.

Close scrutiny of individual shades in the use of conventional motives and of individual peculiarities of language and imagery results in breaking up the seemingly homogeneous mass of classical, i.e. pre-Islamic, verse into groups which can with reasonable certainty be assigned to different schools. By combining the internal indications yielded by the poems themselves with the unfortunately rather sparse historical references, it is possible to establish within certain limits the chronology of the early development.

At present, six artistic schools can be traced in the earlier part of the Jāhilīyah, to include the poets, born between *circa* A.D. 440 and 530. This is not to say that there were no poets who by their very nature defy such classification: the two great outlaw poets, Ta'abbaṭa Sharran and al-Shanfara, are the outstanding examples of such individualistic talents. Most interesting perhaps is that group of poets whose lives centered around the principality of al-Ḥīrah and in whose work Sassanian influence has left some traces. Abu-Du'ād al-Iyādi (*ca.* 480-550) and the Christian ʻAdi ibn-Zayd (*ca.* 545-585), present a strange blend of Bedouin and townsman mentality. Ṭarafah (*ca.* 535-568) and later again al-Aʻsha, brought the refined artistic tradition of another school, whose representatives belong to the clan Qays ibn-Thaʻlabah of the Bakr ibn-Wā'il, to Mesopotamia. Al-Aʻsha is doubtless the supreme master of language among the pre-Islamic poets. The convivial scenes in his *qaṣīdahs* reveal the inspiration of Sassanian poets. Imru'-al-Qays ibn-Ḥujr, a Kindah prince (*ca.* 500-540), the most famous and the most influential Arabic classic poet, was, like Ṭarafah, the author of one of those model *qaṣīdahs*, the so-called *muʻallaqāt*. His contemporary, ʻAbīd ibn-al-Abraṣ, represents the peak of another school.

Toward the end of the sixth century the unification of language and style made a considerable advance. These schools coalesced, as it were, pooling their vocabulary and their imagery. But this development did not go so far as to include groups which may be said to have flourished beside the main stream of Arabic poetry. The most important school of this later period is that of the Hudhali poets, which can be followed from about 550 to 700. One of the motives in which this group specialized is the description of bees and honey. Such descriptions also entailed a certain enrichment of the natural scenery, when the poets became interested in the gathering of the wild honey.

The *dīwān* of the Hudhalites contains a great many poems by people who only occasionally composed verse. It must be realized that side by side with the "professional" poet an enormous number of amateurs or dilettantes at some time or other voiced their feelings or their wishes in poetical form. This accounts for the fact that we always find together verses which are contemporary as to date but not as to stage of development, since, naturally, the non-professional tends to be at least one generation behind his professional colleagues. As these conditions were not taken sufficiently into consideration, they contributed much to the long prevailing conviction of the stagnating uniformity of classical poetry. Backward also, but perhaps culturally rather than technically, remained the popular, or semipopular *rajaz* poetry. The cleavage between *rajaz* and *qarīḍ*, the regular poetry, was keenly felt even at a much later date. The magical connotation of the *hijā'*, for instance, was much longer preserved by the *rajaz* than by the *qarīḍ*.

Although one cannot quite escape the impression that "classical" poetry had very nearly run its course when Muhammad appeared, it is impossible to overlook the fact that he severely injured its natural development. Pietist tradition probably exaggerated his hostility against poets and his alleged saying that the *shi'r* (poetry) was the Koran of Satan is certainly a forgery. He was careful in drawing a line between himself and the poets. But he did this less to combat poetry than to avoid having his revelations confused with the irresponsible utterances of the littérateurs in general and of the soothsayers in particular. The decisive point was that the Prophet undermined the ethos on which heathen poetry was based, and thus weakened, if not annihilated, many of its incentives: best proof thereof are those poets who like

Labīd (*ca.* 560-665?) no longer produced anything of note after their conversion to Islam.

This grandiose attempt to create an Arabic religious and juridical prose, the Koran, shows remarkably few reminiscences of the diction of classical poetry. The imagery of the eschatological prophecies is largely influenced by Syrian homiletics and the origin of the various literary patterns which Muhammad employs in his preaching has not yet been sufficiently investigated, but they can hardly be called Arabic. Only the incoherent and allusive presentation of epic subjects resembles corresponding passages in poetry which, by the way, seems to have reached the level of the real "ballad" only once, to wit, in the widely renowned song of al-A'sha on the faithful Jew, al-Samaw'al. It is somewhat bewildering that neither the religious nor the political issues or events of incipient Islam have had an appreciable repercussion in contemporary poetry. Whenever the great campaigns are mentioned their importance is not grasped; if they are disapproved of, the dislike springs from disinclination to serve or live in foreign lands or to be separated from the clan. That is all. Classical tradition did not provide for discussion of world events and early Islam did not feel any imperative need to develop an adequate form.

The halt in poetical production, caused by the rise of a new civilization, was only temporary. Barely twenty years after Muhammad's death (632) a new upsurge began which ultimately both broadened and deepened the outlook and scope of Arabic poetry. No longer confined to the arid steppes of Arabia proper, the poets responded to the stimuli of the new life and to the cosmopolitan influences which it brought to bear upon them. Philology developed as a conservative force in literature. The general conviction of the gradual deterioration of the age and the feeling of literary insecurity due to the weakening connection of the city people with the genuine Bedouin language also encouraged a continuation along traditional lines. But the gap between reality and literary fiction became too wide and people increasingly came to realize the cultural and political superiority of their age as compared with the Jāhilīyah. The eighth century saw the beginning, the tenth the victory of this new attitude. The importance of this change for literature is obvious.

The main features of the postclassical development of Arabic poetry can conveniently be summed up under the three headings of (a) the development of the form, (b) the motive extension, and (c) the rise of literary criticism and theory.

THE DEVELOPMENT OF THE FORM

The *qaṣīdah* remains the predominant form. Although the discrepancy between the poets' urban milieu and the Bedouin garb of their odes was soon felt and frequently derided, tradition as upheld by the philologists forced the singer to imitate endlessly the classical models. A small group of poets, however, in whom their Bedouin background was still a living force, such as al-Farazdaq (*ca.* 641-728) and Jarīr (d. 728) whose bitter poetical contests (*naqā'iḍ*) gave them both notoriety and fame, the Christian al-Akhṭal (d. 710), and above all, dhu-al-Rummah (d. 719 or 735), brought about an Indian summer of the classical *qaṣīdah*, the beauty of which is undeniable. It is true, Marwān ibn-abi-Ḥafṣah (721-797) and Muslim ibn-al-Walīd (*ca.* 747-803) faithfully carried on the tradition, but their well polished odes are skillful imitations, and the grammarian, abu-'Amr ibn-al-'Alā' (d. 770) is right when he exclaims that dhu-al-Rummah's death marks the end of (classical) poetry. Parallel to the last flourishing of the *qarīḍ* ode, the *rajaz qaṣīdah* took a noteworthy development in the direction of the strictly literary sphere. Al-'Ajjāj (d. 715) and his son Ru'bah (d. 762 or 764) won considerable reputation for themselves by composing long *rajaz* poems, but they did not succeed in wholly removing the stigma that weighed down on the form. The end of the eighth century also brings the life of this movement to a close.

In the meantime a new ideal of education, the *adab*, which

centered on the literary requirements of the *kātib*, the official conducting the state correspondence, had become supreme. The *kātib* was supposed to embellish his letters with poetical and koranic quotations, so he needed collections of appropriate verse, providing for any occasion. At the same time the huge amount of ancient verse still current came to be cumbersome ballast for the ordinary "intelligent layman" whose interest in the old poems was mainly concentrated on their quotable or otherwise familiar highlights. The decline of the genuine ode brought the *qiṭʿah* (fragment) to the fore, that is, any independently developed part of the *qaṣīdah*. Especially the amatory and panegyrical passages of the ode were, from about 770, treated as isolated units. Such *qiṭʿahs* were nothing new; the classical period had known them, but the shift in emphasis was unprecedented.

These tendencies combined to inaugurate a Golden Age of anthologies. East and West vied with each other in selecting verse (and also suitable prose) for the use of the scribe and the layman of literary interests and perhaps also to ensure the preservation of ancient literary treasures. Best known of all is the collection of poetical excerpts made by the famous poet, abu-Tammām (d. 846). Its name, *al-Ḥamāsah* (prowess) indicates with which category of poetry the compiler was primarily concerned.

Metrical innovations beyond those accepted in al-Khalīl's system are rarely attempted and if tried do not find any response. On the other hand the poets frequently turn away from the long meters favored by the classics and prefer to use the lighter and shorter cadenced rhythms, such as *ramal* and *hazaj*.

Outside of ode and fragment, however, a new type of poem appears: the narrative poem in short lines (usually *rajaz*) which rhyme aa bb cc, etc., thus facilitating very extensive "*muzdawij*" ("paired," i.e. in paired rhymes) compositions. Abān al-Lāḥiqi (d. about 815) popularized *Kalīlah wa-Dimnah* in this form and wrote *muzdawij* books on the Wisdom of the Indians, on Fasting, and the like. Ibn-al-

Mu'tazz (d. 908) celebrated the exploits of his cousin, the caliph al-Mu'taḍid (892-902), in the same manner. This type of "historical" or "political" poem became popular and was used, for example, in a poetical feud between Arabs and Byzantines in 966. It survived till at least the sixteenth century, when one Muḥammad ibn-'Abd-al-'Azīz al-Kālīkūti wrote the history of the Portuguese relations with Malabar in a somewhat barbarized *muzdawij* poem.

Folk songs are occasionally referred to, but (in the East) unfortunately never quoted. Abu-al-'Atāhiyah imitates the songs of the Tigris sailors in a poem which has been preserved. In Spain strophic poems were composed before 900. Their various forms were destined to influence strongly the structure of Provençal troubadour poetry. Although the Moslem West always surpassed the East in the development of truly popular songs it can be safely assumed that forms like the *mawāliya* or the *kān wa-kān* which, so to speak, come to the surface only in the eleventh century had been developing over a long period of time. It is, however, of interest that the songs originating during the siege of Baghdad, in 813, while voicing the popular sentiment, are composed in the usual literary forms.

MOTIVE EXTENSION

During the early reigns of the Umayyad dynasty (661-750) Medina became the first center of religious learning and, strangely enough, at the same time the home of the first literary school that was almost exclusively interested in erotic poetry. It is said that the leading figure of the group, 'Umar ibn-abi-Rabī'ah (*ca.* 643-719), only once tried his hand at a *qaṣīdah* in the traditional style. He completely dropped the conventional melancholy attitude and exchanged the impersonal pattern of the *nasīb* for small and characteristic pictures of his own experiences. These he presented with extraordinary grace and in charming and comparatively simple language, frequently inserting vivid dialogues. His trend toward the frivolous was counterbalanced by the somewhat feverish sentimentality in the verses of poets like Jamīl al-'Udhri (d. 701), or the semilegendary Qays ibn-Dharīḥ and 'Urwah ibn-Ḥizām. Popular imagination wove around some of these lovelorn figures romantic legends glorifying their chaste and faithful passion which often leads them to an early death caused by love alone. The general conception of love in these poetical cycles and many a detail of their tearful and heart-rending, yet, in a certain sense, also playful episodes bears the mark of that Hellenistic attitude toward love which animates the Greek novel.

'Umar ibn-abi-Rabī'ah exercised considerable influence on three successive generations. The spiritual resemblance with 'Umar of al-'Abbās ibn-al-Aḥnaf (d. between 803 and 813), one of the greatest poets at the court of Hārūn al-Rashīd (786-809), is unmistakable. But the beginning of 'Abbāsid rule was also marked by the rise of another school of love poetry, inaugurated, as it seems, by a man of Persian descent and widely suspected orthodoxy, Bashshār ibn-Burd (d. 783). His approach was less sentimental, more popular in emotion and expression, and his verses, for which he usually chose the less pompous meters, apparently lent themselves well to singing. The caliph al-Mahdi (775-785) considered his poems a danger to public morals and forbade him the composition of love songs. The difference between his style and that employed by erotic poets like Jamīl was clearly felt by his contemporaries. The tendency toward simplicity of expression appears to have been characteristic of this age, as it recurs in the work of such widely different personalities as the Shī'ite propagandist al-Sayyid al-Ḥimyari (723-789), abu-Nuwās, the greatest of Arabic lyricists (*ca.* 756-810), and the pious abu-al-'Atāhiyah (748-828). Only a few decades later a reaction set in—of which abū-Tammām may be called the standard-bearer—which stood for elaborateness of thought and expression, rich rhetorical adornment and which again gave preference to the heavier metrical forms.

The early 'Abbāsid age also saw the establishment of the religious as a generally recognized field of poetical expression. Never since the Civil War between Mu'āwiyah and 'Ali (concluded 661) had it been entirely wanting. The sectarians, Khārijites and Shī'ites, produced many a moving poetical testimony to their faith; religious arguments entered political poetry; love songs jestingly used the language of theology, and even dogmatic questions were occasionally discussed in metrical form. But it was left to the first generation which was born under the theocratic 'Abbāsid government fully to develop those scattered though promising germs. Abu-Nuwās and abu-al-'Atāhiyah composed their *zuhdīyāt*, poems extolling withdrawal from worldiness and deprecating this world in favor of the hereafter. At the same time, Rābi'ah al-'Adawīyah (d. 801) and other followers of the mystic path addressed their Lord in verse, thus opening one of the most beautiful chapters of Arabic poetry, which was brilliantly continued in the tenth century by the martyred al-Ḥallāj (d. 922).

More and more the poets depended for their subsistence on the munificence of the caliph or the grandees. Before 800 the Barmakid vizier Yaḥya ibn-Khālid appointed Abān al-Lāḥiqi to head a "Department of Poetry" (*dīwān al-shi'r*) where the merits of the panegyrical poems which the poets submitted were judged. While the individual poet might become influential, the social standing of poetry tended to decline. The poets, drawn closer into the life of the court, would act as political mouthpieces of the government. Not to mention lesser poets, a large proportion of the great al-Mutanabbi's (d. 965) *qaṣīdahs* can be classed as "poetical leaders."

Naturally, the poets who were attached to the court described and celebrated whichever interest was paramount in high society. This situation probably accounts for the rise of hunting-songs, *ṭardīyāt*, in which again abu-Nuwās excelled. His poems, like those of the Ḥamdānid prince, abu-Firās (d. 968), introduce a sporting element into their subject which was almost entirely absent in the corresponding parts of the classical ode where the hunter usually sets out to gain his livelihood. The flourishing of convivial poetry and of wine-songs (*khamrīyāt*) again reflects the attitude of the aristocracy and, at times, of the court as well. There is an unbroken line of artistic progress from the wine-songs of the Ḥīran nobleman 'Adi ibn-Zayd, to al-A'sha, to the Christian panegyrist of the Umayyads al-Akhṭal, to the Umayyad caliph al-Walīd ibn-Yazīd (743-744) and to the amazingly versatile abu-Nuwās, perhaps the most inspired of them all. The tradition continues and has its representatives in the West as well.

Their close connection with the political life of their time made some of the poets interested in treating historical subjects of actual importance. Abu-Tammām's ode on the conquest of 'Ammūrīyah (838) may have set the style. Ibn-al-Rūmi (836-889 or 896) followed suit with his elegy on al-Baṣrah when this city was overrun by the Zanj (871). The description of al-Mu'taḍid's deeds by ibn-al-Mu'tazz, the somewhat later abu-Firās' ode in praise of his house, and, in Spain, the *rajaz* panegyric of 'Abd-al-Raḥmān III (912-961) by ibn-'Abd-Rabbihi (869-940), illustrate the permanence of the poets' interest in contemporary events.

The age enjoyed poetical entertainment of all kinds. Side by side with his serious poems, ibn-al-Rūmi composed cooking recipes in verse, while others parodied the time-honored *marthiyah* by writing dirges for their pets.

The ninth century inaugurated a new approach to nature and, therefore, to descriptive poetry. Flowers and gardens are chosen as subjects of lengthy odes; colorful and somewhat forced metaphors are used to render the exquisite beauty of a rose or a narcissus. Abu-Tammām and ibn-al-Rūmi did much to advance the "modern" attitude which again strangely resembles that of the later Greek writers, and al-Ṣanawbari (d. 945) specializes in singing the beauties of the countryside, of spring, the blooming garden and of flowers. Classical poetry had been fond of describing violent thunderstorms, now the charm of still-life is discovered.

THE RISE OF LITERARY CRITICISM AND THEORY

In the ninth century a poet, Di'bil (d. 835), and various scholars, al-Aṣma'i (d. about 831), al-Jumaḥi (d. 845), and ibn-Qutaybah attempted to classify the innumerable poets of both the heathen and the Islamic period. Their "class-books" laid the foundation of all later essays in literary history. The literary biography culminated in abu-al-Faraj al-Iṣfahāni's (d. 967) *Kitāb al-Aghāni* (Book of Songs). A third type of literary study came into being, the *muwāzanah*, the "balancing of one poet against another," represented by al-Āmidi's (d. 987) famous comparison of abu-Tammām and al-Buḥturi (d. 897).

Philology, the needs of the *kātib*, the attempts of the theologians to establish the aesthetic uniqueness of the Koran, and finally a genuine interest in nature and structure of poetry, cooperated in inspiring the first students of literary theory, such as al-Jāḥiẓ (d. 869), al-Mubarrad (d. 898), ibn-al-Mu'tazz and Qudāmah ibn-Ja'far (d. 922). While the first two writers did little more than elaborate on the genuine, semipopular and semilearned criticism which had been current amongst the Arabs for centuries, the latter two must be credited with pioneering in the systematic treatment of the figures of speech. Qudāmah's endeavors to transplant Greek rhetorical thought into Arabic theory failed and the Greek influence faded within one century after his death. But rhetoric and literary theory have remained ever since integral parts of Islamic science.

From the eleventh century onward Arabic poetry could no longer be treated as a single stream of development. The distance between the regional literatures became too great. The process leading to this situation, largely political in its causes, can be observed as early as the ninth century, when Spanish Moslem poetry sounds one or another note not familiar in Eastern verse. A little later, Persia revived her own language. Bilingual poets are characteristic of tenth century Iran, but in the eleventh century the battle was decided and

Persia no longer contributed directly to Arabic poetry. In compensation, Syria, North Africa and Spain began to emulate more successfully Baghdad, which still remained the center of the Islamic universe.

APPENDIX

The following specimens of Arabic poetry have been selected with a view to the needs of the non-specialist reader. They are intended to convey a general impression of nature and scope of Arabic verse and to help to visualize the major phases of the development outlined in this article.

I. 'Abīd ibn-al-Abraṣ (first half of sixth century)

1. Dost thou weep for a vanisht abode, over traces of tents outworn?
   —and is weeping for love-longing the business of one like me?
2. These were their camps when the tribe was gathered all together:
   now are they a wilderness, save for wildings in an empty land.
3. No voices stir there now but the uncouth sound of the wild,
   the cries of the male and female ostriches, dusky herds.
4. Yea, if Ghabrā' al-Khubaibah has become desolate,
   and gained in exchange for our folk other dwellers not equal to those,
5. Yet time was I looked on the whole kin dwelling there in content
   and happy: but what is the passing of days but change on change?
6. After the children of 'Amr, my kinsfolk and my brethren,
   can I hope for smoothness of life? nay, life is a leader astray.
7. But although they have gone, and departed on their way,
   —never will I forget them all my life long, or cease to mourn.
8. Will ye two not stay for a moment to-day, before we part,
   —before long distance, and cares, and variance, have sundered us,
9. To await ladies borne on camels that travel between Tabāla
   and the high land of al-Khall, with the followers trailing after them?
10. When I saw the two leaders of the caravan hasten briskly along,
    a pang seized my breast that they should depart with a heart so light.

Selections I and XI are reprinted through the courtesy of Luzac and Company, London; Selections II, III, IV, VI, VIII, IX, X, XII through the Cambridge University Press and the Macmillan Company, New York.

11. We raised our whips to our beasts, and they skimmed along with us
—our camels with well-knit forelegs, swift and fleet of pace,
12. Plying briskly their hindlegs, as though behind them lay
deserts trackless, forlorn, where they trotted in the forenoon haze;
13. And they brought us to the caravan, our beasts the active and light,
the breastgirth securing the saddle, thick of cheek, quick of step.
14. Then we bent sideways, and entered on talk with women kind
—above them were hangings of striped cloth of Jaišān, with broidered borders;
15. And they turned to us their necks, and the jewels that thereon hung,
with speech that dealt with such things as the careless loves to hear;
16. Then was it as though the East-wind had wafted to us the scent
of a bale of musk, so precious that none could pay its price,
17. Or the fragrance of lavender by the brook-sides of a mead,
where a plenteous shower in the night has washed away dust and grime.

(*Dīwān*, No. 15, translated by C. J. Lyall,
Volume 21, Gibb Memorial Series)

II. Al-Shanfara al-Azdi (sixth century)

1. Bury me not! Me you are forbidden to bury,
But thou, O hyena, soon wilt feast and make merry,
2. When foes bear away mine head, wherein is the best of me,
And leave on the battlefield for thee all the rest of me.
3. Here nevermore I hope to live glad—a stranger
Accurst, whose wild deeds have brought his people in danger.

(R. A. Nicholson, *Literary History of the Arabs*, p. 81)

III. Maymūn ibn-Qays al-A'sha (*ca.* 565-629)

1. Many a time I hastened early to the tavern—while there ran
At my heels a ready cook, a nimble, active serving-man—
2. 'Midst a gallant troop, like Indian scimitars, of mettle high;
Well they know that every mortal, shod and bare alike, must die.
3. Propped at ease I greet them gaily, them with myrtle-boughs I greet,
Pass among them wine that gushes from the jar's mouth bitter-sweet.

4. Emptying goblet after goblet—but the source may no man drain—
Never cease they from carousing save to cry, "Fill up again!"
5. Briskly runs the page to serve them: on his ears hang pearls below,
Tight the girdle draws his doublet as he bustles to and fro.
6. 'Twas the harp, thou mightiest fancy, waked the lute's responsive note,
When the loose-robed chantress touched it and sang shrill with quavering throat.
7. Here and there among the party damsels fair superbly glide:
Each her long white skirt lets trail and swings a wine-skin at her side.

(Nicholson, p. 125)

IV. 'Umar ibn-abi-Rabī'ah (d. 719)

1. Blame me no more, O comrades! but to-day
Quietly with me beside the howdahs stay.
2. Blame not my love for Zaynab, for to her
And hers my heart is pledged a prisoner.
3. Ah, can I ever think of how we met
Once at al-Khayf, and feel no fond regret?
4. My song of other women was but jest:
She reigns alone, eclipsing all the rest.
5. Hers is my love sincere, 'tis she the flame
Of passion kindles—so, a truce to blame!

(Nicholson, p. 237)

V. Jamīl al-'Udhri (d. 701)

1. Awake, O caravan of sleepers, hey, awake!
So I can ask you: Does love kill a man?
2. "Yes," they replied, "it breaks his bones,
leaves him perplexed, chased out of his wits."

(Frg. 2.1,2; Edited by F. Gabrieli, RSO 17.62)

VI. Jamīl al-'Udhri

1. Oh might it flower anew, that youthful prime,
And restore to us, Buthaina, the bygone time!
2. And might we again be blest as we were wont to be,
When thy folk were nigh and grudged what thou gavest me!
3. Shall I ever meet Buthaina alone again,
Each of us full of love as a cloud of rain?

4. Fast in her net was I when a lad, and till
This day my love is growing and waxing still.
5. I have spent my lifetime, waiting for her to speak,
And the bloom of youth is faded from off my cheek;
6. But I will not suffer that she my suit deny,
My love remains undying, though all things die!

(Nicholson, p. 238)

VII. Bashshār ibn-Burd (d. 783)

The caliph al-Mahdi asked Bashshār b. Burd to improvise a few verses on love in which Love would judge the lovers. So Bashshār said:

1. "I make Love a judge between my love and myself; today I acquiesce in such an arrangement.
2. So we assembled; then I said: O love of my soul, lately my eyes have enjoyed little sleep;
3. You punished me and exhausted the strength of my body; have mercy today on him who is smitten with perpetual illness [of the heart].
4. Love said: My pronouncement cannot free you, for illness and suffering are better for you [than health].
5. I said when he had answered me, inspired by passion himself: Passion prompts every judge to practice injustice."

Then al-Mahdi sent word to Bashshār: You have passed sentence on us and we concur. And he ordered that the poet should be given a thousand dīnār.

(*Aghāni* 3.60)

VIII. Abu-Nuwās (d. 810)

1. Ho! a cup, and fill it up, and tell me it is wine,
For I will never drink in shade if I can drink in shine!
2. Curst and poor is every hour that sober I must go,
But rich am I whene'er well drunk I stagger to and fro.
3. Speak, for shame, the loved one's name, let vain disguise alone:
No good there is in pleasures o'er which a veil is thrown.

(Nicholson, p. 295)

IX. Rābi'ah al-'Adawīyah (d. 801)

1. O my Joy and my Desire and my Refuge,
My Friend and my Sustainer and my Goal.
2. Thou art my Intimate, and longing for Thee sustains me,
Were it not for Thee, O my life and my Friend,
3. How I should have been distraught over the spaces of the earth,
How many favours have been bestowed,

4. And how much hast Thou given me
Of gifts and grace and assistance.
5. Thy love is now my desire and my bliss,
And has been revealed to the eye of my heart that was athirst.
6. I have none beside Thee, Who dost make the desert blossom,
Thou art my joy, firmly established within me.
7. If Thou art satisfied with me, then
O Desire of my heart, my happiness has appeared.

(Margaret Smith, *Râbi'a, the Mystic*, p. 55)

X. Abu-al-'Atāhiyah (d. 828)

1. Get sons for death, build houses for decay!
All, all, ye wend annihilation's way.
2. For whom build we, who must ourselves return
Into our native element of clay?
3. O Death, nor violence nor flattery thou
Dost use, but when thou com'st, escape none may.
4. Methinks, thou art ready to surprise mine age,
As age surprised and made my youth his prey.
5. What ails me, World, that every place perforce
I lodge thee in, it galleth me to stay?
6. And, O Time, how do I behold thee run
To spoil me? Thine own gift thou tak'st away!
7. O Time! inconstant, mutable art thou,
And o'er the realm of ruin is thy sway.

(Nicholson, p. 299)

XI. Al-Ṣanawbari (d. 945)

1. Rise and gaze, O Gazelles, the flowerbeds reveal their miracles!
2. The spring has rent the veil which had wrapped their faces divine.
3. Roses like cheeks, narcissus like eyes, which greet the loved ones.
4. Anemones, like silver-mantles, with blank legends;
5. Cypresses like singing-girls tucked up to the knee;
6. One looks like a gentle maiden playing with her companions at midnight.
7. The gentle breeze has made the brook tremble and filled it with leaves.
8. Had I the power to guard the garden—no mean soul would ever tread its soil.

(A. Mez, *Renaissance of Islam*,
translated by D. S. Margoliouth, p. 261 f.)

XII. al-Mutanabbi' (d. 965)

1. Shame hitherto was wont my tears to stay,
But now by shame they will no more be stayed,
2. So that each bone seems through its skin to sob,
And every vein to swell the sad cascade.
3. She uncovered: pallor veiled her at farewell:
No veil 'twas, yet her cheeks it cast in shade.
4. So seemed they, while tears trickled over them,
Gold with a double row of pearls inlaid.
5. She loosed three sable tresses of her hair,
And thus of night four nights at once she made;
6. But when she lifted to the moon in heaven
Her face, two moons together I surveyed.

(Nicholson, p. 310)

BIBLIOGRAPHY

E. Bräunlich. "Versuch einer literargeschichtlichen Betrachtungsweise der altarabischer Poesie," *Islam*, XXIV (1937), 200 ff.

C. Brockelmann. *Geschichte der arabischen Literatur*. Weimar-Berlin, 1898-1902; Supplement, 1937-41.

H. A. R. Gibb. *Arabic Literature: An Introduction*. London, 1926.

I. Goldziher. *Abhandlungen zur arab. Philologie*. Vol. I (1896).

———. "Bemerkungen zur arab. Trauerpoesie," *WZKM*. XVI (1902), 307 ff.

A. González Palencia. *Historia de la literature arábigo-española*. Madrid, 1928.

G. von Grunebaum. *Die Wirklichkeitweite der früharab. Dichtung*. 1937.

———. "Zur Chronologie der früharab. Dichtung," *Orientalia*, N.s. VIII (1939), 328 ff.

———. "The Early Development of Islamic Religious Poetry," *JAOS*. LX (1940), 23 ff.

———. "Arabic Literary Criticism in the 10th Century," *JAOS*. LXI (1941), 51 ff.

———. "Pre-Islamic Poetry," *The Moslem World*. XXXII (1942), 147 ff.

R. A. Nicholson. *A Literary History of the Arabs*. London, 1930.

O. Rescher. *Abriss der arabischen Litteraturgeschichte*. Stuttgart, 1925-33.

N. Rhodokanakis. "al-Hansâ' und ihre Trauerlieder," *SBWA*. CXLVII. (1904), Abh. 4.

G. Weil. " 'Arûḍ," *Encyclopaedia of Islām*.

AL-GHAZZĀLI

NABIH AMIN FARIS

The first half of the fifth Moslem century saw the perigee of Moslem power in the East. What had once been a realm united under a sole Moslem ruler was now a collection of scattered dynasties, not one of which, save perhaps the schismatic Fatimids of Egypt, was capable of imperial sway. Spain and North Africa, including Egypt, had long been lost to the caliphs of Baghdad; Northern Syria and Mesopotamia were in the hands of turbulent Arab chiefs; Persia was split up into the numerous governments of the Buwayhids, whose Shī'ite leanings left little respect for the shadowy caliphs of their time, or was held by sundry petty dynasts, each ready to attack the other and thus add to the general weakness and confusion. The prevalence of schism increased the disunion of the various provinces of the vanished empire. A drastic remedy was needed, and it was found in the invasion of the Saljuq Turks.

These rude nomads, unspoilt by town life and civilized indifference to religion, embraced Islam with all the zeal and fervor of their uncouth souls. They swarmed over Persia, Mesopotamia, Asia Minor, and Syria, devastating the country, and exterminating every dynasty that existed there; and, as a result, they once more united Moslem Asia, from the confines of Afghanistan to the White Sea, under one rule. They drove back the re-encroaching Byzantines, and bred a generation of stalwart Moslem warriors, to whom, more than anything else, the crusaders owed their initial reverses. In short, they rescued a dying state, re-established its power, and gave it a new lease on life.

But these potentates did not and could not give Islam a religious reformation and a cultural renaissance. The need for such a revival did not escape their notice. Indeed, the necessity for an ideological foundation for the revived state was sought by Ṭughril Beg, Alp Arslān, and Malik-Shah.

The task was entrusted to the care of their great vizier, the illustrious Niẓām-al-Mulk. He, therefore, founded and endowed in 457/1065, the Niẓāmīyah school in Baghdad, the first real academy in Islam which made provisions for the physical needs of its students, and the model for later institutions of higher learning. Other schools, bearing the same name, were founded in almost every important city of the realm, such as Nisapur, for example, where the Imām al-Ḥaramayn (d. 478/1085) headed the new academy.

For the most part, however, these schools and academies advocated an education which, though adequate for the growing demands of the state, was wholly unsuitable for meeting the deeper needs of Islam, particularly that of supplying the community of the faithful with a unifying principle of life. It was an education limited to the imparting of knowledge for utilitarian purposes: to secure government employment and to gain position and prestige, comfort and wealth, security and ease.

When the first of these academies was founded, al-Ghazzāli was seven years old. We must, therefore, assume that he was the product of the system which these same schools spread throughout the Saljuq world. He himself attended the Niẓāmīyah school of Nisapur, where he sat at the feet of the Imām al-Ḥaramayn, the greatest and best known intellectual janissary of the time. He was fired by the same zeal and ambition for worldly ends which characterized the Imām, whose favorite disciple he was, until his intellectual attainments threatened to eclipse those of his master. The Imām became secretly jealous of him, and their relations with each other, though always correct, became rather cool. That al-Ghazzāli was the product of this same system of education and that he, likewise, shared in the current trend of seeking it for utilitarian purposes is further supported by his own admission, made later in life, that both he and his brother sought learning for the sake of something other than God, but that He was unwilling that it should be for aught but Him.

Fortunately, however, an early Sufi influence in his life was destined to assert itself, and finally save him from the materialistic mania which had taken hold of the learned men of his time. This influence can be traced to the Sufi in whose care the father of al-Ghazzāli left his sons, Muḥammad and Aḥmad. It was, however, to make itself felt later. In the meantime, al-Ghazzāli's intellectual attainments attracted the attention of Niẓām-al-Mulk. At the death of the Imām al-Ḥaramayn, Niẓām-al-Mulk summoned al-Ghazzāli to his court, and after a period of six years, appointed him a lecturer at the Niẓāmīyah school at Baghdad (484/1091). Little is known of the activities of al-Ghazzāli during these six years. He seems to have spent the greater part of them debating with other scholars, and establishing his reputation as the most learned man of his time.

Four years of teaching at the Niẓāmīyah placed the Baghdad of the great Saljuqs at his feet. Scholars flocked to hear him, and dignitaries courted his favor. His reputation spread far and wide across the world of Islam, and he earned the honorific titles of Imām Khurāsān and Imām al-'Irāq. Above all, the number of his enemies multiplied—which often is the sign of greatness. He was conscious of his own gifts: prodigious memory, keen intellect, a happy gift for expression and an amazing capacity for work. These produced in him an inordinate sense of superiority. He despised his contemporaries and had nothing but contempt for other learned men. He was, as the moderns phrase it, "fixed for life." Yet, he seemed, even to his contemporaries, restless. And then overnight he chucked it all (488/1095). He experienced a sudden transformation of ideas and ideals as thoroughgoing as that of Saul of Tarsus on the way to Damascus. In his own words, as reported by his friend and biographer 'Abd-al-Ghāfir al-Fārisi, "a door of fear was opened upon him, which diverted him from everything else and compelled him to ignore all but God." So complete was the change, that many, including some of his friends, could not accept its authenticity. Even 'Abd-al-Ghāfir entertained some doubts and for a while thought that al-Ghazzāli "had clothed himself with the garment of pretense." Others were more certain and less charitable. 'Abd-al-Ghāfir conducted a personal investigation, which convinced him "that contrary to the prevalent belief, al-Ghazzāli's conversion was sincere and that he came to himself." "The evil spirit of folly, the inordinate desire for rank and position, love of pomp and prestige, and the reprehensible traits which characterized him were transformed into tranquillity, magnanimity and oblivion to conventional formalities. He took on the habit of the saints and devoted himself to the task of guiding people to a deeper concern for the affairs of the hereafter."

The reasons for this abrupt change are not easy to determine. Some scholars have tried to connect the event with the death in 487/1094 of the Great Saljuq Nāṣir-al-Dīn Maḥmūd, who is supposed to have been favorably disposed towards al-Ghazzāli, and the succession of Rukn-al-Dīn abu-al-Muẓaffar Barkiyāruq, who is thought to have been hostile to him. The two brothers had been at war with each other for several years. This attractive hypothesis fails when we note that the crisis in al-Ghazzāli's life took place prior to Rajab 486 (1093). Even if we assign the crisis in his life to the period ending in Rajab 488 (1095), we cannot link his flight, if it indeed were flight, to the accession of Barkiyāruq which took place in 487/1094. Furthermore, the fact that he could place his brother Aḥmad as his deputy in the lectureship at the Niẓāmīyah would militate against the theory that he was in disfavor with the sultan.

It is better, therefore, to examine what he himself had said concerning this period in his life. In reply to an inquiry as to the reasons which led him to discard in turn the methods of the scholastic theologians and traditional authority, as well as the different philosophical systems and rationalism, he said, "From the period of adolescence . . . I have interrogated the beliefs of each sect and scrutinized the mysteries of each doctrine, in order to disentangle truth from error and orthodoxy from heresy. I have never met one who maintained the hidden meaning of the Koran without investigating the nature of his belief, nor a partisan of its exterior sense without inquiring into the results of his doctrine. There is no philosopher whose systems I have not fathomed, nor theologian the intricacies of whose doctrine I have not followed out. Sufism has no secrets into which I have not penetrated; the devout adorer of the Deity has revealed to me the aim of his austerities; the atheist has not been able to conceal from me the real reason of his disbelief. The thirst for knowledge was innate in me from an early age; it was like a second nature implanted by God, without any will on my part. No sooner had I emerged from boyhood than I had already broken the fetters of tradition and freed myself from hereditary beliefs.

"Having noticed how easily the children of Christians become Christians, and the children of Moslems embrace Islam, and remembering the tradition, 'Every child has in him the germ of Islam, then his parents make him Jew, Christian, or Zoroastrian,' I was moved by a keen desire to learn what was this innate disposition in the child, the nature of the accidental beliefs imposed on him by the authority of his parents and masters, and finally the unreasoned convictions which he derives from their instructions.

"Struck with the contradictions which I encountered in endeavoring to disentangle the truth and falsehood of these opinions, I was led to make the following reflection: 'The search after truth being the aim which I propose for myself, I ought in the first place to ascertain what are the bases of certitude.' In the next place I recognized that certitude was the clear and complete knowledge of things, such knowledge as leaves no room for doubt nor possibility of error and conjecture. . . . All forms of knowledge which do not unite these conditions (imperviousness to doubt, etc.) do not deserve any confidence. I then examined what knowledge I possessed, and discovered that in none of it, with the exception of sense-perceptions and necessary principles, did I enjoy that degree of certitude which I just described. . . . I then set myself earnestly to examine the notions we derive from the evidence of the senses. . . . The result of a careful examination was that my confidence in them was shaken.

"Then I reflected in myself: 'Since I cannot trust the evidence of my senses, I must rely only on intellectual notions based on fundamental principles.' But the notions I derived from my senses made the following objections: 'Who can guarantee that you can trust to the evidence of reason more than to that of the senses?' Perhaps there is above reason another judge who, if he appeared, would convict reason of falsehood, just as reason has confuted [the senses]. And if this third arbiter is not yet apparent, it does not follow that he does not exist.

"To this argument I remained some time without a reply. . . . Such thoughts as these threatened to shake my reason, and I sought to find an escape from them. But how? In order to disentangle the knot of this difficulty, a proof was necessary. Now a proof must be based on primary assumptions, and it was precisely these of which I was in doubt. This unhappy state lasted about two months, during which I was not, it is true, explicitly or by profession, but morally and essentially a thoroughgoing skeptic.

"God at last deigned to heal me of this mental malady; my mind recovered its sanity and equilibrium, the primary assumptions of reason recovered with me all their stringency and force. I owed my deliverance, not to concatenation of proofs and arguments, but to the light which God caused to penetrate into my heart—the light which illuminates the threshold of all knowledge."

This is the gist of the story as told by al-Ghazzāli himself. We need not, therefore, seek for his great renunciation an external cause, political or otherwise. The urge for such theories, however, is not confined to modern scholars, but has also lured past generations of learned men. Al-Sayyid al-Murtaḍa preserves for us in his voluminous commentary on the major work of al-Ghazzāli the following explanation for that remarkable conversion. One day, as al-Ghazzāli was preaching, his brother Aḥmad entered the hall and, addressing his brother, said:

> "Thou guidest others, but thou art not guided;
> Thou chidest others, but thou art not chided;
> Whetstone, as thou art, how long wouldst thou
> Sharpen the knife, and yet thou remainest blunt?"

Whereupon al-Ghazzāli forsook his previous ways and renounced the world.

This tale is interesting only in so far as it reflects the intellectual and moral snobbishness of al-Ghazzāli prior to his conversion; it fails to answer the question which perplexed contemporaries and later scholars alike. That question, however, was, as already stated, answered by al-Ghazzāli himself. Dissatisfied with traditional authority, he sought a unifying principle for life in rationalism. Rationalism failed him, and he wandered for two months in the wilderness of skepticism, when at long last, almost miraculously, he came upon the fresh waters of mysticism. Having quenched his spiritual thirst from those waters, his tormented soul was refreshed. He penetrated the veil, and entered upon that state where he could see truth face to face.

Thence he left Baghdad and wandered as a dervish in Syria, Palestine and Egypt, moving between Damascus, Jerusalem, Cairo and Alexandria. He then performed the pilgrimage and returned to Damascus where he taught and wrote. To this period of about ten years belongs the greater bulk of his writings, including his major work, the *Iḥyā' 'Ulūm al-Dīn* (The Revival of the Sciences of Religion). Towards the end of 499/1106 he was prevailed upon to return to Nisapur and assume teaching at its Niẓāmīyah School. But his soul, once freed, did not enable him to remain there long. He did not feel at home in those surroundings; the atmosphere was too oppressive and worldly for a spirit refined by solitude and meditation. Had it not been for the demands placed upon him by his family, he would have, probably, never returned. In less than two years he retired to his birthplace, Ṭūs, where he led a life of seclusion until death claimed him in 505/1111.

In the course of his new life, al-Ghazzāli laid down for himself certain rules of conduct. These are embodied in a short tract entitled *The Ten Rules*, and offer the best summary of his ethics.

The road to hell may be paved with good intentions, but the path to heaven may not be built without them. Al-Ghazzāli, then, insists on intention as the first rule of conduct. As usual he quotes the tradition in support of his position: "Verily, to every man is the intention he hath resolved." This intention should be good and lasting without change. Good in so far as it concludes what it set out to do, and leaves the rest to God; lasting in so far as it continues to be good, and is not dissuaded from its goal by anything worldly, but persists in its resolve.

Unity of purpose is the second rule. Serving God alone is the way he states it. The sign of this service is to be satisfied with nothing but the truth, and to deem all things besides unworthy. "Woe unto him who is subservient unto money." Therefore, let him who would serve the Lord avoid the things of this world, and rest his hopes and aspirations in God. Al-Ghazzāli realizes the difficulty of this rule in a world where man is exposed to want and need and his standards are ruled by false values. Having himself experienced doubt as to the goodness of God, the meaning of life, and the basis of certitude, he warns against doubt as the most vicious of all afflictions. It drove him to the verge of madness. Therefore, "cast away that which breedeth doubt within you, and take hold of that which maketh for strength." Furthermore, man should be physically in this world, but in reality in the hereafter. "Be in this world as a stranger, or a traveler, and regard yourself as dead [to the world]." The outward sign of this state is contentment: to be satisfied with mere shelter against the elements, and with enough to keep hunger from your door. "Sufficient unto a man is a mouthful wherewith he keepeth his body and soul together." Therefore, he that has a loaf of barley should not seek a loaf of wheat, and he that has a mess of porridge should not desire a pot of gold. The sign of the stranger is a light load as he sojourns in alien land, and his mark is his disinclination to weigh himself down with the goods of this world. The sign of the traveler is his prompt response, and his seal is his contentment with what comes his way. The sign that one is dead to the world is to prefer the affairs of the hereafter to the affairs of the present.

The third rule is to conform throughout to truth, and to make bold to differ with oneself by forsaking pleasure and enduring pain, by resisting desire and abjuring luxury and ease. As a result of such discipline, the disciple penetrates the veil, and enters upon that state where he can see the truth face to face. His sleep then becomes wakefulness, his company solitude, his satiety hunger, his high rank abasement, his speech silence, and his plenty paucity.

The babel of religious sects and philosophical thought confused and appalled al-Ghazzāli. To him "this diversity in beliefs and religions, and the variety of doctrines and sects which divide men," were "like a deep ocean strewn with shipwrecks, from which very few can be saved." Worse still, "each sect believed itself sole possessor of truth and salvation; 'each party,' as the Koran puts it, 'rejoices in its own creed.' " He, therefore, urged orthodoxy upon the Moslems. This constitutes his fourth rule: to conform in life to the established practice, and to avoid all innovations, lest one be a faddist, vain in his own ways. For he who is a law unto himself shall not prosper. It might be difficult to understand how such an independent thinker as al-Ghazzāli would advocate a principle which would amount to blind acceptance of authority—one which he himself rejected in practice. It must be remembered that al-Ghazzāli's concern was primarily the people, whose discernment and judgment he did not respect or trust. In the second place he deemed authority, despite its shortcomings, better than anarchy. The unbridled sectarianism of the Protestant churches in the United States, for example, is more degenerate and disturbing than the ossified traditionalism of the Coptic or the Abyssinian Church. And finally, it is not unusual for a great soul to seek refuge against perplexity and bewilderment in the authority of an established orthodoxy, be the person al-Ghazzāli, or Newman or even Heywood Broun.

In the fifth rule al-Ghazzāli recognizes the evils of procrastination and warns against them, urging steadfast zeal and determination. In the sixth he reminds his fellowmen of their duty to acknowledge their inability (*'ajz*) to accomplish anything without the help of God, but warns them not to use this as pretext for laziness in good works and neglect of independent action. Side by side with this sense of dependence they should cultivate humility and lowliness, and show respect and regard to their fellowmen.

In the seventh rule al-Ghazzāli preaches a doctrine of salvation by faith. He calls it the rule of true fear and hope. One should not feel secure in the superiority of well-doing, but should rest one's hope in God. This sounds like a faint echo of the Pauline doctrine, and reminds us of the words, "For by grace are ye saved through faith; and that not of yourselves: it is the gift of God; not of works, lest any man should boast." It is not unlikely that al-Ghazzāli, who boasted of investigating every system, had access to the writings of Paul. But whatever influence there was, it must have been unconscious. Or could it be inherent in the nature of their parallel religious experiences?

In the eighth rule al-Ghazzāli recommends a life of devotion and prayer. He is sure that to neglect devotional exercises is to shut oneself from the only source of spiritual power. The eighth rule leads to the ninth, that of continual observation and watchfulness (*murāqabah*). This is the first of the mystical states (sing. *ḥāl*). He who persists in watching and observing his own heart for God, and banishes therefrom everything but God, will find God and His grace, and certainty besides. He will move from groping to tranquillity, and from tranquillity to reality, through the will and power of God. His meditation will then increase, until he attains true faith. Thence he will be absorbed in God, wherein is the substance of faith. He will then say, "I have seen nought without seeing God therein, exalted above all in His subsistence, existing through His will and power, according to the contemplation and presence of the heart." The outward sign of this rule is to be courteous to other people, and discriminating in the choice of friends and companions. The Prophet said, "My Lord hath taught me, and hath taught me well."

The tenth rule is consecration to a knowledge wherein one would see God. It should be pursued with diligence, both outwardly and inwardly. Its outward sign is perseverance in good works, since he who thinks that he can do without good works is a moral bankrupt. God, besides whom there is no other god, said, "If ye love me, then follow me: God will love you."

The major work of al-Ghazzāli, however, which established his position in Islam as the greatest religious figure after Muhammad, is the *Iḥyā' 'Ulūm al-Dīn.*

The work itself is divided into four parts. This is no mere accident. Desiring to ensure for his ideas the widest circulation possible, al-Ghazzāli modeled his *Iḥyā'*, only in form, after the most popular books of the day. These dealt with jurisprudence, and were always divided into four parts, one for each of the component parts of the discipline, namely the Koran, the *sunnah* (the usage of the Prophet as recorded in tradition), catholic consent, and analogy. Al-Ghazzāli was not the first Moslem writer to employ this device. He himself alludes to the *Taqwīm al-Abdān* (Tables of Physiology) of ibn-Jazlah (d. 493/1100), which, like the earlier *Taqwīm al-Ṣiḥḥah* (Tables of Health) of ibn-Buṭlān (d. 455/1063), was a medical work modeled, for the purpose of gaining a wider audience, after the then very popular astronomical tables. Each of these four parts of the *Iḥyā'* was called *rub'* (quarter). The first deals with the Acts of Worship (*'ibādāt*), the second treats of the Usages of Life (*mu'āmalāt*), the third discusses the Destructive Matters of Life (*muhlikāt*), and the fourth expounds the Saving Matters of Life (*munajjiyāt*). The first two deal with the outward forms of worship, while the last two treat of the inner nature of religion.

Each of these four "quarters" contains ten books (sing. *kitāb*). The quarter on the Acts of Worship comprises the following:

1. The Book of Knowledge
2. The Articles of Faith
3. The Mysteries of Purity
4. The Mysteries of Prayer
5. The Mysteries of Alms
6. The Mysteries of Fasting
7. The Mysteries of the Pilgrimage
8. The Rules of Reading the Koran
9. On Invocations and Supplications
10. On the Office of Portions

The quarter on the Usages of Life comprises the following:

1. The Ethics of Eating
2. The Ethics of Marriage
3. The Ethics of Earning a Livelihood
4. On the Lawful and the Unlawful
5. The Ethics of Companionship and Fellowship with the Various Types of Men
6. On Seclusion
7. The Ethics of Travel
8. On Audition and Grief
9. On Enjoining Good and Forbidding Evil
10. The Ethics of Living as Exemplified in the virtues of the Prophet

The quarter on the Destructive Matters of Life comprises the following:

1. On the Wonders of the Heart
2. On the Discipline of the Soul
3. On the Curse of the Two Appetites—The Appetite of the Stomach and the Appetite of Sex

4. The Curse of the Tongue
5. The Curse of Anger, Rancor, and Envy
6. The Evil of the World
7. The Evil of Wealth and Avarice
8. The Evil of Pomp and Hypocrisy
9. The Evil of Pride and Conceit
10. The Evil of Vanity

The quarter on the Saving Matters of Life comprises the following:

1. On Repentance
2. On Patience and Gratitude
3. On Fear and Hope
4. On Poverty and Asceticism
5. On Divine Unity and Dependence
6. On Love, Longing, Intimacy, and Contentment
7. On Intentions, Truthfulness, and Sincerity
8. On Self-Examination and Self-Accounting
9. On Meditation
10. On Death.

In these forty books which make up the four quarters of the *Iḥyā'*, al-Ghazzāli has preserved the summation of medieval Moslem thought. For this reason, it occupies a unique position throughout the Moslem world. This position is best described by the words of al-Nawawi, famous thirteenth century scholar, who said, "Should all other Moslem writings be destroyed, the *Iḥyā'*, if spared, would make up for all the loss."

But before attempting to estimate the lasting contribution of al-Ghazzāli to Islam in particular and to religious thought in general, it is necessary to determine the extent of his originality. He himself acknowledges his indebtedness to several Sufis whose writings he studied immediately after emerging from his crisis. Among the five he names, we may single out two: abu-Ṭālib al-Makki (d. 386/996), author of the *Qūt al-Qulūb*, and al-Ḥārith al-Muḥāsibi (d. 243/857), author of several mystical works. The pages of the *Iḥyā'* reflect definite and extensive dependence on the *Qūt al-Qulūb*, both in content and form. Passages are quoted verbatim, though always expanded and enriched by illustrations and examples. Al-Ghazzāli's religious experience was, however, more profound, and, therefore, his writings were more convincing, and his contribution greater.

His first contribution to Islam was that of bringing the problem of education into organic relation with a profound ethical system. He saw that the temporal gains which the Saljuqs had achieved would not endure without a corresponding ethical and moral reawakening; he even declared that those gains were purely materialistic, and, therefore, should not endure. The remedy he prescribed was education, not limited, like that which the best minds of his time advocated, to the imparting of knowledge for utilitarian purposes, but one which would also stimulate the moral consciousness of the individual.

In the realm of religion, he grafted mysticism, which had hitherto been deemed as unorthodox, to Islam, and established its orthodoxy. His mysticism vitalized the law by making personal religion and individual experience a part of Islam. His orthodoxy safeguarded the faith against unbridled emotionalism. Through his writings he led the Moslems back from scholastic labors upon theological dogma and minutiae to a living contact with the Word. Through them he brought philosophy, which he regarded merely as *thinking*, and philosophical theology within the range of the ordinary man. He freed Islam from the dead formalism of scholastic literalism, and quickened it by the warmth of the living spirit. And it was exactly this warmth for which Islam was groping. And this humbled and chastised man, who was cursed as a heretic in Baghdad, Damascus, Jerusalem, Cairo, North Africa and Spain, became the Authority of Islam (*Ḥujjat al-Islām*). He brought Islam back to life, revitalized the law, and breathed into it a spirit of warmth and kindliness.

But the influence of al-Ghazzāli extended beyond the

walls of Islam. His works were partly translated into Latin before the middle of the twelfth century. Raymund Martin had access to al-Ghazzāli's *Tahāfut al-Falāsifah* (The Incoherence of the Philosophers), a polemic against the Philosophers and scholastics of Islam, and incorporated a great deal of it in his *Pugio Fidei.* Henceforth al-Ghazzāli's arguments in favor of the *creatio ex nihilo* and his proofs that God's knowledge comprises particulars, as well as that of the dogma of the resurrection of the dead, were employed by Christians in many scholastic treatises. His mental and religious attitude appealed to Christian scholars from the moment his writings became accessible to them.

Another work of al-Ghazzāli, which treats of the place of reason as applied to revelation, presents many parallels in its arguments and conclusions with the *Summa Theologica* of Thomas Aquinas. This can hardly have more than one explanation, since the *Summa* and the *Pugio Fidei* were both written at the request of Raymund de Pinnaforte, General of the Dominican Order. The similarity of some chapters in both is suggestive. Some of the more important questions on which Aquinas and al-Ghazzāli agree are the value of human reason in explaining or demonstrating the truth about divine things; the ideas of contingency and necessity as demonstrating the existence of God; the unity of God as implied in His perfection; the possibility of beatific vision; the divine knowledge and the divine simplicity; the names of God; miracles as a testimony to the truth of the utterances of prophets; and the dogma of the resurrection of the dead.

Another source for Aquinas' familiarity with the writings of al-Ghazzāli was Maimonides, who drew his Peripatetic theories from the *Maqāṣid al-Falāsifah* of al-Ghazzāli. Aquinas refers in *Contra Gentiles*, iii. 97, to a Moslem theologian quoted by Maimonides. That theologian is al-Ghazzāli.

Intellectually, al-Ghazzāli was probably a man of lesser stature than Aquinas, but his personal contribution to theology was more considerable than that of the Christian theologian; and both had much in common. Their intentions, sympathies and interests were essentially the same. Both endeavored to state the case for the opposition before they pronounced judgment; both labored to provide a reasonable statement of their faith; and both found happiness in the mystical apprehension of the divine which they confessed made their earlier strivings seem as nothing.

In the East, Bar Hebraeus (d. 1286) seems to have come under the direct influence of al-Ghazzāli. This influence is clearly reflected in the former's *Book of the Dove* and *Ethikon*. In fact the same relation which exists between al-Ghazzāli and abu-Ṭālib al-Makki exists between Bar Hebraeus and al-Ghazzāli. The religious experience of this brilliant dignitary of the Jacobite Church parallels that of al-Ghazzāli. Like al-Ghazzāli, he went through a religious crisis which made him appear before himself no longer as the head of a time-honored church but as a poor and humble beggar for religious light, a soul which on its way unto the union with God had only reached the stage where light is still dim and shadows prevail.

Al-Ghazzāli's influence on medieval Judaism was even greater than his influence on Christian scholasticism. This was brought about mainly through his ethical teachings. He approached the ethical ideals of Judaism to such an extent that some supposed him to be actually drifting in that direction. His works were thus eagerly studied and used by Jewish writers, and several borrowed extensively from them. In particular, al-Ghazzāli's *Mīzān al-'Amal* was translated into Hebrew and clothed in Jewish garb by substituting biblical and talmudic quotations for koranic and ḥadīth citations.

To the followers of Islam as well as Judaism and Christianity, the life and works of al-Ghazzāli offer an inspiration and an object lesson in personal religion. His last words before death closed his eyes give the best key to his whole transformed and remarkable personality. After performing his ablutions and prayers, he asked his brother to hand him his shroud. He took it, kissed it, and laid it on his eyes and said, "I hear and obey the command to go unto the King."

He dropped his bag and eased his weight,
He tossed his bowl from which he ate;
He shed his shoes and freed his feet,
His course to run, his Lord to meet.

BIBLIOGRAPHY

E. E. Calverley. *Worship in Islam.* Madras, 1925.

Claud Field. *The Confessions of Al Ghazzali.* London, 1909.

D. B. Macdonald. *The Religious Attitude and Life in Islam.* (Chicago, 1909), chaps. viii-x.

———. "Life of al-Ghazzāli with Special Reference to his Religious Experience and Opinions," *Journal of the American Oriental Society.* XX (1899), 71-132.

———. "Book 8 of Rub' II of the *Iḥyā' 'Ulūm al-Dīn* (on al-Samā')," *Journal of the Royal Asiatic Society.* 1901-1902.

———. "Book 4 of Rub' IV of the *Iḥyā' 'Ulūm al-Dīn* (on Love of God)," Hastings' *Dictionary of Religions.* II, 677-80.

George H. Scherer. *Ayyuha 'l-Walad,* Ar. text and Eng. tr. Beirut, 1933.

Margaret Smith. *Studies in Early Mysticism in the Near East.* London, 1931.

———. *An Early Mystic of Baghdad.* London, 1935.

———. "Al-Risālat al-Laduniyya," Eng. tr., *Journal of the Royal Asiatic Society.* 1938.

A. J. Wensinck. *Bar Hebraeus' Book of the Dove.* (Leyden, 1919), pp. cxi ff.

———. *The Muslim Creed.* Cambridge, 1932.

CRUSADE AND JIHĀD

JOHN L. LAMONTE

THE RELIGIOUS MOTIVATION IN THE CRUSADES AND THE MOSLEM WARS AGAINST THE LATINS IN SYRIA IN THE TWELFTH AND THIRTEENTH CENTURIES

War aims and war issues are always controversial matters. In the excitement and heat of preparation for war certain aims and motives are emphasized which the colder light of later reason often reduces to considerably less importance than they seem to have had at the moment. Even where the motives seem entirely clear cut there are always found to be subsidiary war aims which contribute towards bringing about the condition of actual war. The general rule may be laid down that the ideological aim is emphasized in order to gain popular support, although the economic and political motives may be in reality more potent factors than the ideological which receives so much publicity.

No issue is more calculated to stir up ordinary citizens than that of religion. There is something fatal about religious zeal which makes men anxious and willing to risk their own lives in return for the dubious pleasure of exterminating others who differ with them on some detail of their definition of the attributes of the deity or the proper method of conducting his worship. In ancient days when each tribe had its own particular deity, the various gods were invoked to support the ambitions of their followers, and the defeat of the tribe involved the loss of prestige of the god whose power was not great enough to assure his people success in their attempts to seize the lands and goods of their neighbors. The gods of Carthage went down with the galleys of the Punic fleet; had Carthage won, Baal might well have topped the hierarchy of the Roman pantheon. *Vox populi vox dei est*: it is no great step from the invocation of the god to aid in the ambitions of the tribe or nation to the idea that the desires of the people are the will of the god. I dare say that the good Carthaginians were quite convinced that Baal willed them to fight the Romans; certainly the Athenian Empire involved the glory of Athena; throughout antiquity the gods often participated personally in the struggles of their followers and if after Homeric times they made fewer personal appearances, they were none the less concerned. Saints and archangels commonly fought in the Christian armies in the early days; *In hoc signo vinces* was employed by Constantine in a thoroughly secular conflict, and the Germans in the first world war announced proudly "*Gott mit uns.*" In the present conflict, having abolished God, the Germans cannot well invoke Him, but they have substituted Germanism as a God-concept, and their zeal for its glory is as passionate as that of the devotees of any more orthodox religious sect. To many devout people today the struggle with Nazism is colored largely by the fact that in preserving democracy and destroying the Nazi peril they are defending their religion and the principles of the Christian faith. Perhaps the cooperation of the Japanese with the Nazis can in part be explained on the grounds that they have always been emperor worshipers and so do not find their religion undermined. And the Italians have for so many centuries been so close to the worldly representatives of Christ that they fail to take very seriously attacks made upon the bases of His power on earth.

Of all religious wars the crusades are undoubtedly the most celebrated. On the battlefields of Syria two great religions engaged in bitter conflict; Christ struggled with Muhammad where earlier he had wrestled with the Devil. "*God wills it*" was the war-cry of the First Crusade. Mob hysteria affected the men who heard Pope Urban's impassioned address at Clermont no less than it did the eminent French gentlemen who gave away all their manorial rights in the hysteria of brotherly love on the famous night of August 4, 1789. Urban's speech was singularly provocative and persuasive; to the disgrace of Christendom infidel hands were polluting the Holy Sepulcher and the other sacred shrines of Palestine, these places must be restored to Christ; pilgrims to the East had been persecuted, the roads must be opened and kept free to them (a doctrine as appealing to that audience as the freedom of the seas is to us today); the cruel race of the Turks were perpetrating atrocities on the Oriental Christians (atrocities and outrageous incidents have never failed to stir men up to violence). Nor did Urban neglect the gains, temporal as well as spiritual, which accrued to the crusader; salvation awaited those who gave their lives for the cause, the rich cities of the Promised Land would be the reward of those who lived to conquer them. The pope did not mention the value to the papacy of a huge army marching under his orders or the effect which it would undoubtedly have on the emperors to see the popes so amply armed. He did not mention that the Church had suffered at the hands of the secular power and that the crusade would be a useful reminder to the empire that the Servant of the Servants of God could yet command. Like any good propagandist Urban stressed the ideological aims of the crusade; peace among Christians and death to the enemies of the faith was his message; and the result was wholly satisfactory. Carried away by his oratory, the audience wept and cheered; crosses were hastily made and affixed to their garments; men of all stations and ranks hastened to pledge themselves to the holy war. The effectiveness of the preaching of the crusade by the agents commissioned by the pope "to carry the word to all peoples" is attested not only by the celebrated passage of William of Malmesbury, but by the fame of Peter the Hermit. The peasants' crusade, emotional, ignorant and ineffective, is the one really wholly religious part of the First Crusade. While many of the leaders who participated in the "crusade of the princes" were undoubtedly moved by essentially religious considerations, there were others who went more for the things of this world than for the glory of God. The motives of Godfrey, who sought forgiveness for his earlier sins and salvation for his soul, are not to be questioned; Robert of

Normandy and Robert of Flanders were probably inspired largely by religion, though there was also, I believe, the factor that they had in the crusade a chance to become heroes; but no one can suggest that Bohemond of Tarento went for any reasons other than the desire to found a principality in the East, and Raymond of St. Gilles, that old veteran of the Spanish wars, also had an eye for the fair lands of Syria. Their followers were probably motivated by any number of reasons; some went out of purely religious fervor, some left to escape the monotony of their daily existence or the sharp tongues of their wives, some took the cross out of pure love of adventure, some just went along because it was being done. But I think it is safe to assume that then as now the bulk of the fighters were stimulated by the idealistic aims which the leaders too professed, and that to the great mass of the participants the First Crusade was essentially a religious war.

And what of the Moslems they were setting out to conquer? They too had a tradition of a holy war, the *jihād*. Their earliest conquests—that inevitable expansion of the virile Arabian race—had been made under the guise of the extension of the faith. They too had "carried the gospel unto all nations" and had made conquests and converts simultaneously. Under the early caliphs Islam had taken the offensive against the lands of the infidels, and the *jihād* had carried the banner of the Prophet from the Pillars of Hercules to the borders of India. The crusade was merely the Christian counteroffensive and it was but reasonable to expect that Islam, attacked, would rise united to ward off the blow directed against the lands of the Prophet. Had religion been the dominant motive in the minds of the Moslems, as many writers would have us believe, this is what they would have done. The actuality was quite otherwise.

Viewed from the Moslem side, the crusades were but distressing incidents in the long history of the struggle for Syria. They were major wars and as such loom large in the Moslem chronicles of the period, but they were never the vital affairs that Western writers would make them appear.

At first practically ignored by the caliphs, the crusades never disturbed the seats of power in Islam as did the Turkish or Mongol conquests, they were never important enough to produce real unity in the Islamic world. And why should they have been? They were of greater importance to Christendom than to Islam and they never succeeded in producing Christian unity.

All historians of the crusades now agree that one of the chief factors in the success of the First Crusade was the dissension and inability to cooperate in the face of a common danger shown by the Moslem rulers of Syria when the Christian forces arrived in the East. The political geography of late eleventh century Syria was a crazy quilt of semi-independent states. At the opening of the century the country had been divided between the Byzantine Empire and the Fatimid caliphate of Cairo. But the Saljuq invasions had destroyed this balance and had left practical anarchy throughout Syria.

Alp Arslān's campaign of 1070-1071 is usually thought of only in terms of the battle of Manzikert where he destroyed the Byzantine forces, but it also hit at the Fatimid power, for the Saljuqs as a result of that campaign conquered not only southern Anatolia and northern Syria but pushed south to take Damascus and Jerusalem from the Egyptians. In the decade after Manzikert Syria was split into a multitude of small states, some owing allegiance to the sultan, many wholly independent. The chief power in Syria and Palestine was Tutush, the younger brother of the sultan Malik-Shah, who conquered for himself Damascus, Jerusalem, Acre and most of Palestine and southern Syria, and who stood as a buffer and a rival between the Saljuqs of Iconium and the Fatimids of Egypt. In 1086 Tutush defeated Sulaymān ibn-Quṭlumish of Iconium in a battle for Aleppo and seemed about to make himself supreme in Syria, only to have the fruits of victory wrested from him by the arrival of Malik-Shah, who appropriated unto himself the cities of the north, appointing loyal emirs in Aleppo, Edessa and Antioch.

When Malik-Shah died in 1092, Tutush tried to avail

himself of the opportunity presenting itself in the civil war which broke out between the sons of the sultan. He quickly forced the rulers of the Saljuq cities to accept his rule and even reached eastward for the sultanate itself in 1094; but Barkiyāruq, the eldest son of Malik-Shah, succeeded in establishing himself in the sultanate at the expense of his brothers and drove his uncle back into Syria. Tutush however still held Damascus and Aleppo, while his vassals Thoros, an Armenian, and Suqmān ibn-Urtuq held Edessa and Jerusalem respectively. At his death in 1095 Tutush's sons Riḍwān and Duqāq inherited Aleppo and Damascus, but the Fatimids invaded the south and drove the Urtuqids out of Jerusalem in 1096. Barkiyāruq seems to have been fairly indifferent to events in Syria, and was satisfied to have but a vague suzerainty over the sons of Tutush, though he did support his general Karbuqa who conquered Mosul from the 'Uqaylids and became the chief agent of the sultan in the west.

The above rapid sketch of events in Syria can give but a very inadequate picture of the confusion which existed when the crusaders arrived. Few of the Turkish princes recognized either the sultan or each other, all were rivals and all sought their own increase at the expense of their neighbors; Qilij Arslān of Iconium, Karbuqa of Mosul, Riḍwān of Aleppo, Duqāq of Damascus, the Fatimid governors of Jerusalem and Ascalon, the Armenians in Cilicia, the Dānishmands in Cappadocia and the Urtuqids, who had removed to Diyār-Bakr, were all pulling against each other and were all mutually distrustful. Real cooperation among them was impossible; the crusaders needed meet them only one by one.

The first campaigns of the crusaders were against the Saljuqs of Iconium. In collaboration with the Byzantines they captured Nicea, then defeated the Turks in open battle at Dorylaeum. Although sensing vaguely the threat of the invasion, the emirs of Syria rather rejoiced in the defeat of their northern rivals and lifted no hand to assist them. Then the crusaders arrived before Antioch which they besieged. Yaghi-Siyān, the emir of Antioch, was the vassal of Barkiyāruq and on bad terms with both Riḍwān and Duqāq; only from Mosul could he expect, and only from Mosul did he get, any assistance. True, certain troops from Aleppo and Damascus joined the expedition which Karbuqa led to the relief of Antioch, but they are said to have deserted in the hour of battle and left Karbuqa to defeat. And while the crusaders were engaged around Antioch, ambassadors from the Fatimid caliph came bearing offers of alliance against the Turks! Meanwhile Thoros of Edessa had gladly received the Franks into his domains and cast off his vassalage to his Moslem suzerain; the Armenian princes of Cilicia did likewise, and the various Christian peoples, Maronite, Jacobite, Nestorian and Armenian, all rendered the crusaders valuable assistance in their conquest. As for the Arab emirs, they preferred to pay tribute to the conquerors and to let them pass through their territories, hoping perhaps that they would be defeated by the stronger forces which they would encounter farther south. In the confusion of the last century the people had grown used to a rapid change of masters: Byzantine, Turk, Arab, Frank—it mattered little to them whom they served; the Christian population did hope for somewhat better treatment at the hands of coreligionists and so aided the invaders, but the Moslem population was largely apathetic and its leaders were too impressed with the invincibility of the Franks and too unwilling to risk reprisal by giving aid to each other to offer any effective resistance.

It is quite true that throughout the period of the Frankish occupation of Syria there were constant wars between the Christian and Moslem states; while there were intervals of peace between campaigns, war was the normal state of affairs and there are few years in the annals of the kingdom of Jerusalem that do not have mention of some sort of hostilities. But these incessant wars were not in the least religious wars. The annals of any feudal state of Western Europe are just as full of petty wars as are those of the crusader states. The issue was the political control of Syria; no power could successfully dominate Syria without control of the seacoast nor could the people of the coast dominate without control of the interior; consequently there was bound to be constant conflict between the inhabitants of the opposing states. That this is true is amply proven by surveying the whole picture of Syrian politics. There were certainly as many wars between conflicting Moslem states as there were between Moslem and Christian; there were probably as many civil disputes among the Christian princes as there were wars with the infidels. Furthermore neither religion hesitated to ally itself with men of the opposite faith against their own coreligionists. Unholy alliances of Christians and Moslems characterized the history of the Latin colonies in Syria.

The Western Christians who settled in Syria soon learned to get along with their Moslem neighbors at least as well as they did with their Christian fellows, and men of both faiths learned to respect the others for the qualities they possessed. Adapting themselves to the Oriental mode of life, the Latins quickly adopted the costumes and customs of the Orientals and the rude manners of the Franks were refined through contact with the more sophisticated peoples of the East. The Moslems too came to admire the courage, loyalty and chivalry of their religious opponents when they had any chance to observe these traits. Friendly intercourse was common between princes of both faiths; the hunting agreements and the sports competitions are familiar to all readers of Usāmah's *Memoirs*. Among the lower classes constant association in business and in the routine of daily life soon obliterated any religious animosities; intermarriage wiped out the racial and religious differences; in the Frankish cities there developed a cosmopolitan society, of which mute evidence can still be seen in the remains of Gothic churches surrounded by Oriental buildings. This fusion of East and West produced a civilization which was, in many respects, superior to that of any other country of the time, and in which may be detected the germs of some of the finest developments of the Renaissance.

A sharp distinction must always be made between the tolerance of the Syrian Franks and the religious fanaticism of the crusaders newly come from the West. Elsewhere I have tried to point out this essential difference in the point of view, and have shown that the Eastern Franks got along with their Moslem neighbors better in many respects than they did with their Western allies. Even the Christian archbishop, William of Tyre, lamented the disruption of amicable relations with Egypt which ruined the trade, and in the councils of the kingdom of Jerusalem it was always the barons most recently arrived from the West who advocated war with the Moslems. An exception to this must of course be made of the military orders of the Templars and Hospitalers, but these were semimonastic orders definitely pledged to carrying on the holy war under all conditions and at all costs. The professional religious of both sides always urged the holy war; it is with the secular rulers that this discussion deals. The chronicles of the Eastern and Western Latins reflect their attitude towards the Moslems; while Western writers like Ambroise, the chroniclers of the First Crusade or Jacques de Vitry are full of abuse in their references to the Moslems, the Eastern Frankish writers, like the continuator of William of Tyre or Philip de Novara are remarkably free of religious prejudice.

Grousset seems to feel that this toleration was a sort of moral degradation and that later generations of Syrian Franks were, to use the phrase of Jacques de Vitry, "an evil and perverse generation, wicked and degenerate," but the lack of religious fanaticism seems to me rather a sign of increasing civilization, and in spite of the expressed opinions of such eminent authorities as de Vitry and Grousset, I cannot find any unusual signs of moral decay in the Syrian Franks of the later twelfth and thirteenth centuries.

Nor am I at all sure that the religious zeal of the First Crusade lasted even through the lifetime of the men who led it. Men of the first generation learned that "their neighbors had much in common with themselves" though it is quite true that they "regarded all Moslem Syria as an unoccupied promised land" as far as attempts to capture it were concerned. But I do not feel that the attempts to capture Moslem lands were due at all to the fact that they were Moslem lands; it was merely that the generation of the First Crusade were out to conquer principalities, and the land in general was held by Moslems, wherefore it was from Moslems that it had to be taken. The career of Tancred, one of the great heroes of the First Crusade, and one whose cruel and bloody slaughter of the Moslems in the sack of Jerusalem brought joy to the heart of Raymond of Aguilers, gives ample proof that the leaders of the crusade, in pushing forward their expansionist policy, were following purely secular aims and were willing to compromise when necessary with their Moslem opponents. Tancred was determined to create as large a state as possible, and whether he took it from Moslem, Greek, Armenian or fellow Frank mattered not at all to him, and he spent fully as much time and energy in trying to take Laodicea and other Christian cities from the Greeks and Armenians as he did in fighting the Turks. Nor does the career of Baldwin de Burg, especially in his Edessan days, refute this general thesis.

One would naturally expect the first period of Frankish conquest in the years immediately following the First Crusade to be the most marked by really religious wars, but even in this period we find some of the best examples of interreligious alliances. The confusion which the crusade brought to Syria gave an impetus to the Moslem princes to attack each other and to capitalize on the difficulties of their neighbors who were attacked by the Franks. In 1101 while Riḍwān of Aleppo was defending himself against Tancred he was attacked by Jamāl-al-Dawlah of Ḥimṣ, and as early as 1105 Baktāsh, the brother of Duqāq of Damascus, allied with the Latins against Duqāq. Riḍwān of Aleppo was always more concerned with his struggle against his brother in Damascus than he was in fighting the Latins; and in 1105 he agreed to pay tribute to Tancred in order to free his hands for a war which he was undertaking in Mesopotamia. If the Moslems were engaged in fratricidal strife, the Christians were hardly less so; we have already noticed that Tancred fought the Greeks and Armenians; he also carried on a long struggle with Raymond de St. Gilles, with Baldwin of Edessa and Joscelyn de Courtenay. In the course of these wars both aides allied with Moslems, Tancred assisting Mawdūd in his capture of Mosul.

This Mawdūd had been sent to Syria by his brother the sultan Muḥammad ibn-Malik-Shah with the definite purpose of driving the Franks out of Asia. It was the first definite attempt of the sultan to unite the Moslems in a holy war against the Christians, and although for a time in the years 1110-1113 Mawdūd succeeded in forming a coalition of the Urtuqids of Māridīn and Ṭughtigīn of Damascus which combatted a temporary Christian union, the effort was too great and the alliances too unstable on both parts. Baldwin of Jerusalem and Tancred both helped Baldwin de Burg free Edessa from a Moslem invasion, but they were soon quarreling among themselves. By 1115 we find Damascus and the Urtuqids allied with the Franks in conflict with the armies of the sultan, which were led by the lords of Aleppo, Ḥimṣ, Hamadhān and Shayzar. The death of Lu'lu' of Aleppo in 1117 brought on a civil war in which the rulers of Ḥimṣ, al-Ruḥbah and Māridīn, struggled for the control of Aleppo. When they discovered that the only person who was gaining anything was Roger of Antioch who had taken the occasion to plunder Aleppan territory, the Moslems united under the leadership of Īl-Ghāzi of Māridīn long enough to rout Roger, but the coalition which so badly defeated the Franks in 1118-1119 broke up after the death of Īl-Ghāzi and his nephew Balak, and by 1125 civil war was again rife among the Moslem princes. In that year Aleppo very nearly fell to the Franks who were allied with the famous rebel Dubays ibn-Ṣadaqah of al-Ḥillah, who had shortly before threatened Baghdad itself, and it was only the prompt action of Āqsunqur al-Bursuqi of Mosul which saved the city.

From this brief survey it will be apparent that the Frankish states, even in the first period of the conquest, entered into the complicated network of Syrian politics no differently than did the various Moslem emirs. Occasionally the Frankish states did ally against a Moslem coalition, but never was there found complete cooperation among the Moslem powers to expel the Western infidels. The rival caliphates of Baghdad and Cairo could never get together, and as frequently as not alliances and wars cut across religious lines entirely.

Traditionally the *revanche* of Islam begins with the career of 'Imād-al-Dīn Zangi ibn-Āqsunqur. But Zangi should under no circumstances be considered as the protagonist of the *jihād*. The conquest of Edessa, although according to Kamāl-al-Dīn it had long been near to the heart of the atabeg, was, as Kamāl-al-Dīn clearly states, undertaken only as an afterthought and due to the urging of the emir of Harran who pointed out the ease with which it could be captured. W. B. Stevenson says of Zangi: "The conquests he aimed at were chiefly from Moslem rivals. It must be concluded that he deliberately abstained from attack on the Latin states. While he built up his power he desired to be free from the risks of serious war with them. . . . His attack on Edessa in 1144 was . . . by no means characteristic of the events of his reign. It seems that he himself regarded it as a departure from his own policy, undertaken at the instigation of another."

The record of Zangi's wars, and they were many, show this to be true. So far was he from the perfect religious champion that he allied in 1132 with that archrebel and persecutor of the caliphate Dubays ibn-Ṣadaqah (whom we have already seen allied with the Franks) in an attack on the sacred person of the caliph al-Mustarshid. He engaged in an almost ceaseless struggle with Damascus, and his conquests of Ḥamāh, Ḥimṣ and Aleppo and his wars with the Urtuqids were all of greater importance to him than fighting Christians. And that even though Edessa was directly in his line of expansion and, after his conquest of Aleppo, divided his own territories. He was not even averse to allying with the Latins if it suited his needs.

After his capture of Edessa in 1144, Zangi did not follow

up his victory by occupying the Edessan territory which still resisted, but abandoned it and turned his attention to the east where he campaigned in the region of Khilāṭ and the upper Euphrates. That Zangi's conquest of Edessa is a turning point in the history of the Latin states in Syria cannot be questioned. It precipitated the Second Crusade, which by its dismal failure did much to relieve the minds of the Moslems of their fear of the invaders from the West; further it marks the first step in the process of the Moslem reconquest of the land; but it cannot be said to mark any innovation in Moslem policy. Zangi conquered Edessa because it rounded out his territories and because it seemed an easy prey. The Latins allied with Anar of Damascus because Zangi seemed to both of them to constitute a menace to all of his neighbors, and both parties profited by the alliance. It was only in after years that the conquest of Edessa was seen to be the crowning glory of Zangi's career. At the time, and in his own opinion, the capture of Edessa was less significant than the conquest of Aleppo and Ḥimṣ, but later historians, intent upon increasing the glory of the founder of the dynasty, emphasized that conquest which seemed to make him the champion of all Islam against the unbelievers.

But if Zangi did not devote his attention primarily to the wars with the Latins, the same cannot be said for his son Nūr-al-Dīn who succeeded him at Aleppo. Many historians, who admit that Zangi was not the hero of the religious wars that he is sometimes depicted, still insist that in Nūr-al-Dīn Islam found a pious and sincere champion whose chief desire was to rid the land of the infidels. Nevertheless I am inclined to doubt if even Nūr-al-Dīn was especially interested in religious war per se. It is perfectly true that he spent the better part of his life in conflict with the Franks, but this can easily be explained when we remember that he inherited only the western part of his father's domains and that the presence of his brother Sayf-al-Dīn Ghāzi in Mosul effectively blocked any hopes of expansion in that direction. Nūr-al-Dīn had no interests in Mesopotamia, his only hope of expansion was towards the west and south in the direction of the Latin states, Damascus and Egypt. And if he fought the Franks, he also conquered Damascus and sent his armies into the lands of the Fatimid caliphs. If he often fought the Franks it was because they stood in the direct line of his natural expansion; not religion but the desire to augment his domains in the only direction possible guided his policy in his relations with his Latin neighbors. I do not claim that the religious aspect of the war was not appealing to Nūr-al-Dīn, who was a man of natural piety and sincere in his religious beliefs. But I cannot believe that a survey of his activities does not prove that his main motive was political and that the religious was at best only a subordinate element, to be exploited for home consumption but not to be taken too seriously.

Nūr-al-Dīn's first campaigns were directed against his closest neighbor and one who he knew would take advantage of any opportunity to attack him. In order to campaign against Antioch he made an alliance with Damascus. The fact that Europe had armed and despatched the Second Crusade against him naturally made him anxious to secure himself against expected aggression on the part of the Franks. When the crusaders, instead of helping the prince of Antioch against Nūr-al-Dīn, turned their attack against the previously friendly Damascus, Nūr-al-Dīn was ready to assist his new ally against them, and there can be no doubt that the threat of his approach was one of the determining factors in causing the crusaders to abandon the siege of Damascus. In 1149 he was engaged in a campaign against Antioch but dropped it when Sayf-al-Dīn died and he thought it advisable to seize Mosul. After ensconcing a younger brother at Mosul, he next turned to Damascus where the death of Anar offered opportunities for profitable intervention. It is worthy of notice that at this time he offered friendship and alliance to the Latins if they would assist him in the capture of Damascus. In 1150 he was again drawn to the north, where he invaded the former Edessan lands largely to prevent their absorption by Mas'ūd of Iconium, and in this campaign he was satisfied to occupy only a few districts in order to put a limit to the expansion of the northern sultan and to show his own claims in that region. In 1155, after he had completed his conquest of Damascus and felt himself free of worries on his southern frontier, he returned to Edessa and took most of the territory, capturing it not from the Latins but from the Turks of Iconium. How anxious he was to avoid war with the Latins while he still had Moslem enemies to cope with is shown by his treaty of 1156, whereby he agreed to pay to Jerusalem the tribute which Damascus had previously rendered as the price of the Latin alliance. When war finally broke out between Nūr-al-Dīn and the Franks in 1157 it was due to an unprovoked attack on the part of the Latins.

The Franks had been following a policy of political opportunism throughout the period since the loss of Edessa. When the Second Crusade came to the East for the sole purpose of recapturing Edessa, it had been diverted by internal rivalries and by the selfish policy of the Jerusalemite Franks, who opposed campaigning in the north, into an attack on Damascus, although for several years the Latins and Damascenes had been in close alliance. In the years immediately following the crusade the kingdom of Jerusalem was torn by civil war between King Baldwin III and his mother Queen Melissende, and when that struggle had been settled by the defeat of the queen and her partisans, King Baldwin turned his attention to the conquest of Ascalon which he took from the Egyptians in 1153. The capture of Ascalon was the last important acquisition of territory made by the kings of Jerusalem, and it was secured at the cost of some minor Syrian border places which Nūr-al-Dīn took while the Franks were campaigning in the south. But the great blow came the following year when Nūr-al-Dīn occupied Damascus and presented a united frontier all along the eastern border of the Latin states. Nor did the northern Franks show greater political acumen than their southern brethren. While Baldwin was fighting the Egyptians and losing his eastern frontier posts to Nūr-al-Dīn, Renaud de Châtillon, the new prince of Antioch, became engaged in a series of conflicts with the princes of Armenia, the emperor of Byzantium and the Turks of Iconium.

The struggle with Nūr-al-Dīn was resumed by King Baldwin in 1157 when he made a plundering expedition across the border. Desultory war followed; then in 1159 was arranged a joint expedition of the Franks and the Byzantines, and the presence of the Emperor John Comnenus at the head of a large army made the matter a serious one for Nūr-al-Dīn. But Comnenus seemed more anxious to assure his control over Armenia and Antioch than to make any serious inroads into Moslem territory, and the campaign was abandoned when the sultan agreed to surrender a number of prisoners taken in earlier battles. Chalandon has suggested that the emperor found Nūr-al-Dīn a valuable check on the Latins who were willing to accept the suzerainty of the empire when threatened from the east, and that he deliberately did not push the campaign. At any rate a truce was arranged and Nūr-al-Dīn was free to perform the pilgrimage to Mecca which he had been planning for some years past.

With the death of Baldwin III and the accession of his brother Amaury to the throne of Jerusalem in 1163 events took a new turn. Amaury had been count of Jaffa and of Ascalon since its capture and was especially interested in the southern developments. A golden opportunity was offered to him to increase his power and prestige in the south by a civil war which broke out in the enfeebled Egyptian kingdom, and, urged on by the Hospitalers, Amaury plunged his kingdom into a series of wars with Egypt. The war in Egypt was a struggle for position between Ḍirghām and Shāwar, rival candidates for the post of grand vizier; the waters were too troubled not to attract fishermen and both Amaury and Nūr-al-Dīn turned covetous eyes southwards. Informed of the virtually defenceless condition of the kingdom, Amaury seized the pretext that the Egyptians had failed to remit the tribute which they had been paying regularly since 1160, and launched an expedition into the land of the Nile. The ancient river again protected its people; its floods compelled Amaury to retreat, but the king had scouted the country and seen what easy prey it would be. Meanwhile Ḍirghām had driven out Shāwar, who had fled to Damascus to seek the aid of Nūr-al-Dīn. Persuaded chiefly by his general Shīrkūh, the sultan authorized an expedition to reinstate Shāwar; in 1164 the Syrian army triumphantly invaded Egypt, restored Shāwar to his position of vizier, and then sat down in the country to enforce the fulfillment of the many promises which Shāwar, in his exile, had so glibly made. The vizier, anxious to be rid of such overwhelming allies, appealed to Amaury to help him drive out the Syrians, with the result that a second Latin invasion took place in 1164. Shīrkūh was forced to accept Amaury's terms that both invaders should withdraw from Egypt, but the Latins paid heavily for their increase in prestige by the loss of further border fortresses which Nūr-al-Dīn took while the Frankish armies were engaged in the south. From Antioch to Egypt the war raged along the frontier of the Latin states and all the permanent gains were made by Nūr-al-Dīn. In 1167 both sides again invaded Egypt and again both sides withdrew. The following year Amaury led a fourth army into the south and this time reached and besieged Cairo itself, but Shāwar again called in Shīrkūh and the Latins were forced to withdraw. Shīrkūh entered Cairo, deposed Shāwar and proclaimed himself vizier for the Fatimid caliph. When he died only a couple of months later, his place was taken by his nephew Ṣalāḥ-al-Dīn Yūsuf ibn-Ayyūb, the celebrated Saladin, who continued to govern Egypt in the dual rule of vizier to the caliph and governor for the sultan Nūr-al-Dīn. The Latins, this time assisted by the Byzantines, made a miserable attempt to intervene, but their timing was bad. They were severally defeated and the whole expedition collapsed before Damietta; Saladin was supreme in Egypt and the encirclement of the Latin states was complete.

Had Saladin acted with perfect loyalty towards his master, the Latin states would probably have fallen during the lifetime of Nūr-al-Dīn, but the ambitious governor preferred to pursue a more independent policy and failed entirely to cooperate with the sultan. In 1171 he was strong enough in Egypt so that he no longer felt it necessary to retain the puppet caliph, and at the death of al-'Āḍid the caliphate was left vacant, the prayers being said in the name of the 'Abbāsid caliph of Baghdad. Thus even the religious schism between the Sunnite and Shī'ite caliphs, which had materially aided the Christians in their earlier conquests, was ended, and Christendom was confronted with a technically united Islam. The change was accepted with remarkable indifference by the mass of the Egyptians, although there were a few sporadic revolts in favor of the Fatimid house, one of which involved the Latins, even bringing a crusade from Sicily which failed to take Alexandria. The troubles in Egypt served chiefly as an excuse for Saladin not to join Nūr-al-Dīn in his campaigns against the Frankish states. While both Moslem princes continually attacked the Latins, Saladin saw to it that they never campaigned at the same time, always withdrawing from a given locality before Nūr-al-Dīn could arrive there, and always finding it impossible to join his master when summoned. Saladin may have feared that Nūr-al-Dīn meant to replace him in Egypt; he may have realized the extent of his own ambitions and have known what he would do were he in Nūr-al-Dīn's place. There seems to be no evidence that Nūr-al-Dīn suspected the loyalty of Saladin for some time, as Saladin was eloquent in his professions of abject servitude to the sultan; eventually, however, the discrepancy between the words and the actions of his general convinced Nūr-al-Dīn that he could no longer be trusted and the sultan was preparing an expedition against Saladin when he died in 1174.

Nūr-al-Dīn's accomplishments in the weakening of the Latin states in Syria caused him, as we have seen, to be hailed as one of the great protagonists of the *jihād*, but it should be evident, even from this brief sketch of his career, that his wars were consistently directed at the single goal of establishing his dynasty over a united Syria. He interfered in Mosul only to secure it for members of his family, but in the west he persistently tried to extend and to fill out his frontiers. He fought against the Saljuqs of Iconium with as good gusto as he did against the Franks of Antioch to secure his northern frontier; he expanded into Moslem and Latin Syria impartially, taking what he could to round out his possessions, and his most significant conquest by far was that of Damascus. In fact, like his father, he seems to have avoided war with the Latins if he could as well expand at the cost of his Moslem neighbors, but, blocked as he was on the east, he had of necessity to seek his conquests in the west and south, whether the enemy be Moslem or Christian, Arab, Turk or Egyptian, Greek, Armenian or Latin. The conquest of the Latin states was dictated by geography and should have preceded the more remote conquest of Egypt; circumstances gave him Egypt—it was inevitable that he or his successor should fill in the gap and secure the "outlet to the sea" for his landlocked empire. Egypt gave him what was most needed for the reduction of the Frankish cities—a navy and a coast to base it on, but it was Saladin who was to receive the profit therefrom.

The death of Nūr-al-Dīn coincided in point of time with that of Amaury of Jerusalem. The internal difficulties of Jerusalem, which found itself subject to a series of regents for a king invalided by leprosy, offered a golden opportunity for Saladin to strike at once against the enemies of the faith. Had Saladin been the religious fanatic he is sometimes portrayed, it is reasonable to expect that he would have begun his expansion at the expense of the divided and weakened Franks; a Frankish war might have proven easier than the conquest of Moslem Syria, but Saladin preferred to secure his position in Moslem Syria before attacking the Latins. They would be conquered, but they would have to wait their turn and the convenience of the conqueror.

When Nūr-al-Dīn died he left his empire to his eleven

year old son; the emirs of the various cities proclaimed themselves regents for the boy and at once began a struggle for power. Saladin, supported by the wealth of Egypt, was from the first the strongest of the contestants; he occupied Damascus in 1174, proclaiming himself the guardian of the boy-sultan and then advanced on Aleppo. The emir of Aleppo invoked the assistance of both the dreaded Assassins and the Franks, but the allies were defeated by Saladin in the battle of Ḥamāh in 1175, after which Saladin threw off the mask, suppressed the little king and openly proclaimed himself sultan, seeking and obtaining recognition of his title from the caliph of Baghdad. The campaigns which he fought against the Franks in 1175-1176 were only a part of the general war which he was conducting against Aleppo and its allies; by the end of 1176, having reduced all of Syria with the exception of the city of Aleppo and the territories of the Assassins, he felt free to return to Egypt and to plan the reduction of the offensive Latins. But while the Latin wars occupied him continuously from 1177 to the end of his life, Saladin never gave them his exclusive attention. In 1182 he finally captured Aleppo; in the same year he campaigned in Mesopotamia; in 1185 he signed a four year truce with the Latins in order to attend to affairs in Mesopotamia and secure his suzerainty over the Zangid prince of Mosul.

It would be wearisome and useless to go into any details concerning Saladin's conquest of the kingdom of Jerusalem. The local situation within the Latin state was such that it demanded intervention; no politician who was worth his salt could have refrained from seizing the opportunities offered by the internal dissensions of the Franks. Two distinct parties had developed within the Latin state, the one composed chiefly of the native Frankish nobility under the leadership of Count Raymond III of Tripoli and the Ibelin brothers; the other, the so-called "court party," made up largely of recent arrivals to the East and led by Guy de Lusignan, the husband of Princess Sibylle, Girard de Ridefort, the Master of the Temple, Joscelyn de Courtenay and Renaud de Châtillon. The party of Count Raymond consistently urged keeping on as good terms as possible with Saladin; they saw that the hope of the country lay in accepting from the sultan a position of vassalage and knew that Saladin would respect his treaties. The other party was the party of war, their attitude was that of the Western crusaders and of the religious orders. Joscelyn, it is true, had been born and brought up in the East and his personal hatred for Raymond and his private ambitions dominated his judgment; Renaud was always the inveterate enemy of the Moslems and the champion of a policy of expansion, the fifteen years he had spent in a Moslem prison having failed to acclimate him to the East or to soften his bigotry.

It was the Franks who really precipitated Saladin's conquest of Jerusalem. We have already seen how inevitable it was that the sultan should reduce the coast after he had secured the hinterland, but Saladin might have been willing to permit the Franks to occupy their lands under his suzerainty had they not provoked him to action by deliberate affronts and attacks. The worst offender was Renaud, who not only twice attacked and pillaged Moslem caravans during times of truce, but who shocked and scandalized all Islam by a foolhardy and fruitless raid into the Red Sea against the holy cities of Mecca and Medina in 1182-1183. This mad raid not only convinced Saladin that the Franks should be evicted from the East, but cost the Latins the alliance of the Zangid prince of Mosul who refused longer to be allied to such sacrilegious unbelievers. Even then, although he loudly proclaimed the *jihād* and called on all Moslems to support his war against the Christians, Saladin would undoubtedly have compromised with any of the Franks except Renaud himself. Against Renaud the sultan took a mighty oath, which he fulfilled when he decapitated him after Ḥaṭṭīn, but he entered into a truce and alliance with Raymond of Tripoli, even after he had embarked on his final war against the Franks.

In his whole conquest of the Latin kingdom Saladin never showed himself a religious fanatic. His clemency and chivalry were the wonder of his contemporaries and brought him the praises of historians from his own day on, and in his treatment of the conquered population he exercised a restraint and consideration which was in direct contrast with the normal accepted brutalities of medieval warfare. His policy of escorting refugees from the captured cities to the Christian stronghold of Tyre was quixotic for it concentrated his enemies and eventually prevented him from being able to capture Tyre itself. Throughout the entire conquest, Saladin acted as though he were trying consciously to render himself acceptable to his future subjects and to lay the foundations for a state in which both religions would dwell together under the rule of the sultan. One is tempted to speculate as to what might have been the result had Europe not responded to the appeal for the Third Crusade. Certainly the Christians of Syria would have been no worse off under the mild rule of the Ayyubids than they were in their own continual anarchy, and they might have been spared the horrors of the Mamlūk conquest. Many of the Syrian barons had already shown that they would as soon serve Saladin as Guy de Lusignan, and even Conrad de Montferrat, the hero of the resistance of Tyre, subsequently offered to hold the kingdom of Jerusalem as a vassal of the sultan.

The period of the Third Crusade was undoubtedly one of almost strictly religious war. While neither Philip Augustus nor Richard Lion Heart were motivated as much by religion as they were by the desire to gain glory through Eastern conquests, and while both probably went on the crusade primarily because it was "the correct thing to do," the crusade was, on the whole, Europe's answer to the fall of Jerusalem and the reappearance of the Holy War as a potent factor in politics. To Saladin it was a direct challenge to Islam to defend its conquests from the Christians and he exploited to its best advantage the unifying value of the common cause of religion. But even in this war chivalry played as large a rôle as religion; the legends of the chivalrous contacts of Richard and Saladin have their basis in fact although the two monarchs never met face to face. Throughout, their relations were those of two gentlemen competing in a major sport and there can be no doubt but that Richard's sorrow in not capturing Jerusalem was far more humiliation that he had not won his goal than any great grief at not being able to rescue the Holy Sepulcher. The terms of the treaty which closed the crusade show clearly the essentially secular and chivalrous concept of the war, both sides were to prepare for a renewal of the conflict when each had recuperated from their present exertions and the Christian pilgrims were to be allowed free access to the shrines of Jerusalem under convoy by Moslem troops.

Thus even in this period when religion really dominated the Moslem policy there was always a secular aspect to the war; religious prejudice never produced blind fanaticism on the part of the leaders. Saladin's object was to destroy the political power of the Franks, it was never to exterminate the Christians; the goal of the Zangids had been reached and surpassed in the political unification of Syria and Egypt; the aim of Saladin was to preserve the empire he had conquered.

The twelfth century was the great age of the crusades; the thirteenth century history of the Latin states in Syria is usually considered as an epilogue. For the continued existence of the Latin states, their reorganization after the Third Crusade and their ability to keep alive throughout almost a century of constant travail, was due wholly to the rivalries which divided Islam and prevented any ruler from again uniting Syria into a single powerful state. When the Egyptians did finally secure supremacy over their eastern neighbors the time of the Latin states had come and they were liquidated. That it did not happen sooner was merely because they were no longer any threat to the Moslem powers and because the Moslems were so busy among themselves that they had no time to spare for the Latins. Throughout the twelfth century, especially in the first half thereof, fear of European reprisals in the form of new crusades stayed the hands of the Moslems from attacking the Christians until they were well established in their powers at home. The Latins were found to be useful buffer states between the Moslem monarchies, they were harmless and to a certain extent useful; until the major issues were settled no one had the time to bother with them. In this we can perhaps find a parallel to the situation of Sweden today.

Of course there were crusades throughout the century which might have brought the Latin states real help and in part have re-established them as important factors in Eastern politics. But the thirteenth century crusades only sufficed to keep up the hopes of the Syrian Franks without seriously embarrassing the Moslems. The crusade of St. Louis is a notable exception to all that has been said about secular motivation, but it did not materially improve the situation of the kingdom of Jerusalem.

Western Europe had poured forth men and money on the crusades of the twelfth century; the early thirteenth century crusades received a creditable enough support; but by the middle of the century Europeans were thoroughly sick of the whole business. Even the papacy had on the whole lost interest in the Holy Land and from 1208 on the war against the heretics at home took precedence in the minds of most popes over the crusades against the Moslems. Men and money which had been raised for the Eastern crusades were diverted by the popes to the European conflicts; crusades became the recognized weapon of the popes in dealing with their secular enemies and the nadir of crusading idealism was reached at the very close of the century when Boniface VIII launched a crusade against the house of Colonna. Against the rival cardinals the pope spent men and treasure; for the sufferings of the East he had only crocodile tears. Among the nobility the fashion of crusading was gradually passing out of style; having reached its height in the time of the Third Crusade. Crusading continued to be a popular pursuit of the nobles through the early years of the next century and the Fourth Crusade did attract the cream of the chivalry of France. That this crusade was launched from a tournament is somewhat indicative of the attitude of most of the participants, but that it forgot all about Jerusalem and became a glorious adventure of conquest in the Byzantine Empire was evidence of changed mores. The Latin Empire of Constantinople and the Latin states of Greece proved more attractive to Western knights than did Syria, and even Syrian Franks left their homes to partake of the adventure in the north. Among the lesser folk who had contributed so largely to the ranks of the earlier crusades all interest in the movement died out. The *non-croisé* bested the *croisé* as in Rutebeuf's dialogue; men stayed home, tended their gardens and secured the spiritual benefits of crusading through the acquisition of indulgences.

At the very end of the twelfth century had occurred a crusade, really more a continuation of the Third Crusade than a separate movement, which might well have changed the course of history. Emperor Henry VI projected a great expedition which should have brought under his control not only Syria and the former kingdom of Jerusalem but also the Byzantine Empire. The plans for this tremendous undertaking were well laid; after securing the allegiance of the kings of Cyprus and Armenia, Henry sent the first divisions of his army to the East, but before more could follow the emperor died and all his schemes collapsed. Henry VI is one of those rare fortunate souls who died in the flower of his youth and promise; historians can freely speculate on what might have been had he but lived to carry out his dreams, but history cannot be written in the pluperfect subjunctive and nothing at all came of the plans which the emperor had made.

On the other hand the Moslems had not followed up the impetus given them by Saladin and completed the reduction of the Latins. At Saladin's death his lands were divided up among his sons, Egypt, Damascus and Aleppo becoming the seats of three separate states and, instead of cooperating to drive out the Franks, the brothers promptly engaged in dynastic wars which were only terminated when Sayf-al-Dīn (Saphadin), Saladin's brother, got control of the lands of his nephews and made himself sole sultan. The reign of Sayf-al-Dīn from 1202 to 1218 was a period of peace and recovery for the Latin states, for Sayf-al-Dīn was inclined to be friendly towards the Franks; he had been the personal friend of Richard and his marriage to Richard's sister had once been seriously discussed. Between Sayf-al-Dīn and Jean d'Ibelin, the regent of Jerusalem, a firm truce was arranged during which both parties devoted themselves to the settling of their internal affairs. This state of amity might well have continued had it not been that just before the death of the sultan the truce was broken by the Franks, who were forced into a renewal of the wars by the arrival of fresh crusaders from Europe under the command of Andrew of Hungary. This first division of the Fifth Crusade, which campaigned in Syria in 1218, did little if anything to benefit Jerusalem and went back home before the bulk of the crusaders arrived in the East at all.

When the major part of the host did arrive, it was directed against Egypt, which had passed by inheritance to al-Malik al-Kāmil, one of Sayf-al-Dīn's sons. The strategy of the Fifth Crusade was sound; military considerations had shown that Jerusalem was extremely difficult to take and the idea was conceived that an attack on Egypt, which was far more accessible, might force the sultan to give up Jerusalem as the price of peace. The crusaders accordingly aimed their attack on Damietta at the mouth of the Nile; and true to the expectations the sultan did offer Jerusalem in return for Damietta. But the papal legate Pelagius overruled the desire of the secular leaders to accept these terms and demanded the complete defeat of the Egyptians with the capture of Cairo itself. Led by Pelagius, the army marched inland as far as al-Manṣūrah at the junction of two branches of the Nile where, trapped by the Nile floods and the Egyptian arms, the crusaders were forced to surrender all that they had captured in return for the sultan's safe conduct back to Syria.

In his troubles with the crusaders al-Malik al-Kāmil had received the support of his brother al-Malik al-Muʿaẓẓam of Damascus, but as soon as the danger was passed the brothers began quarreling over the division of the empire. Al-Muʿaẓẓam called in as allies the Khwārizm Turks; al-Kāmil turned to the West and secured the alliance of Frederick II, sultan of Sicily and emperor of the Holy Roman Empire, a sworn crusader.

The crusade of Frederick II is unique in the history of religious wars. Personally an agnostic, tolerant of all religions but intolerant of heresy, which smacked to him too strongly of insubordination towards constituted authority, Frederick was by temperament the last person imaginable to lead a crusade. He had taken the crusader's vows when he assumed the crown of the Empire in 1215 but had successfully stalled off fulfillment thereof until too late a date to be of any assistance in the Fifth Crusade. Hoping to interest Frederick in Jerusalem and stimulate his zeal, the pope in 1225 arranged for the emperor's marriage with Isabelle de Brienne, the princess of the crusader kingdom. There can be no doubt but that his marriage did arouse Frederick's interest in the kingdom, but his reaction was one of which the pious pope could never have conceived; to the pope interest in Jerusalem must be expressed by means of a crusade; to the practical and irreligious emperor interest was best expressed by securing possession of the kingdom in the most efficient manner possible. The manner was suggested to him when al-Kāmil appealed to Frederick for help against Damascus—the emperor would receive the Holy City as the price of his military aid to the sultan. He at once set about preparing for a military expedition to the East; his means were slightly unorthodox, for the emperor was going crusading, as the ally of a Moslem prince, in a fleet manned largely by Moslem sailors.

Then al-Mu'aẓẓam died and al-Kāmil no longer had any need for his Western ally. The Egyptians invaded Syria, overrunning the southern provinces, while from the north came al-Ashraf of Mesopotamia, another brother, proposing a division of the Damascene provinces whereby he should receive Damascus itself while al-Kāmil took the south. The sultan was therefore in no mood to give up to Frederick the major portion of his newly acquired plunder in return for assistance which he could not use. But Frederick had made his plans and intended to see them carried out. While an advance contingent went on to Syria in 1227, the main host of his army assembled at Brindisi where they quickly fell victims to disease, the emperor himself being among those affected. However, despite his illness, Frederick took ship but was compelled by the seriousness of his malady to put back into port; he explained the cause of his return to Pope Gregory IX but that irate prelate, who saw in the affair only seasickness and an excuse for again deferring the sailing, promptly excommunicated him. Had Gregory but known of Frederick's treaty with al-Kāmil he might not have suspected the sincerity of Frederick's intentions to go, but he would certainly not have withheld the excommunication. When the emperor, recovered, subsequently set sail, the pope forbade the expedition as it was canonically impossible for an unreconciled excommunicate to participate in a holy crusade; Gregory did not know how unholy Frederick's expedition really was.

The size of the emperor's army was not large enough for him to hope to accomplish anything through force of arms, and the patriarch of Jerusalem, the Templars and Hospitalers, most of the clergy and some of the barons of the Latin kingdom refused to cooperate with him. His best chance, and the one he took, was to emphasize his nuisance value, since only through negotiation had he any hope of securing his demands. Fortunately Frederick found in al-Kāmil an urbane, worldly, tolerant individual, much like himself, and one who could appreciate his position. Moslem historians report that the emperor frankly told the sultan that it was largely a matter of "saving face at home" and that he would not have demanded Jerusalem if it was not necessary for him to secure it to save his position in Europe. Albeit reluctantly, the sultan agreed to a treaty whereby Frederick was given the city of Jerusalem, in which, however, Moslems retained certain special areas and in which both religions exercised complete freedom of worship and pilgrimage. The patriarch of Jerusalem reacted to this infamous treaty by promptly placing the Holy City under the interdict and forbidding good Christians to set foot in it, an order which the emperor and his immediate followers disregarded altogether.

Perhaps it is a mistake to refer to this expedition of Frederick's as a crusade; certainly it does not fulfill the definition of a crusade as a military expedition, undertaken under the auspices of the papacy, for which spiritual benefits are promised to the participants. While it was the only crusade, except the first, which succeeded in getting possession of Jerusalem, and if judged by its results was by far the most successful of any of the later crusades; yet no stretch of the imagination could possibly make of it a religious war on the part of any of its participants. Both Frederick and al-Kāmil were distinctly in advance of their times as regards religious toleration; both represented that small group which, through contact with men of the alien faith, had learned to disregard religion and treat their politics as a purely secular matter. The inhabitants of Syria in general shared this point of view, but neither Christendom nor Islam as a whole were ready for so intelligent a solution of the problem.

The period following the campaign of Frederick II was one in which both Moslems and Christians in the East engaged in civil wars almost to the exclusion of foreign conflicts. In reading the *History* of Philip de Novara, the best authority for the happenings in the kingdom of Jerusalem in the years 1230-1240, one would gain the impression that foreign affairs were virtually nonexistant, so concerned is the author with the internal struggle. When Moslem wars did occur the Franks participated as allies of one Moslem power against another, and the Moslems were themselves too taken up with their private disputes to attempt any concerted action against the Latins. Even the great military orders, those sworn enemies of Islam, so far forgot their vows that they allied shamelessly with Moslems against other Christians and especially against each other, the Templars joining with Damascus against the Hospitalers and Egypt. Some of the bloodiest battles of the period were fought between the forces of the rival orders.

Far worse than these were the wars which raged between the citizens of the various Italian communes. Pisans, Venetians, Genoese, Marseilleise and Catalans fought each other in all the ports of the East, shifting alliances but always struggling for political and commercial supremacy. In the "War of St. Sabas" more than twenty thousand men were estimated to have been killed in Acre in the year 1257-1258. This war, which started as a local quarrel between Venetian and Genoese colonists, eventually came to include the Franks as well, the Venetians being supported by the commune of Acre, the king of Cyprus, most of the Frankish nobility, the Templars, Teutonic Knights, Pisans, and Provençals, while the Genoese were assisted by the lord and citizens of Tyre, the Hospitalers, the Catalans and the *Anconitani*. Both Acre and Tyre suffered heavily from the destruction of property within their walls as well as from the disruption of trade, and it was not until 1277 that peace was finally concluded between the last contestants, and the Venetians were readmitted into Tyre.

Nor were the Latin nobles less mutually belligerent. Antioch was torn by civil war for the better part of the century, its princes fighting at one time or another with the kings of Armenia, the Hospitalers, and their own vassals the lords of Gibelet (Byblos, Jubayl) and Botron (Batrūn). The struggle between the Ibelinians and the imperialists occupied the kingdom of Jerusalem for over a decade, and had not long been settled by the final expulsion of the imperialists when a dynastic struggle for possession of the throne broke out, involving in its later stages the kings of Cyprus and the agents of Charles of Anjou, king of Sicily. Fortunately for the Latins the Ayyūbid kingdoms of Egypt and Syria were engaged in no less bitter conflict and the emirs of the various lesser cities took the occasion of the major struggle to engage in private wars among themselves. The history of the crusades of Thibaut of Champagne, king of Navarre, and Richard of Cornwall in 1239-1240 show how these civil wars could involve even crusaders from the West and render their assistance nugatory.

Thibaut began his crusade with an attack against the Egyptians. In a battle near Gaza his forces were routed and many of the leaders taken prisoner. Invited into an alliance by the emir of Ḥamāh, Thibaut advanced towards Ḥimṣ only to find that his ally had made peace, leaving him stranded. The crusaders were approached by the Templars with offers of alliance from the sultan of Damascus, who promised to restore the castle of Ṣafad and other strongholds which he had captured, if the crusaders would assist him in a campaign against Egypt. The alliance was agreed upon and the combined Frankish-Damascene army moved south to Jaffa, but the Hospitalers, inveterate enemies of the Templars, had cooked up a rival scheme and approached Thibaut with proposals for an alliance with Egypt against Damascus, in return for which the Egyptian sultan offered to return all the prisoners captured at the recent battle of Gaza. It should be noted that Ṣafad and the castles restored by the Damascenes were all the property of the Templars, while among the prisoners to be released by the Egyptians was the Master of the Hospital. Thibaut, who seems to have been more than a little confused about the whole business, accordingly opened negotiations with Egypt, at the same time adhering to his alliance with Damascus. Then, apparently feeling that he had adequately fulfilled any crusader's vow he had taken, the count suddenly left Jaffa and returned to France. His place as leader of the crusade was taken by Richard of Cornwall, who arrived in the East soon after Thibaut's departure. Richard signed the treaty offered by the Egyptians, and proceeded to refortify Ascalon. This completed, he too returned to Europe, leaving the Syrian Franks hopelessly divided between the two alliances.

The fall of the imperialists in Tyre who had favored the Egyptian alliance in 1243, plus a victory over the Egyptians won by the Damascenes and Templars, strengthened the hands of the Damascene party among the Latins, but Egypt allied with Karak and a general war broke out along the borders. Karak then sold out Egypt and joined Damascus, the Latins wholly accepted the Damascene alliance and Egypt made a counteralliance with the Khwārizm Turks. The city of Jerusalem, which had been held by the Latins since 1229, was captured by the Turks in 1244 and the allied Damascene-Latin army was decisively defeated at Gaza, the Latins bearing the brunt of the losses. The victorious Egyptians pushed on and took Damascus itself in 1246, thus ending the rivalry between the branches of the house of Ayyūb. But even in the Egyptians' year of victory the new menace which was to threaten their control over Syria first appeared; the Mongols, emerging from the steppes of Asia, raided northern Syria, forcing the prince of Antioch to pay them tribute.

Before proceeding to a discussion of the Mongol-Egyptian struggle, which dominated the scene in Syria for the next quarter century, it is necessary to stop and observe the one expedition of the century which can really be called a religious war. In 1244, during an attack of sickness, St. Louis of France had taken the cross. The army which he led to the East was almost exclusively French and was brought together entirely by the power and persuasiveness of the king. No political motives need be sought for this crusade. St. Louis' natural piety and his desire to rescue the Holy Land was the only cause, and the crusade itself was the response of the chivalry of France to the beloved monarch who ruled in what has been well termed "the Indian summer of feudalism." Almost last among men Louis longed for the delivery of the Holy Sepulcher and was willing to waste the strength and wealth of his kingdom in the holy cause. Galahad was not purer in his quest for the Grail than was Louis in his quest for the Sepulcher: and like Galahad Louis was alone in his perfection. If one can judge from Joinville (and what better authority could we ask?) chivalry and feudal loyalty rather than religious zeal animated the knights who accompanied the king. Joinville would follow his lord to the gates of Hell, but he would not have sought the road alone.

The story of St. Louis' crusade is so well known through the rich narrative of Joinville that we need not stop long over it here. The conquest of Damietta, the march up the Nile, the battle of al-Manṣūrah and the defeat and capture of the king are all familiar episodes in a well-known tale. Louis' four years in Syria, after his release from Egypt, accomplished practically nothing; the crusade on the whole was a dismal failure. Nor was Louis' second attempt, the ill-fated crusade of 1270 which was diverted to Tunis, more productive of benefit for the Latin East. The death of the sainted monarch in the camp at Tunis removed the one power which might have exerted itself to assist the Eastern Franks, and left them to their own devices. The last real crusader entered the heavenly Jerusalem in lieu of the earthly one which he so ardently sought.

More important than the crusade of St. Louis was the revolution which took place in Egypt in 1250. At the death of the Ayyūbid sultan, a palace revolution brought to the throne the first of the Mamlūk rulers, establishing the dynasty which was to bring Egypt to the zenith of her medieval prestige and power. But the Mamlūks had hardly begun to establish their power in Syria when it was challenged by the invasion of the Mongols, who swept through the Middle East under the command of Hulagu. Emerging from the heart of inner Asia, the Mongols, in what has been termed the first *blitzkrieg*, quickly overran Iran and Iraq, destroying the caliphate of Baghdad and massacring the population of that once glorious city in 1258. Even the terrible Assassins were swept out of their stronghold of Alamūt by the wild warriors of the Khan, and Aleppo and Damascus were an easy prey for them. The Mongols exploited to its fullest advantage the "war of nerves," spreading the fear of their name through the countries which they had marked down for conquest and backing up the legends of their cruelty and invincibility with deeds of atrocity which shocked and terrified the more civilized peoples. In Syria, as in Russia and Iraq, kingdoms and principalities were swept away in a torrent of conquest and slaughter; nothing seemed able to withstand their destructive advance.

And Christian Europe rejoiced in the victories of the Mongols. The fact that they were on the whole friendly to the Christians, that there were among them many Nestorian Christians, that Hulagu himself had a Christian wife, and that Kitbugha, the general who took command in Syria when Hulagu was called back to Siberia was himself a Christian made the popes and the rulers of Western Europe look upon them as allies in a common struggle against Islam. The idea of a great European-Mongol alliance which would crush out the Moslem states was a favorite one with the popes for many years and numerous embassies were exchanged between Europe and the courts of the khans, of which the embassies of John of Piano Carpini and William of Rubriquis are only the most celebrated. Only Frederick II among the rulers of the West sensed the real menace of the Mongol advance and urged a crusade against them, but Frederick was himself distinctly suspect in the eyes of the papacy, and was known to be in alliance with the Egyptians; the pope preferred to invoke the crusade against Frederick and to negotiate an alliance with the Asiatic barbarians. The idea of the Mongol "crusade" was responsible for much of the blundering which marked the Oriental policy of the popes in the late thirteenth century and which resulted in the complete loss of the kingdom of Jerusalem. Many modern historians seem to have fallen under the same spell, Grousset, for example, lamenting loudly the failure of the Syrian Franks to assist wholeheartedly the invasion of the Mongols. To me it seems that the very assistance which they did give the Mongols was the thing which brought on the destruction of the Latin states, and that a policy of friendship with and vassalage to the Mamlūks would have been the only way of maintaining their existence in Syria. For even admitting that the extermination of the Latin states was an essential aspect of Egyptian policy, it should be remembered that those cities which allied with the Egyptians against the Mongols were permitted to survive long after those who had abetted the Mongols were destroyed, and that the Mamlūks did not attack Christian towns while the towns lived up to their treaty obligations.

The Syrian Franks were hopelessly divided in their attitude towards the Mongols, as they were in everything else. The kings of Armenia and the princes of Antioch-Tripoli became the vassals of the invaders and gave them tribute and military assistance, but the lords of the more southerly cities wavered between the advantages of the Mongol and the Egyptian alliances, Julian of Sidon, John d'Ibelin of Beirut, John de Gibelet, the Templars and the citizens of Acre favoring the Egyptians.

The first decisive battle between the Mongols and the Mamlūks was fought at 'Ayn Jālūt on September 3, 1260. The Mongols, led by the Nestorian Kitbugha, were supported by troops from Armenia and Antioch, while the southern Latins gave at least passive assistance to the Egyptians. In this battle the defeat of the Mongols was complete, Kitbugha was killed on the field and his army scattered; the victorious Mamlūks pushed on for the reconquest of Damascus and Aleppo and the northern Christians were subjected to a punitive campaign to warn them against the folly of supporting the enemies of the sultan. But the Mongols still held Mesopotamia and the north and only waited a favorable opportunity to recoup their losses.

Meanwhile, the great sultan Baybars al-Bunduqdāri had usurped the throne of Egypt, after assassinating his predecessor Quṭuz. Baybars' conquests at the expense of the Latins cause him to be remembered as one of the great champions of Islam, but it is rather as the founder of the greatness of Mamlūk Egypt that he deserves a place in history. Although a pious Moslem, he was no more motivated by religion than were any of the sultans who preceded him, and his conquest of the Latin states was simply the inevitable step in the aggrandizement of Egypt. That his was not a *jihād* is evidenced by his eagerness to secure the friendship of Christian monarchs, Charles of Anjou-Sicily, James of Aragon, Alphonso of Castile and Michael Palaeologus of Constantinople all being sought by him as allies political or commercial. Like Saladin he combined his wars against the Latins of Syria with conquests from rival Moslem powers, and his wars include campaigns against the Ayyūbid princes of Syria, the Assassins of the Lebanon, the Īl-Khāns of Persia, the Berbers of North Africa and the Nubians. It was as part of his policy to secure the predominance of Egypt, rather than from respect for the office, that in 1261 he established in Cairo the 'Abbāsid caliph, whose capital at Baghdad had been destroyed by the Mongols; Baybars found the orthodox caliph a useful tool in securing his position against Fatimid pretenders.

Baybars' conquests in Latin Syria were made chiefly in the years 1256-1268. Caesarea, Arsūf and Jaffa, several of the castles of the Orders, and even mighty Antioch were captured and delivered over to plunder. Grousset has pointed out that one reason for the great success of Baybars was the fact that, unlike Saladin, he fought with professional soldiers and did not have to take into account the rights and privileges of a feudal army. He was able to keep his men in the field for longer campaigns than was the great Ayyūbid and so was able to carry on more extended and remote campaigns.

In 1270-1272 the last European offensive on behalf of the kingdom of Jerusalem was led to the East by Prince Edward (later King Edward I) of England. It was the only part of St. Louis' second crusade to reach Syria at all, and it succeeded in accomplishing nothing more than to antagonize the sultan and precipitate the fall of mighty Crac des Chevaliers and other Latin strongholds.

Even in these last crucial years the Latins could not refrain from civil war: Charles of Anjou, who had purchased the title of Jerusalem from Marie of Antioch, a contender for the throne who had been passed over in 1268, took the control of Acre in 1277 in alliance with the Templars and in opposition to Hugh of Cyprus, to whom the High Court had awarded the throne. Charles had followed the Eastern policy of Frederick II and was the friend of Egypt, as we have seen; his governors in Acre assisted the sultans and consistently kept on good terms with them, Eudes Pelechin, governor of Acre, signing a ten year truce with Qalāwūn as late as 1283.

The death of Baybars in 1277 gave the Syrian Franks only a short respite, for Qalāwūn, who ascended the Egyptian throne in 1279, vigorously prosecuted the war which his great predecessor had left unfinished. His first major victory was won in 1280 over a Mongol army which invaded Syria only to be wiped out at Ḥimṣ, a victory which broke forever the effective power of the Mongols in Syria. After this success all the lords of the southern Latin cities hastened to make treaties with the sultan, but it was too late—Qalāwūn could not afford the risk of having the Christians again attempt to assist the Mongols. The chief conquest of his reign was the city of Tripoli, which was indulging in a petty civil war over the succession to the throne of Bohemond VII, in which one side called in the outside help of the Genoese and the other summoned the sultan. Qalāwūn came, but there was nothing left in Tripoli when he departed (1289). After the fall of Tripoli there was comparatively little that needed to be done to complete the expulsion of the Franks from Syria; Acre, Beirut, Sidon, Tortosa and a few isolated castles were all that was left to the Latins. Qalāwūn died in 1290 before he had finished "mopping up," but the final work was done by his successor al-Ashraf Khalīl, who captured Acre in May 1291. The immediate cause of the attack on the city was a raid into Moslem territory made by some Western crusaders who had just arrived at Acre, and who thus broke the truce, giving the sultan an excuse to destroy the city. After the fall of Acre the other Latin towns surrendered; the kingdom of the crusaders was ended, the unification of Syria was completed.

The fall of Acre did not produce any great repercussions in the West. The popes wailed but no crusade was launched to try to revive the defunct kingdom. Publicists went into great details about the proper manner of conducting a new crusade but nothing much came of them. The end of the crusaders' kingdom did not of course end the wars between Christians and Moslems; the kings of Cyprus, those insular heirs of the kingdom of Jerusalem, engaged in fairly frequent wars with the Egyptians, one of which, Pierre I's conquest of Alexandria in 1365, has been dignified with the title of crusade. But these conflicts much more nearly resemble raids than holy wars, and the Mamlūk conquest of Cyprus under Sultan Barsbāy in the fifteenth century was inspired, not by religious zeal, but by the fact that the Cypriots sheltered and succored pirates who preyed on the Egyptian commerce.

Similarly the expeditions which were sent out to check the advance of the Ottoman Turks have sometimes been called crusades. The crusade of Nicopolis in 1396 in part deserves that appellation for it was a combination of chivalrous adventure, religious mysticism and practical politics. But with the exception of Nicopolis these expeditions attracted few who did not have a personal secular stake in the matter, and it is hard to see in them other than political and economic wars. Religion continued to be invoked in every struggle in which men of different faiths were involved; every war against the Turk was a crusade, every war against the Christians was a *jihād*, but it was only so called because of the emotional appeal of the religious excuse and to secure popular support for the war.

The great difficulty in discussing these matters lies in the attitudes of the contemporary chroniclers of both religions. Both Christian and Moslem historians play up the religious elements in interreligious wars; both extol the piety of the leaders who fought for the faith; both ignore practical causes in stressing the one with the greatest popular appeal. And of course the official documents which were used to stir up enthusiasm for the wars are no check on the chroniclers, for they, even more than the historians, give only the ideological aspect of the case.

In conclusion, then, let me reiterate my thesis. In the twelfth and thirteenth centuries, in the age of the crusades and of the *jihāds*, religion played the same rôle that political ideology does today; neither Christian nor Moslem, with a few notable exceptions, invoked religion save as a cloak for secular political ends, but it was the ideological banner under which men fought and for which men can always be counted on to die. Religious fanaticism, in the age of the crusades, was an important and valuable stimulant; it was seldom a prime cause or dominant motive.

BIBLIOGRAPHY

L. Bréhier. *L'Eglise et l'Orient au Moyen Age: les Croisades.* 5th ed. (Paris, 1928).

The Chronography of Bar Hebraeus, tr. E. A. Wallis Budge. Oxford, 1932.

C. R. Conder. *The Latin Kingdom of Jerusalem.* London, 1897.

The Damascus Chronicle, tr. H. A. R. Gibb. London, 1932.

René Grousset. *Histoire des Croisades.* 3 vols. (Paris, 1934-36).

P. K. Hitti. *History of the Arabs.* 2nd ed. (London, 1940).

E. J. King. *Knights Hospitallers in the Holy Land.* London, 1931.

S. Lane-Poole. *Saladin.* New York, 1898.

———. *History of Egypt in the Middle Ages.* London, 1901.

D. C. Munro. *The Kingdom of the Crusaders.* New York, 1935.
Recueil des historiens des Croisades. Several vols. (Paris, 1843 *seq.*).
R. Röhricht. *Geschichte des Königreichs Jerusalem.* Innsbruck, 1898.
W. B. Stevenson. *The Crusaders in the East.* Cambridge, 1907.
G. Zananiri. *L'Egypte et l'équilibre du Levant au Moyen Age.* Marseille, 1936.

FOURTEENTH CENTURY JERUSALEM AND CAIRO THROUGH WESTERN EYES

HENRY L. SAVAGE

Historians are coming more and more to realize that much of the thought that proved productive of change in the history of Western Europe was thought borrowed from Eastern thinkers. But if modern historians have not always been aware of that fact, ecclesiastical and university administrators were quite conscious of it in medieval days. Saracen learning was dreaded as disturbing to the curriculum of the medieval university and the pattern of thought taught therein. Time would fail me if I attempted to enumerate and expatiate on how the Umayyad capital of Cordova, and, to a lesser degree, the cities of Egypt as well as those of what is now Iraq, made themselves preceptresses of the Western world in architecture, mathematics, medicine and music.

Eastern learning became current in the West chiefly through the crusades, those movements more or less continuous, which from the eleventh to the fourteenth centuries brought the warriors and then the merchants of the Occident, in war or in the chaffering and huckstering of the bazar, against Oriental opponents as keen and as canny as themselves.

War and economic rivalry, or the desire for profitable trade, were not the only means by which Moslem and Christian states became acquainted with one another. There was the far closer link of pilgrimage, a link that was at times melted by the flare-up of hostilities, but never allowed permanently to remain so in medieval times, and productive of far greater understanding and benefit between Europe on the one hand and the Levant on the other. As we know very well, armed force meets only armed force in reply, whereas many more doors are open to those who "pass all in peace." During the course of the medieval centuries pilgrims were passing into Palestine by various routes, and with more or less difficulty, as the case might be, but still passing and, in the majority of cases, returning to their homes—to the profit of their own souls, let us hope, but certainly to the enlightenment of their neighbors and to the general and gradual improvement, physical and mental, of medieval life.

Let us follow the footsteps of one such pilgrim. I will not prolong the introduction: He is Ogier, eighth baron d'Anglure. The town of Anglure, in which was situated the chief stronghold of the family, lies some thirty miles in a slightly southeast direction from the town of Epernay and some twenty-five miles southwest of Troyes in what is now the Department of Marne. It was, then, however in the royal province of Champagne, and Ogier, its lord, though not a powerful provincial magnate, was certainly a man of importance.[1] There had been a crusading tradition in his family, one of his ancestors having accompanied his feudal lord, the Count of Champagne, on the crusade led by Philip Augustus and Cœur de Lion in 1190, and then, as if once were not enough, set out from his ancestral fields in 1199 upon the crusade which ended with the capture of Constantinople and the foundation of a Frankish dynasty there (*S.V.*, pp. xxx-xxxiii). Tradition says that this ancestor had once been taken prisoner by the great Sultan Saladin himself, and his life spared by the grace of that monarch upon condition that he adopt as arms a coat *d'or semé de sonnettes d'argent soutenues de croissants de gueules*, and that the eldest son of the family should in the future bear the name Saladin. It may be that the crescents recall the crescent of the Turkish Sultans, but whatever the value of this story, it is a fact that the name Saladin was borne by several members of the family who stemmed from that crusading Ogier. Certainly the war cry used by the family, *Damas*, "Damascus!" would seem to recall Ogier's fighting days in Syria.

[1] The latest edition of the *Saint Voyage de Jherusalem*, which gives the story of Ogier's journeying, is that edited by F. Bonnardot and A. H. Longnon, in *Société des Anciens Textes Français*, Vol. X, Paris, 1878. All references are to the introduction or text or indices of that edition. Previous editions were printed in 1621 and 1858.

Perhaps it was the dash of crusading blood in his veins that sent our Ogier off on his *saint voyage*. If one has brisk and stirring ancestors one is, often as not, disposed to brisk and stirring deeds. Yet there may have been another reason for the journey. There is in the *Archives nationales* of the French government a royal pardon to Ogier under date of October 12, 1391, for a rather seamy action.

The pardon tells us that at the close of an Easter day in 1385 three retainers of the Sire d'Anglure asked him for an evening off. In a village near Epernay they had stopped at an inn, and there were struck with the beauty of the innkeeper's wife, Colette. Without further ado they trussed her up on a horse and carried her to a château of Ogier's called *le Thoult* nearby—quite wisely, for the Dame d'Anglure must have been at the family seat at the time. On the next day, early in the morning, Ogier happened, by chance, to have gone to mass at a nearby church with a relative, and then to have returned to his Château du Thoult. Upon his arrival there, he met one of the retainers and asked him whence he had come, where were the others and where they had been to remain so long away. The retainer replied, "Go to your chamber and you will know well enough!" Ogier did so and found there Colette, who was warming herself by the fire. He asked, "My friend, who has brought you here?" Colette named one of his retainers. Ogier replied in an amiable tone, "My friend, you are well come, 'tis fitting that I speak to you," took her by the hand and led her into his closet. And soon after he brought her again into his chamber where there was a fire burning, and commanded his people and the officers of his household that they give her meat and drink. Meanwhile, Colette heard the voice of her mother, who had found out the whereabouts of her daughter, followed her up and was now calling without in a loud voice: "False and wicked knight, you have my daughter within your castle." When Ogier had asked, "What is it I hear?" Colette had answered, "'Tis my mother, for God's sake let me go away with her." And straightway he took her and delivered her to her mother, saying these words, "Dame, you have said your daughter was here, if this be she, take her, for I have not known her; God knows that."[2]

Colette departed, but some two years later, egged on by her mother and husband, brought suit against the lord of Anglure. It was against this suit that Ogier sought and received a royal pardon "pour consideracion des services qui lui et ses predecesseurs ont faiz a nous et aus nostres es guerres de nostre royaume."[3]

There would be little point in retelling this sordid story were it not for the possibility that it may have had something to do with the pilgrimage which Ogier undertook ten years later. It would show little knowledge of life in the Middle Ages to suppose that our friend was overcome with shame for what he had done, and that the memory of his past conduct aroused feelings of remorse, and drove him to accept the cross, pick up the pilgrim's staff, and take the long road that led to Jerusalem. One who reads between the lines of the story and notes the cool and careful planning of this little coup, reads Ogier as one who did what he did with full awareness, as one who would have shouldered the consequences of his action with embarrassment, perhaps, but without any emotional upset. Medieval noblemen were accustomed to express their passions as and when they felt them and, if necessary, with a high hand.

Yet the case must have been a notorious one from whose repercussions Ogier heard. The pardon puts the best face it can upon his conduct, but even in its colorless and official language the whole business sounds badly. An admitted attack and a lie to cover it! Life with the Dame d'Anglure could not have been pleasant after such an escapade—and the low voice of his confessor must often have counseled that he atone for this and other misdeeds of his past life by an act of exemplary devotion.

That this crime of Ogier's had aught to do with the jour-

[2] *Saint Voyage*, pp. lxix-lxx.

[3] *S.V.*, p. lxxi.

ney is surmise only. Yet it is not an unlikely surmise. Perhaps consciousness of his own imperfections accounts for the mildness of his criticism of Turk and Saracen.

But now to the voyage upon which Ogier launched himself in 1395. The account of it is to be found in two mss., one (Ms. Fr. 15217) in the Bibliothèque nationale, and the other written down in the neighborhood of Metz, now in the Library at Epinal (Ms. No. 189). Both are paper mss. of quarto size, containing other works besides the narrative with which we are concerned. The account of Ogier's journey and return begins with these prefatory sentences: "*Cy apprès s'ensuit le contenu du saint voyage de Jherusalem et le chemin pour aller a Saincte Catherine du mont de Synay et ainsi a Saint Anthoine et Saint Pol es loingtains desers de Egipte; lequel saint voyage a esté* [*Ms. 189E estre*] *fait par monseigneur d'Anglure et autres de sa compagnie en la*[*n*] *mil. iij.*^{c} *.iiij*^{xx}. *et .xv., en et par la maniere qui s'ensuit.*"

Having gotten Ogier started, let us not delay him too long by further detailed explanations. We shall pass over the service of consecration for one about to make a pilgrimage, so beautifully and graphically described by Sir George Sitwell. We can be almost certain that Ogier and his fellow pilgrims, having heard mass, were escorted to the bounds of the parish by their fellow-parishioners. Though thus protected by God's blessing, Ogier probably did not neglect certain earthly precautions—he may have carried letters of credence or introduction vouching for his identity and importance, for he seems to have received certain courtesies which only his position in his own land could have won for him.

Ogier and his party[4] left Anglure on horseback July 16, 1395, proceeded through Burgundy and Savoy, passed below Mont Cenis, into Piedmont, through Asti into Pavia (July 31). Leaving Pavia on August 3, they arrived in Venice on

[4] Besides Ogier, these were his father-in-law, Simon de Sarrebruck, next, a knight of Artois, Pierre de Nortquelmes, probably a vassal of Ogier's, and third, the writer of the narrative, a servitor of the house of Anglure.

August 9. After a side trip to see at Padua a tournament which never came off, as both contestants made peace—presumably to Ogier's disgust—they sailed from Venice August 30.

We shall not chronicle their stops in the Mediterranean. Suffice it to say that leaving the island of Rhodes (September 20) they stopped at Beirut (September 24), where an opportunity to go ashore and "take in" all the relics there to be seen was given. One cannot fail to observe that all the features of a tourist cruise in the twentieth century were well understood in the fourteenth.

Ogier's comment on Beirut sounds somewhat like the reflection of the bored and tired tourist: "Beirut is a fine city, but it used to be finer than it is at present—and only Saracens live there." The ship cleared Beirut the twenty-sixth of September and stood off Joppa on the thirtieth.

The pilgrims must have been glad to get rid of their sea legs, but apparently Joppa held no joys for them, for the account, after recalling that it was there that St. Peter resuscitated Tabitha, and informing us solemnly that there it was that the same apostle did some deep-sea fishing, then adds sourly that on the mountain pilgrims are accustomed to sleep in a chapel of St. Peter, where there's nothing in a decent condition.

On October 4 the party, having taken the Joppa road that passes through Rama (Mod. al-Ramlah), descended the path which led into a walled portion of the Castle David, or Tower of David, now the citadel of modern Jerusalem, but a structure that long antedates pilgrim, crusader, and Moslem. Here they were immediately in front of the Joppa gate, waiting for permission to enter. The hour was vespers, i.e. shortly before sunset.

"Soon afterwards we left that place, all of us on foot, and by permission of the lieutenant of the Sultan entered the holy city of Jerusalem at the hour of low vespers,[5] and were

[5] *Vespres basses*, in a free translation, "at vespers, while the sun was sinking." For the idiom, see T. Johnes' *Essay on the Works of Froissart*, London,

harbored and lodged in the Hospital where at present it is customary to lodge the pilgrims."[6] The writer, *more medii aevi*, makes no attempt to express the feelings that must have stirred in their bosoms as they passed through the gate in the fading light.

Ogier and his companions had traveled up on donkeys or mules (*asnes*), horses being forbidden all pilgrims by the Moslem overlords of Palestine. This rule, if intended as a gesture of contempt for the Christian faith, was, to use a modern psychological term (a very bad one, be it said), easily "rationalized" away by pilgrims. The Master himself had made his triumphal entry into Jerusalem upon this humble animal; the disciple was not above his Master! Nay, where the Master rode, the disciple must walk, so that to show his own unworthiness the pilgrim dismounted and entered the city *tout a pié*. Furthermore, entry into Jerusalem, whether donkeyback or by shanks' mare, was, for Christians, possible only through the Joppa gate.

Bright and early (*trois heures avant le jour*) the pilgrims were routed out. The medieval pilgrim business had nothing to learn from Associated Tours or Thomas Cook. They went fast. The first day's tour started out from before the Church of the Holy Sepulcher, under the guidance of the *frere gardien* of that church, who, we are glad to learn, was "*moult bonne et honneste personne*," and took the pilgrims through a number of streets where there were what Ogier called "*sains lieux*" (holy places) to be visited. Thus in moving away from Mount Zion, on which the Church of the Holy Sepulcher is situated, the pilgrims came upon the house where "the sweet Virgin Mary learned at the school"; and in the same street the house of Pilate where Christ was falsely accused and judged to death, to which all entry was forbidden

1801, p. 118, "Sometimes he adds to these words of *prime, tierce, none, vêpres*, the epithet of *basse*, to mark that the time of these hours was near closing." But see also the word *bas* in Tobler-Lommatzsch, *Altfranzös. Wörterbuch*.

[6] Ogier probably is referring to the Hospital of St. John the Baptist belonging to the Knights Hospitalers, the chief reception-place of Roman Catholic pilgrims in medieval times.

Christian pilgrims.[7] On the east side of the city, and at the outlet of the street which passes the north wall of the Haram is the gate of St. Stephen near which the first martyr suffered. It is a place "*toute de roches*," and there the pilgrims saw one rock higher than the rest on which sat St. Paul, "who guarded the vestments of tyrants while they stoned St. Stephen."

The trip continued at lightning speed. In quick succession came "Jessemany" where our Lord was taken when Judas kissed him at the hour of midnight, "with glaives and lanterns," *le Mont d'Olivet*, *Bethfagé* and the sacred sites of Mount Zion. From the Mount of Galilee (a part of the Mount of Olives), opposite *Bethfagé*,[8] the pilgrims could see the lamps shining, for day had not yet dawned, in the building erected on the site of the Jewish temple—the Dome of the Rock, often wrongly called the Mosque of Omar, and in the Temple of Solomon (Mosque of al-Aqṣa)—a "*tresnoble chose a veoir*," as Ogier's scribe tells us. Entry into the Dome or its precincts was, of course, impossible for Christian pilgrims. Their dragomen told them that twelve thousand lamps were lit regularly, except twice in the year, probably at the Mawlid, the anniversary of the Prophet's birth, and at the end of Ramaḍān (or possibly at al-Aḍḥa, Feast of the Sacrifice), when thirty-six thousand shone forth.

Visiting continued, apparently for the rest of the day, and the pilgrims, retracing their steps to the vicinity of the Church of the Holy Sepulcher, saw a number of spots on Mount Zion associated by legend and tradition with the Catholic faith, if not with "true religion." First, in an angle

[7] "En icelle maison n'entre nulz chrestians pelerins, et est l'entrée dudist hostel murée" (*S.V.*, p. 15). Entry was probably forbidden because of the danger of riot and destruction. The Moslems, quite rightly, were ever on the alert to prevent popular disturbances caused by quarrels between the various Christian sects or effervescence of religious mania; cf. the account of Father Felix Fabri's visit to the Church of the Holy Sepulcher (1485) quoted in Watson's *Jerusalem*, pp. 259-60.

[8] Actually the Dome of the Rock would be invisible from the village of *Bethfagé*. Ogier evidently would have us understand that the pilgrims saw it from the slope of the Mount of Olives over which the road to *Bethfagé* runs.

between two walls, was the place where the Paschal Lamb that was consumed at the Last Supper was roasted, and in the same place was the water warmed with which Christ washed his disciples' feet. In the Church of Saint Saviour, erected on the site of the house of Annas, the stone covering of the high altar was the identical stone which covered the sepulcher of our Lord, on which sat the Angel whom the three Marys found when they came to anoint the body of their Master. As they left the Church of Saint Saviour and approached the Church of Notre Dame, converted into a mosque after Ogier's visit, their guides pointed out to them an open spot which held two great stones. On one of these our Lord was accustomed to sit when he preached to his disciples and the Virgin sat on the other. Somewhat farther on is the place where St. John the Evangelist said daily mass before the Virgin after the Ascension of our Lord into Heaven. I have mentioned the exhibition of these sites as evidence of how far legend could carry belief. Whether their guardians or custodians fully and firmly believed that the events of sacred story happened and its personages acted on those spots and in the manner in which they related them, we do not know. If I did not remember Chaucer's Pardoner, I should say that they probably gave full credence to what they related. But there is no doubt whatever that the Sire d'Anglure and his father-in-law, his retainer, and his faithful chronicler, and many another pilgrim, believed all they were told and would have believed more had it been told them.

The day, that busy October 5, wore to an end, but its climax was yet to come. At the hour of Vespers the pilgrims assembled before the Church of the Holy Sepulcher, prepared to pass the night within it, a night to be spent in devotion and pious observance, for many of them the most solemn night of their lives. As they assembled, the Moslem officials who were to supervise their admission sat on large blocks of polished marble on either side of the church door, their faces carefully averted. When the crowd had assembled, they opened the doors with their keys and admitted the pilgrims, two by two, looking at those who passed before them very keenly. Of those officials Fabri tells us "that they are greatly skilled in the art of physiognomy, and that as soon as they looked upon any man, they perceive his station in life, his disposition, and his desires."

Within the church, our party saw a flight of eighteen steps to a level where there were two altars and between them the "proper place where our Lord Jesus Christ was crucified, and suffered death and passion for human lineage." There was the hole in the rock, made to support the cross, and the hole was "all round"; there was that portion of the rock that split when the Saviour's blood fell upon it. The fissure made by the precious blood is a deep one, and at the bottom of it one can see the head of a corpse, which some say is that of our first father, Adam.

Any student of the Jerusalem of the Middle Ages, will find it profitable to read *Le Saint Voyage* much more carefully than any student has yet done. As an instance of what can be learned, there is an account of the Holy Sepulcher which is of archaeological value: in brief we know definitely that on October 5, 1395, the Sepulcher was very like a Gothic chapel, whose pavement was of marble, that it was vaulted, richly ornamented (i.e. with carving), painted, and decorated with figure, animal, or grotesque sculpture;[9] so that to western eyes, at least, it was a "very noble and very devout place." But our narrator is careful to tell us that the aperture where the cross had been placed, and the rock to its right that had been split by the fall of the precious blood, were not covered by the marble pavement.

When the approach of day made it possible for mass canonically to be said, high mass was celebrated. Before it Ogier and his companions had made their confessions, and at it they received communion. Ogier tells us that at the numerous chapels of the church pilgrim-priests were saying numerous low masses. At the close of the high mass, which

[9] Gothic builders knew when and how to use color, not only on woodwork but also on stone.

ended at 8 A.M., Father Fabri tells us that the Saracen guardians came to turn the pilgrims out. Ogier corroborates the fact of their dismissal, but puts the time of it much later, at nones.[10]

But we must hasten on as fast as our pilgrims. Reasons of expediency forbid us, as they forbade them, to tarry longer than a day in Jerusalem. On the sixth of October they were in Bethlehem, on the seventh in Jerusalem again, whence on the ninth they departed for the Jordan and the Dead Sea, returning to the city by way of Bethany to view the house of Lazarus on the eleventh. The next day was spent in Jerusalem, and on the thirteenth they departed for Bethzel (Bayt-Jāla) near Bethlehem, to equip themselves for the long journey to the Monastery of St. Katherine at Sinai, and after that to Cairo and the boat home.

At Bethzel one stopped only to equip himself with wine for the journey. This the "consul of Jerusalem" (the official of the district charged with the duty of overseeing the subsistence and lodging of pilgrims and of levying the tribute which each one had to pay to the Soldan) delivered to them. Ogier's narrative tells us that the wine ration, so necessary for a Frenchman or Italian, was a matter that had to be looked to, for wine was not the most plentiful commodity in the country and there was much chance of being overcharged for it. In Bethzel the Christians "of the Girdle," or Christians of St. Thomas,[11] had become expert winegrow-

[10] P. 25: "Le landemain jusques a heure de nonne, que les portes nous furent ouvertes par des Sarrazins." By earlier Roman and by Eastern usage nones was at 3 P.M.; by modern Roman use at noon. We do not know here the time of its celebration.

[11] Epinal Ms. adds *et sont crestiens greique* to explain Paris Ms. *chrestiens de la saincture*. The "Christians of the Cincture" (*Saincture*), i.e. those of the confession of St. Thomas, the apostle of India, so-called because St. Thomas received the "ceinture" or girdle which the Virgin let fall at her Assumption. See *Encyclopædia of Religion and Ethics*, ed. J. Hastings, article on "Syrian Christians," XII, 178-80. Professor Hitti is of the opinion that the reading of Epinal Ms. is to be preferred to that of the Paris Ms. He believes that even in Ogier's day the Malabar Christians in Palestine were few. Mr. Khalidi suggests that the Christians of the Girdle may have been the native Christians of Arabia whom Ogier confused with the Malabar Christians.

those they had intended to see. Another pilgrim, Ludolph von Suchem, gives practically the same list of holy places upon his pilgrimage of 1336-1341. Such itemized lists, and there are a number of them besides that of Ludolph, prove that Ogier or his amanuensis were not unduly credulous or superstitious above other men. Like many another traveler, ancient or modern, he and his party were probably determined to see all that they had paid their money for, and you will remember that Ogier himself may have had quite private reasons for wishing to visit every shrine and site that he could to secure whatever pardon or remission of purgatorial pain that particular relic or site could of itself confer upon the devout petitioner. His scribe's enumerations are no sign of excessive religiosity or a nature warped by prolonged preoccupation with another world.

Indeed, like Thoreau, who found one world enough at a time, Ogier is at his best in the one he once inhabited. In his narrative the particular holy site that he saw or shrine before which he prostrated himself is more often than not introduced by the word "item," as, for instance, "*Item, en la sainte cité de Jherusalem tout près de la place du Saint Sepulcre, est la maison en laquelle saint Jehan l'Euvangeliste fut nez.*" In other words he is checking off—possibly for reasons of his own, possibly for the eye of his confessor—matters of obligation. So much religious business was his and his companions' to perform, and the "items" register its due performance. It is when he is not concerned with shrine-visiting that he interests us most.

He is no literary artist. He had not been bred as a *scriptor* or clerk, but as a seigneur. Though there is every reason to believe that the *Voyage* was written at his direction and under his supervision, it is probable that another than he labored over the task of getting it down on parchment or paper.[12] His gifts lay in other fields than those of artistic

[12] I have wondered whether the regularity of the author's entries, the careful record of each day's events, is not to be accounted for by the supposition that the scribe read to his lord each day the entry of the preceding day. There

ers. Ogier tells us that they cultivated the vineyards "where those good wines grew," and he and his relished their product. "Know well," he tells us, "that one can call them good wines." The trade was evidently a very prosperous one for the Christians of the Girdle outnumbered the Saracens in Bethzel.

A nine-day stop was made at Gaza for other supplies, less attractive, perhaps, to our travelers, but certainly more necessary for the long desert journeys that lay before them. Through the agency of their dragomen, who must have saved them money, the party was equipped with biscuit ("unleavened bread"), asses and the harness for them, goatskins to carry water, and tents. On the twenty-fourth of October they were off, their faces set towards the deserts of the south.

Time fails us in which to describe the Monastery of St. Katherine, nestled down among the rocky peaks of the Sinaitic range, Jabal Mūsa and Jabal Kātrīn, but one miracle is worth retelling. On Jabal Kātrīn, the body of St. Katherine had for many years reposed, after its miraculous transportation by angelic hands from the site of the saint's martyrdom in Alexandria. On that summit of Jabal Kātrīn the rocks lie in piles, one upon another, and long telltale streaks of white reveal where the birds had rested upon them. On all the neighboring stones those streaks appeared, but on the stone where the angels laid their holy burden, there were no such streaks. The birds recognized sanctity, if men did not.

They left St. Katherine on November 10 and entered Cairo on November 22.

Cairo astonished our travelers by its size and beauty and by the general air of prosperity which its streets and houses displayed. Even today travelers tell us that life in Damascus and Cairo runs more gaily and freely than in somber Jerusalem, and that the grim appearance of the Jewish capital, perched high upon its rocks, recalls the fierce passions that have raged in it to such sad consequences; whereas Cairo of the level plain shows its visitors space, air and the play of unshadowed light. The city was so extensive that they spent a third of the night in which they entered it in passage from the gate to their lodging place. Had they entered by day, their progress would have been much impeded by the crowds of people who jostle one another in the narrow canyonlike streets.

The number of the mosques astonished them. Ogier's chronicler was informed that there were twelve thousand in all. Each mosque had its pool for ceremonial ablution, but those pools were not for everybody: the rich used the pools, and the poor the river. The beauty and cleanliness of these mosques, their numerous lamps and marble doors, astonished Ogier's party, who admitted that Saracen "*oratoires*," unlike Gothic chapels in the entire absence of sculpture, painting or gilding, could still be beautiful in the simplicity of white unpainted plaster. No less astonishing and unexpected were the numerous fountains of water scattered throughout the great city, and the beauty of exotic flowers and strange trees.

Stranger, however, than flowers or trees were the animals in the Sultan's menagerie. One elephant in particular among the Sultan's six arrested the attention of the French aristocrats. He had "a blackish skin, ears large as a small windmill vane, pendant and soft like those of a hound, eyes small and round. He was very big, very high, and had a short neck. He could not reach the earth because of his height; but for his snout; he has a sort of tube directly at the end of his snout, just like a pig, which hangs down almost to the ground, and with this tube this elephant takes his food from the ground and carries it to his mouth. Likewise, when he wishes to drink, he fills that tube with the water which is placed before him, and when he has drunk to his satisfaction, he lets the remainder of the water fall to the ground. And when this elephant blows air, he resounds by that tube more powerfully than any trumpet in the world could do, and his voice is loud and terrible to those who are not accustomed to it. Also there spring from his jaw two teeth like a boar's, which are very long and stout. And know that we would not know how to write properly for you of his size and height, but the bed of litter which is made for him to lie down on is easily two feet high at the least [measurement], 25 feet in length, and in breadth some 12 feet. This great elephant was chained by the feet.

"Also in another place in the city we saw five other very strange and outlandish beasts which are called 'giraffa.' These animals are very large and marvelously tall, the neck very long, and they carry the head high, and to us it seemed that they might very well take their food from the longest lance one could carry in these days, especially the tallest giraffes. The two forelegs are higher than the hind ones, the skin like a deer's, the horns like those of a roe buck, about a half foot high, and the feet like a deer's."

On the twenty-fourth of November the four travelers on fine riding mules (Ogier cannot refrain from commenting on their condition and gait), with a dragoman named Cocheca, and no others, rode out to see the "granaries of Pharaoh," i.e., the Pyramids.

Our diarist speaks first of the optical illusion which makes one who is in "Old Cairo," some twelve miles distant from the Pyramids, believe that they are close at hand. When the party reached the vicinity of the three to which they were wending, its members thought that they had seen nothing more marvelous in the course of their travels. Ogier ticks off the reasons why they seemed so impressive. First, because of their huge basal extent, necessitated by the fact that they are not circular but have four sloping sides. Secondly, because of their height, very large below and very pointed above; so pronounced, in fact, that if a man were at the apex, he could hardly be seen, no more than a crow at the top of a steeple. Thirdly, because of their masonry, the skillful cutting of the mammoth monoliths of which they are built up. Our diarist assures us that the Pyramids were built by the Pharaoh whom Joseph served in order to preserve and guard the food against the famine predicted by Joseph when he interpreted his monarch's dream. But while he repeats what his dragomen told him, he is not without the seeing eye—perhaps we had better say the "smelling nose": "There is," he tells us, "a hole at the base of the pyramid, as we stood close to it on the ground, not the height of a man. It is a dark place, and smells badly too, because of the animals who inhabit it." Legend cannot sweeten reality.

I shall have to pass over without mention the visit that our pilgrims made to the Coptic monasteries of St. Anthony-on-the-Nile, St. Anthony-in-the-Deserts and St. Paul, a visit vividly described and quite worthy the attention of the student of the churches of the East. I shall have to pass also over the journey down the Nile, and the sight of a crocodile and the description of the gardens of Alexandria. Cairo and Alexandria move our diarist as Jerusalem did not. Yet I suspect that even the beauties of Alexandria and the good wine to be found in its "funduqs" were beginning to pall a little, for he tells us that on Thursday, December 21, "*Nous entrasmes en une nafve pour retorner en nostre pays.*"

And now what of this man whose path in the Islamic Levant we have followed through the autumn days? How has the new world, whose ways were so far removed from his ways, whose thoughts from his thoughts, affected him? Has it weakened or confirmed old beliefs? Has it led to a different attitude towards men whose ways were different?

A hasty and cursory reading of the *Saint Voyage* might give a reader the impression that Ogier and his fellow-pilgrims were so blinded by superstition, so credulous of all that was told them that their minds were closed to other ways of thinking, and that consequently they have little to tell us of the ways of the East in the late fourteenth century.

Ogier and his companions, it is true, left France as good Catholic Christians. They went "*par devocion*," to confirm and strengthen the faith, much or little, that they already had. Relics and holy places they must see, and see them they did. But the tours on which they went were the regular tours which all pilgrims took, and the sights they saw were invention. He was no literary mystic like Lull; no itinerant speculator like Count Keyserling. He had been trained by war and hunting to look quickly and sharply and to notice small details. We must look upon him, then, as an observer of Eastern customs and practices, for as such he must claim whatever importance history has given him. From him, then, we are not to expect long, priest-inspired disquisitions on the superiority of Christianity over Islam—that superiority to him was a nondebatable question—but an objective account of the Moslem and Christian life in the great cities of the Levant and in the desert in the year of grace 1395 and of the Hijrah 797-798.

To the pilgrims who came in large numbers to Palestine and Cairo the Moslem rulers do not seem to have been hostile. From the tax on the Palestinian pilgrims the Soldan received a good revenue, and one can be well assured that he would have been unwilling to lose it. Indeed, it is interesting to note that Ogier and his company passed freely through Palestine at a time when the Turkish sultan must have received notice that the Christians of the West were assembling their forces in Hungary against him, with the conquest of Jerusalem as one of their eventul objectives. Provided they paid the tax, did not quarrel among themselves, as the various sects were always on the point of doing, and did not profane by their unhallowed feet the shrines of Islam, pilgrims worshiped in peace by the full rites of their respective churches, and came and went as they pleased.

Ogier encountered one prohibition which must have been irritating to Christian pilgrims, but which he seems to have accepted as perfectly understandable: the denial of entrance to such holy sites as were the object of Mohammedan as well as of Christian veneration. He tells us that to certain holy places on the Mount of Galilee (part of the Mount of Olives) no Christian may go "because of the Saracens," although it is said that pardons are to be received there. He

would have been plenty of time when the party, having naught else to do, would have been glad of such a *passe-temps*.

comments also on the conduct of the Saracen guardians of the Haram or Temple enclosure, who "as soon as they see a Christian coming up to the street that leads to the Temple, cry out at him and make him turn back, even though he be in no ways going to see the Temple."

Islam is scrupulous about the sanctity of her shrines, as Sir Richard Burton knew well. Ogier himself found out this fact in Cairo, when he wanted to visit the mosques, whose beauty was such that they seemed to be "*belles eglises de chrestiens*," but he gave up his wish "for fear of the Saracens who would not suffer it."

Ogier notices that Jerusalem was then, as it is now, divided into residential quarters. "Jerusalem is a great and beautiful city," he tells us, "although it is kept in a vile and filthy manner by the Saracens, with which it is so crammed that it is marvelous." In it are fine streets, well vaulted by fine stones, with windows above which give light everywhere throughout, and on top of these vaults are other streets by which one goes commonly from one lodging to another; that is, "the Saracens go, and no other people, for the Christians of the Girdle and the Jews who dwell in the holy city have certain places and streets where they reside."

Of the various races and creeds to be found in the Holy City, Ogier tells us only enough to make us wish that he had told us more. In Gaza, he informs us, there dwell on a certain street a sort of miscreants who are called Samaritans, and of them there cannot be alive in the world more than a thousand, so we were told, and so Our Lord ordained at the prayer of Moses. It is slightly unscriptural to make Moses responsible for limiting the number of the Samaritans.

Ogier then obligingly goes on to tell us how we may recognize a Samaritan when we see one. "The difference by which one can know all the various races of the land we have been describing is this: the Saracens are recognizable because they wear the white linen *kafieh* on their heads—the Saracens of Arabia are recognizable because they have and wear the white *kafieh* on their heads, but always have the head of this headdress wound round their neck and shoulders. The Christians of the Girdle are recognizable because they wear the coloured *kafieh* of a blue shade, and the Jews a yellow one. The Samaritans, that kind of race of which I have spoken above, are recognizable because they wear a *kafieh* of a peach-flower colour clearer than sanguine. And in all the attire and ornaments of all the races named there is no difference of manufacture or any other usage between any of them, except only the differences of *kafieh* aforenamed."

During all his trip Ogier was within the caliphate of Egypt, for he informs us that the Soldan who resided for the greater part of his time in Cairo, was "*seigneur d'Egipte, de Surie, d'Arrabe, et de Mecha vers Inde et autres terres estranges.*"

Atiya calls our attention to the fact that pilgrims were not usually permitted by the Mamlūk sultans to go far beyond the limits of Cairo and of the twin city, Babylon or Old Cairo, lest they learn the secrets of the Indian trade route. In Ogier's case this rule was not enforced, for he was allowed to go up the Nile on a visit to the Coptic monasteries of St. Anthony and St. Paul. The fact that he did so, Atiya believes to be proof that the Mamlūk administrators were convinced that he and his were genuine and honest pilgrims.

Of the non-Roman forms of Christianity that he found in the East, Ogier and his scribe are naturally more tolerant than they are of Islam. Indeed, I think I can see in his account evidence that his charity towards his fellow-Christians of other folds grows warmer as his contacts with them increase.

He notes that at the parvis of the Church of the Holy Sepulcher the four chapels of Notre Dame, St. John the Evangelist, Mary Magdalene and St. Michael, are appropriated respectively to the Greek Orthodox, the Armenians, the Indian Christians and the Abyssinians. Today the Virgin's chapel has disappeared or changed its name, the Magdalene has become two chapels, one dedicated to St. John and the Magdalene and the other to the Forty Martyrs, both in the possession of the Greek Orthodox Church; the other two are in the possession of the same bodies whom Ogier records as holding them. Ogier notes what is still true today, that the Abyssinian Christians (of the Coptic Church) still celebrate their services high up at the top of the Church of the Holy Sepulcher. The East does not change much.

To ecclesiastics of the Roman Church, the Greek, Coptic and Malabar Christians were in schism, and therefore to be regarded as the Church today regards Protestants. If questioned, Ogier would doubtless have voiced that view, for he was a fourteenth century layman and believed what his church commanded him to believe. But I have yet to find in his narrative an opprobrious or discourteous word upon the practices or services of the schismatic churches (schismatic, i.e. to the Roman Church). True, he calls the Samaritans "miscreants," but the word had not then our modern connotation of "scoundrel," but simply the sense of "unbeliever, infidel," and such the Samaritans certainly were.[13] Ogier's term probably implies no more than that they professed no Christian creed. Certainly the sincere devotion and the genuine kindness of the Coptic monks at the monasteries of St. Anthony and St. Paul opened his eyes to the fact that holiness and goodness could not be confined by creedal boundaries: "Within this abbey there are resident and living a hundred brethren and more, who maintain a very holy and excellent life, for at no time do they drink wine or eat flesh or fish, nor do they dress in linen. And in truth they show well that they are good folk, for they make very good cheer for pilgrims, and give them what they can collect of victuals very willingly, without asking for any return. These brethren of whom we speak are called Jaccopites [Jacobins], for they are circumcised, and then baptized as we are, and chant and perform the service very devoutly in their own

[13] They held no Christian creed, being monotheists. See *Encycl. Religion and Ethics*, XI, 161-67. The sole survivors of this sect are to be found today at Nablus (Shechem), where their numbers have steadily decreased.

language, and do not perform the service of Our Lord according to our usage or that of the Greeks, but have another different usage somewhat similar to that of the Christians of the land of Prester John [Abyssinian Christians], as some have told us."

No less kindly are the monks of the related house of St. Paul: "In this abbey . . . are about sixty brethren residing, who, to our thinking, are like to the brethren of St. Anthony, to wit in kindness and in their garb; for they made us very good cheer, and received us very gently and kindly, and prepared for our fare, with all speed, such goods as God had lent them. And though it must have been midnight when we came and entered at the abbey door, yet most of these good brethren arose, and were as assiduous in serving us and bringing hot dishes, as though each one of them were going to get one hundred ducats."

Ogier left the East, as he had come to it, in full communion with and obedience to the Roman Church, but the Coptic brethren had opened his eyes, enlarged his tolerance, and broadened his charity.

> For modes of faith let graceless zealots fight;
> His can't be wrong whose life is in the right.

Here, then, is the very seamark of our utmost sail. Thus much had the East done to one man of unimaginative mind and quite conventional habits. If we multiply many, many times what the East had changed in Ogier, we shall be able to imagine, even though vaguely, what its effect upon the West had been and was continuing to be. *Ex Oriente lux!*

Ogier sailed from Alexandria on Tuesday, December 21, about midnight. After several stops, and the delay in Cyprus caused by the death of his father-in-law Simon of Sarrebruck, they landed at Venice on May 23. And now an interesting coincidence! Between May 23 and May 29 (the last date being that of their departure from Venice) they met the great Enguerrand VII, Sire de Coucy and his son-in-law Henri de Bar, who were on their way to Buda where that crusading force was assembling which in the fall of the same year was to be so disastrously routed by the Turkish sultan Bayazid I at Nicopolis.[14] Ogier received from those distinguished noblemen letters which they wished delivered to France. I am sure he duly posted them. The road home doubtless had its dangers of brigands and of broken bridges, but, if they materialized, they could have held little terror or wonder for those who had passed through the Arabian and Egyptian deserts. On June 22, 1396, they arrived at the Château d'Anglure in time for dinner. Perhaps there is a smirk of self-satisfaction on Ogier's face as he utters his last words to us: "May the Grace of Our Lord Jesus Christ be the guard of all Christians who make, and will make, this holy pilgrimage, *and who have made it*,[15] and give to us all Paradise. *Amen*!"

[14] Atiya (*Crusade of Nicopolis*, pp. 52-3) does not know how Coucy got to Buda from Venice, whether over the Brenner Pass or by galley to Segna (in Croatia). To have gone over the Brenner from Venice would have made him retrace his steps somewhat, and we have extant in ms. the minutes of that meeting of the Venetian Senate which considered and granted the request of Coucy that a galley be assigned to him and his party for the crossing of the Adriatic; see J. Delaville Le Roulx, *La France en Orient*, Bibl. des Écoles Françaises d'Athènes et de Rome, Paris, 1886, II, 25. It is probably upon that minute that the late H. Lacaille (*École des Chartes: Positions des thèses soutenues par des élèves de la promotion de 1890*, Mâcon, 1890) bases his statement "ils s'embarquent à Venise," though it is also possible that he knew of other confirmation. See the writer's "Eng. de Coucy and the campaign of Nicopolis," *Speculum* 14. 423.

[15] Italics my own.

BIBLIOGRAPHY

A. S. Atiya. *Crusade in the Later Middle Ages*. London, 1938.
L. Eckenstein. *A History of Sinai*. London, 1921.
P. K. Hitti. *A History of the Arabs*. 2nd ed., London, 1940.
Sir G. R. Sitwell. *Tales of My Native Village*. Oxford, 1933.
C. M. Watson. *The Story of Jerusalem*. London, 1912.

For enlightenment on the topography of Jerusalem and for information about the peoples dwelling in the regions traversed by Ogier I am deeply grateful to N. A. Faris, P. K. Hitti, and I. R. Khalidi, my fellow-members of the Summer Seminar of 1941.

THE COURSE OF ARAB SCIENTIFIC THOUGHT

EDWARD J. JURJI

In the year of our Lord 1268, Bar Hebraeus—Primate of the Syrian Jacobite Church—arrived at the intellectual center of Maraghah in Persia to deliver a set of lectures on Euclid. Several years later this illustrious historian of science, celebrated as the last classical author in Syriac literature, reappears at the same seat of learning, also under Islamic auspices, in order to teach Ptolemy in Arabic. In this personage and event there is a symbol of the universal aspect of Arab scientific thought, transcending racial, historical, geographical and religious barriers. Islam and the Arabic language are the two ostensible factors in the creation of that gigantic melting-pot in the center of whose orbit rise the scientific leaders of the Arabic-speaking world.

Not Arab by birth nor Moslem by persuasion, the majority of the learned men were nevertheless Islamic insofar as they lived and labored in the shadow of that faith, and Arab since they used Arabic in the transmission of their ideas. The geographic dimension of this scientific movement is noteworthy. It extends from the confines of China to the shores of the Mediterranean, and from the Atlantic Ocean to the Indian. Looking back at its complete record one may say that it reflected the light of the Hellenic sun, when its day had fled, and that it shone like a moon illuminating the darkest night of medieval Europe.

Some bright stars in the Arab firmament lent their own light. All this process of illumination: moon, stars and reappearing sun, alike, fades at the dawn of the new day. They had heralded the Renaissance. Since they had their share in the direction and introduction of vital ideas in both the East and the West, it may be claimed that they are with us still. They continue to fire the imagination of some fifty million Arabic-speaking people. They shed their immortal luster on the culture of two hundred and seventy-five million Moslems.

The perpetual independence of the Arabian is a theme that stands at the core of the vast reorientation of scientific thought that will presently be discussed. It is patent that the kingdoms of South Arabia were successively subdued by the Persians, Abyssinians, North Arabians and Turks. Even the holy cities of Mecca and Medina have bowed under a foreign tyrant. It is common knowledge, too, that the Roman province of Arabia embraced the peculiar wilderness in which Ishmael and his sons must have pitched their tents in the face of their brethren. Yet these and similar exceptions are local and temporary. The body of the purely Arabian nation has escaped the yoke of the most intransigent aggressor. The war machines of Thutmose III, Ramses II, Sargon II, Nebuchadnezzar, Alexander, Pompey, Trajan and Napoleon never achieved the conquest of Arabia. The Turks and others might exercise a shadow of jurisdiction, but Arab pride is reduced to solicit the friendship of a people whom it is dangerous to provoke, and fruitless to attack.

Small wonder, therefore, that no field in the world of the Middle Ages ever witnessed so unquestioned a reign of supreme thought. Due to his practical attitude and broad universal outlook, the Arab succeeded where others had utterly failed. To the baffled amazement of the civilized world it was left to him to leave an imperishable impress on the scientific mind of man. In the hands of a host of unforgettable writers the Arabic language, with its astonishing elasticity, became a vehicle for precise, direct expression, reminiscent of the style of Voltaire in French and Macaulay in English. The language that ranks so high for purposes of eloquence and poetic flight now readily lends itself to the demands of exact and positive expression.

Out of their different circumstances of life the wielders of the new scientific style traveled their numerous pathways till they met together at a single crossroad. Common to most of them was the unwearied attempt to simplify and to make lucid. Herein resided their own unchallengeable genius. They could, despite certain persistent opinions to the contrary, make generalizations and propound a subtle synthesis. They had a stolid mastery over their materials, necessary in creative work. They could classify and enumerate, above all they possessed untarnished the simple gift of orderliness. They, like the Greeks before them, could address themselves to some particular phase of the subject without forgetting the whole.

For a long time interpretation was their legitimate monopoly. Soaring high above the mean levels of confusion they did not seem satisfied till full proof and concrete evidence had been meticulously offered in their writings. And whereas their books often read like modern school and college manuals, they do reveal a deeper insight into ultimate reality. Theirs was a penetrating and incessant search for the Absolute, transcending the limitations of the sensate and operating in the realm of higher values. Herein lies a hitherto unnoticed facet of the Arab scientific tradition, by virtue of which they were soon to cover themselves with enduring honor. Their names are joined to those that constitute the corps of international toilers across the ages who have fought for the liberation of the mind from the burdensome shackles of darkness and ignorance.

On one common ground at least did theological and scientific philosophical thought meet. Giving effect, it may be, to the rejuvenated principles of the Neo-Platonists, Arab scientific thought kept the sanctuary of the Divine securely guarded, and interposed between Him and His creatures an order of sublime spiritual potency. Thus did they unerringly seek to bridge the gap between the Intelligence, which is the first image of unity, and the soul, whose fathomless nature undergirds the doings of men. Of the Almighty, they openly stated that they could not tell what He is, only what He is not. The highest point, beyond which strictly philosophical inquiries did not penetrate, was the Active Intellect—a sort of soul of the world in Aristotelian garb—the principle which inspires and regulates the developments of humanity, and in which lies the goal of perfection for the human spirit.

Never in the course of human culture was there so romantic a drift of scientific thought; none so well known in detail; and none more frequently misunderstood by historians of medieval thought. One may consistently trace the typically Arab patterns of scientific thinking to some origin in Hellenistic mentality. Taken alone, that inevitably fails to help the seeker of the truth arrive at a mature understanding of the subject. That method breaks down because Hellenistic culture itself was transmitted to the Arabs in manifold ways. Other ingredients helped to alter radically the quality of the Greek heritage. No interpretation of the whole integral phenomenon is ever complete that leaves Arab spontaneity out of consideration.

By the tenth century of the Christian era, the Arabs came to find that their language, Arabic, was not only the language of Revelation, of diplomacy and polite intercourse, but also of science. They had by now at their disposal a great fund of generally excellent translations of all the most famous philosophical and scientific writings of the Greeks. The Arab mind, clear and scintillating, and the Arabic language, nervous, virile and rich, both actually and potentially had become a repository for men's highest thought. The old Arabs were an acute and observant people, and for all natural objects which fell under their notice they had appropriate and finely differentiated words. To render the medical works of the Greeks into their own tongue they had, of course, in many cases to invent new terms translated or imitated from the Greek. But they already possessed a fairly copious astronomical vocabulary, which, moreover, they were fond of using in ordinary life, even in poetry.

Perhaps our chief concern ought to be with the individual man—the seeker after knowledge—in whom this compelling movement of scientific thought incarnates and perpetuates itself.

In theory the giants of Arab science won their battle over the theologians by trying to exalt God beyond the limits of the metaphysical and scientific conceptions of law, form and matter. At the same time they stood aloof from the vulgar doctrines attributing a causality to things. Thus they deemed they had left a clear ground for the possibility of miracles.

These men seem to have flourished between the times—between Greek decay and the Renaissance. For when we speak of Arab science most students who are acquainted with the subject understand that reference is being made to the extensive body of scientific and medical doctrine enshrined in books, written in the Arabic language, but which is for the most part Greek in its origin, though with Indian, Persian and Syrian accretions, and only in the sense set forth above the product of the Arab mind. Its importance, as has long been recognized, consists not so much in its originality as in the fact that in the long interval which separated the decay of Greek learning from the Renaissance it preserved the most faithful traditions of ancient wisdom.

The men who bore the brunt of this persistent thought wave summed up in themselves the meaning of science. From them Europe derived not only the philosophical and scientific ideas which they themselves had largely imbibed from others, but, what is even more noteworthy, the secret of their dynamic energy and power. The rendition into Arabic of the Greek masterpieces, whether directly or through intermediate Syriac versions, was effected for the most part under the enlightened patronage of the early 'Abbāsid caliphs at Baghdad, between the middle of the eighth and the ninth centuries of our era. The work was accomplished by skillful and painstaking scholars who were for the most part Syrians, Hebrews, or Persians, of the Christian, Jewish, Zoroastrian or pagan faith.

In other words, Hellenistic thought and culture reached the Arabs through the Syrian Church, the Zoroastrians of Persia, the Jews and the pagans of Harran. The Arabs were that part of the Islamic community which by its mere presence served as a powerful solvent of exotic influences. It is true that the typically Arab scientific thought was often compromised by the patronage of those whom the orthodox Moslem doctors decided to regard as heretics. In spite of this censure it has left quite a distinct and enduring imprint on Moslem theology. After a checkered career in the East, Arab scientific thought passed over to the Western Islamic community in Spain, where a new set of men gave it the earmarks of a specialized development. Therewith it made a deeper impression on Christian and Jewish thought than on the Moslems themselves. Other men of science finally carried the great cause into northeast Italy where as an anti-ecclesiastical program it prepared the way for the rebirth of the classics.

This main line of endeavor was not the sole department in which Arab scientists won their acclaim. It is not even the main arena where intellectually they fought. All along the line their science branched off into new avenues of exploration in the majestic realm of constructive thought. The richest fruits of their labor must be sought in these side issues: in the scholasticism which, in Islam, Judaism and Christianity was a reaction against the fundamental faith—yet not without benefits; and in the medical, chemical and scientific studies of the Middle Ages, which received their fullest measure of enlightenment from Arab science.

Such was the caliber of those men who soon became the custodians of thought in the civilized world. The type of man at the helm did not permit the clash between science and philosophy long to be averted. Moslem theologians had transformed the use of words into the science of the word (*kalām*). Like the scholastic doctors of the Roman Catholic Church they made speculation the major concern of theology. It soon became evident that the practice of natural reason, with the concomitance of Greek science—now naturalized in the Arab mind—would inevitably drag the exponents of free thought into open conflict with the adherents of the principles of revealed truth. The ensuing battle acquired a somewhat strange accent, produced by the queer anomaly that the individual thinker had to perform at one and the same time both the role of philosopher and that of scientist. The division between the two realms—always more ephemeral than real—was never totally consummated. In consequence, men like Maimonides, pursuing a quasi-philosophical procedure, sought first to reflect how things ought to be in order to support, or at least not to contradict, their preconceived opinions. When their minds were made up with regard to their imaginary system, they declared that the world was not otherwise constituted.

Parenthetically it must be observed at this point that the much lauded Greek philosophy, incorporated in Arab thought, was not always a blessing. It often backfired in the hands of those who manipulated it. Greece introduced man's thought to the prospect of controlling nature. She lured him with the concept that science is at the center of things, and the far more perverted notion that man is the measure of all things. It followed with perfect logic, therefore, that the world had merely to be analyzed, organized and dominated by man. In the realm of ethical relationships and morality Socrates developed the idea of conscience. The individual needed a demon to balance his actions and that balancer was conscience. This was the acme of Greek thought and it was a far cry from the nobler teachings of Islam which came infinitely closer to the implications of biblical revelation. For the gods of the Greeks were the projections of great men, but not always good men. Indeed what Greece bestowed upon the Arab and the Moslem was not always bread but quite as often a stone.

The battle raged on. What especially exercised the wits of these thinkers were the dogmas of creation, Providence, and the doctrine of Divine omnipotence. They sought desperately to assert for God an immediate action in the making and sustaining of the world. But they seemed to overreach themselves on every front. They maintained that each change in the constitution of atoms is a direct act of the Almighty.

When the fire burns, or the water moistens, the terms used merely express the habitual connection between one thing and another. It is not the man that throws a stone who is its real mover: the Supreme Agent has for the moment created motion. If a living being die, it is because God has created the attribute of death. The body remains dead because that attribute is unceasingly created. It is needless to say that the scientific mind that leaned too heavily on the legacy from Greece was tempted to drop the whole problem of the unknown, leaving it unsolved, or more likely to repudiate its eternal character. With Averroës many men of science came to see in metaphysics of the foregoing description the very negation of science itself.

Here the question may appropriately be raised as to where Arab men of thought obtained the predisposition for their remarkable outpouring of interest in science and the philosophy of science. In order to answer this question adequately it is not enough to go back to the ninth Christian century when the Arabs came into possession of those resources of science and speculative thought which did not reach the Latins until the twelfth. One must rather start in the early Christian centuries when both within and without the fold of the Church, the Platonic tone and temper had already taken firm root throughout the domains of the Near East. Indeed some of these Greek forces had foreshadowed the coming of Christianity itself. Their total impact was strongly felt in the work of the early Church Fathers; their impulse went into the making of the human element that underlay the writing of the New Testament and the Septuagint. They played a leading role at the historic councils of the Church and in the formulation of the creeds and doctrines of orthodox Christianity such as the Trinity, the Holy Spirit and the incarnation. Much of this heritage was canalized into the Arab mind by the Syrian Christians.

With the passage of time the Neo-Platonic school came gradually to find in Aristotle the finest exponent and expositor of philosophy and scientific thought. During the sixth and seventh centuries, Aristotle became embodied in the teachings of the Peripatetic school of thought whose ideas gained wide circulation among the interpreters of the Eastern Church. Of these, John of Damascus is preeminent, largely because he knew how to make scientific thought subservient to theological interests. In the hands of less doughty churchmen, however, Peripatetic studies became the source of sordid heresies.

The Church of the Nestorians and that of the Monophysites, in their various monasteries, carried on, from the fifth to the eighth century, the study of the earlier part of Aristotle's logical *Organon*, as well as his *Categories*, *Hermeneutica* and Porphyry's *Isagoge*. The second 'Abbāsid caliph, al-Manṣūr (d. A.D. 775), was the greatest patron of Nestorian physicians. He invited them to Baghdad and facilitated their residence therein. He encouraged them to teach and train men. He took special interest in the task of purveying scientific thought through the translation of philosophical and scientific works from Greek, Syriac and Persian. But in all these enterprises he was surpassed by the caliph al-Ma'mūn (d. A.D. 833) under whom the apogee of Greek influence was reached. Thus it came to pass that under the caliphate, during the eighth and ninth centuries, versions of Aristotle's principal works were made into Syriac, and thence into Arabic. In the course of time the names of some of these translators were to be heard in Latin halls of learning. That was certainly true of Joannitius (Ḥunayn ibn-Isḥāq, A.D. 809/10-873) whose translations and those of his associates formed the foundation of the Arab canon of knowledge which dominated medical thought almost to modern times.

The story of Arab men of science has an earlier start and in an unthought-of province. "The first doctor of the Arabians," mentioned by the colorful biographers, was al-Ḥārith ibn-Kaladah (d. *ca.* A.D. 634). An elder contemporary of the Prophet, whose mother was Muhammad's maternal aunt, he became the first scientifically trained man in the Peninsula. He completed his studies at the great Persian medical school of Jundishapur and had the honor of being consulted by the great Persian Kisra (Greek Chosroes) who harbored and protected the Neo-Platonist philosophers driven into exile by the intolerance of the Emperor Justinian. Al-Ḥārith was succeeded in the art of healing by his son al-Naḍr.

Turn to other men who ushered in the sunrise epoch. In A.D. 772, an unknown Hindu astronomer came to Baghdad, whose foundation was no more than ten years old, bearing two treatises on mathematics and astronomy respectively. The latter consisted of the earliest Hindu scientific works dealing with astronomy, the so-called *Siddhantas*, better known to the Arabs as *al-Sind-hind* in the translation of Ibrāhīm al-Fazāri (d. *ca.* A.D. 777), incidentally, the first Moslem to construct an astrolabe on the Greek model. The translation laid the basis of the study of Arab astronomy. If it had no other significance save the introduction of the Hindu numerals into Arabic, and thence through the works of al-Khwārizmi (d. *ca.* 850) as "Arabic numerals" into the West, enough would have been accomplished to justify its inclusion among the epoch-making books of all time. In the following century al-Khwārizmi became the foremost figure in Arabic mathematics. His name is the source of the word "algorism" and his standard book called *al-Jabr w-al-Muqābalah* (Restoration and Equation) gave rise through the first word of its title—*al-jabr*—to our "algebra." Among later mathematicians influenced by al-Khwārizmi are 'Umar al-Khayyām, Leonardo Fibonacci of Pisa (d. after 1240), and Master Jacob of Florence, whose Italian treatise on mathematics, dated A.D. 1307, comprises, as does one of Leonardo's works, the six types of quadratic equations cited by the Moslem mathematicians.

The process whereby those Arabic numerals took root in Europe was incredibly slow. The antiquated Roman numerals and abacus persisted till the early part of the thirteenth century. The new system of numeration first came into common use in Italy. In A.D. 1202 Leonardo Fibonacci, who was taught by an Arab master and had traveled in North Africa, initiated the use of the symbols by the publication of a book which became a landmark, since it inaugurated the new technique and laid the cornerstone of European mathematics. With the discard of the old-fashioned mode of writing the progress of arithmetic was assured. The agelong bonds had been broken at last. The zero and the Arabic numerals are at the basis of the modern science of calculation.

To return to algebra. In the Orient there is evidence of an early interest in problems which would now be solved by algebraic operations. The Chinese were able to solve the quadratic equation in pre-Christian times. The Hindu works of Brahmagupta (*ca.* 628), Mahavira (*ca.* 850), and Bhaskara (*ca.* 1150) contain a large number of problems solved by algebraic method, and show considerable versatility in analysis. In the Arab world, particularly in Baghdad of the caliphs, two traditions of mathematical thought converged, the first from the Greek sources, the second mainly Indian. The result was embedded in such textbooks as those of al-Khwārizmi, abu-Kāmil (*ca.* 900) and al-Karaji (*ca.* 1100). Of these the algebra of al-Khwārizmi had the greatest influence upon European mathematics, having been translated by Robert of Chester (*ca.* 1140) and other medieval scholars.

No less striking was the transformation wrought in astrology and its offspring, astronomy. Notice has already been taken of the open sesame character of the newborn Hindu signs in the field of calculation. More than half a century had yet to elapse before the pioneer astronomers made their bow, led by al-Farghāni, abu-Ma'shar (Albumasar) and al-Kindi, styled "the philosopher of the Arabs" because he was the only ranking thinker of pure Arabian descent. Albumasar was born at Balkh, flourished in Baghdad and died (886) in Central Asia. His principal findings permeated Latin mathematics in translated form. His name became a legend. It turned up as the subject of *L'Astrologo* by Gian Battista del Porta (1606), a play which was adapted in *Albumazar* by Thomas Tomkis, staged before the English monarch, Charles I, in 1614, and revived by John Dryden (d. 1700).

The banner of astrology and astronomy was also lifted high by Muhammad ibn-Jābir al-Battāni (Albategnius, d. 929), born a Ṣābian pagan in the Iraqi hamlet of Battān. He made astronomical observations at al-Raqqah in Iraq, and Antioch, Syria. He corrected some of Ptolemy's results, previously taken on trust. He compiled new tables showing by calculations the orbit of the sun, moon and certain planets. Perhaps independently of Aryabhata (born at Pataliputra on the Ganges, A.D. 476), he introduced the use of the sine in calculation, and particularly that of the tangents. He proved the possibility of annual or sun eclipses and accurately computed the obliquity of the ecliptic, the duration of the tropical year and seasons and true mean orbit of the sun. His best known tables, *al-Zīj al-Ṣābi* (Rome, 1899), preserved in manuscript form at the Vatican Library, was published by Melanchthon—the associate of Martin Luther—at Nuremberg in 1537 as *De Motu Stellarum*, in a blundering Latin translation by Plato Tiburtinus (*ca.* 1116), annotated by Regiomontanus. A reprint of it appeared in 1645. The Escurial Library near Madrid possesses a manuscript of some value by Albategnius on astronomical astrology.

It is clear that the Middle Ages were not really dark in the sense that certain narrow medievalists report. These historians have often erred in their pronouncements on the course of scientific thought in the Middle Ages, showing us only the darkest side of the period. An exaggerated emphasis upon the least progressive elements and exclusive preoccupation with the limited domain of Western thought are responsible for this gross injustice. The truth of the matter is that that stretch of history was not as dark as our ignorance of it. Simply because its greatest achievements were made by Easterners is no valid excuse for its deprecation. The unbiased verdict of history decrees that from the second half of the eighth to the end of the eleventh century, Arabic was the scientific language of mankind. During that period, anyone with ambition to be highly cultured had to study Arabic, just as today whoever desires intellectual advancement must start by mastering one of the great Western languages.

Were anyone to say to you that the Middle Ages are sterile, quote to him one of the names already mentioned or any of the following: al-Rāzi, Thābit ibn-Qurrah, al-Fārābi, Ibrāhīm ibn-Sinān, al-Mas'ūdi, al-Ṭabari, al-Bīrūni, ibn-Sīna, al-Ghazzāli, al-Zarqāli. Nor would it be hard to augment considerably this array of magnificent names. These men had no contemporary equivalents in the West. In their day the most original and most pregnant works of science were composed in Arabic by them. Obviously they were endowed with a great talent of native scientific aptitude. They made stimulating studies in mathematics, astronomy, chemistry, physics, technology, geography and medicine. Their culture radiated from a number of nuclei which were distributed all the way from Spain and North Africa to Central Asia. Having first emerged in the regions of the Fertile Crescent—Syria and Iraq—they were soon to place the entire civilized world in their debt as their ideas acquired two new fields of operation, in the Mediterranean Crescent—from Asia Minor and Syria in the East, through North Africa, to Spain in the West; and in the formidable Asiatic Crescent extending all the way from the Near East to the great lands of the Far East, from Turkey, Persia, Afghanistan and Arabia to China, India, Indonesia, Malaya and the Philippines.

To the east of salt Lake Urmiyah in the northwestern Persian province of Ādharbayjān stood the city of Maraghah, noticed in the first paragraph of this chapter. There Hulagu, who had ravaged Baghdad in 1258, delighted to take his residence in time of peace. He had crushed the Arab capital ruthlessly but its scientific thought had a way of living on. Under the Īl-Khānid Mongol dynasty which he set up, his Arabic-writing Persian scholars made distinct contributions in astronomy and mathematics. The center of their activity was the famous observatory and library of Maraghah headed by the illustrious Naṣīr-al-Dīn al-Ṭūṣi (d. A.D. 1274). The seventy-five years of this regime in Persia gives brilliant testimony to the way in which Arab science was reborn alike in the lives of friend and foe. The instruments at the observatory were much admired and included an armillary sphere, a mural quadrant and a solstitial armil. Here in honor of Hulagu, Naṣīr compiled new astronomical tables which gained popularity throughout Asia, even in distant China. It is noteworthy that the foundations of this short-lived observatory are still extant.

Arab science had also created new centers in the West. The scientific life which expanded in Toledo in the twelfth century was in many respects reminiscent of the translation period in Baghdad some three hundred years earlier. Just as the caliph al-Ma'mūn installed the "House of Wisdom," so Archbishop Raymond founded under the direction of Archdeacon Dominico Gundisolvi a School of Translation which flourished in Toledo until the thirteenth century. The part of the polyglot Christian and Ṣābian translators of Baghdad was performed here by the Jews who ordinarily commanded Arabic, Hebrew, Spanish and sometimes Latin. The converted Jew translated many mathematical, astronomical and astrological works of the Arabs into Latin, as the Ṣābian Thābit ibn-Qurrah had turned those of the Greeks into Arabic. Gerard of Cremona did for the Latins what Ḥunayn ibn-Isḥāq did for the Arabs in translating the works of the philosophers, mathematicians, physicists and physicians.

Sicily must not be forgotten. Controlled by the Arabs for a hundred and thirty years, it came under Norman suzerainty in A.D. 1091, and proved a fertile center for the cultivation and diffusion of Arab science. Among the population, Arabic and Latin were in constant use as vernacular dialects, but some scholars, particularly Jews, also knew the literary forms of these languages. The kings, from Roger I to Frederick II, Manfred and Charles I of Anjou, drew learned men to Palermo regardless of language and religion. Here, as in Toledo, a staff of learned translators began to make Latin versions from Greek and Arabic. These translations dealt mainly with astronomy and mathematics. In medicine no important translations were accomplished in Sicily during the twelfth century. In the subsequent century, during the reign of Charles of Anjou (1266-85), we meet the renowned Jewish translator "Faragut" of Girgenti and his translation of al-Rāzi's *Continens*.

The Jewish scholar, Moses of Palermo, was trained as a Latin translator in the service of King Charles. Of his works we know only the version of a pseudo-Hippocratic work on the diseases of horses. Michael Scot (d. 1235), favorite of Frederick II, translated into Latin from Arabic and Hebrew versions the entire biological and zoological works of Aristotle, particularly the abstract of *De Animalibus* with Avicenna's commentary which he dedicated to the emperor in 1232. It is commonly recognized that the interest of Frederick II in zoology was even keener than his interest in optical questions. But it was not merely moral support and encouragement that he contributed. He went so far as to compose a book on hunting, *De Arte Venandi*, based upon Michael Scot, particularly his translation of Aristotle's zoology.

Neither Maraghah nor Toledo or Palermo ever would have attained any grandeur as centers of scientific distribution and thought radiation but for the preparatory spadework so diligently executed in the translation period (A.D. 750-900) and followed immediately thereafter by the flowering of scientific creativity (*ca.* 900-1100). The treasurehouses of Arab science accumulated in the course of the formative stages are just beginning to reveal themselves. In Istanbul alone there are more than eighty mosque libraries containing tens of thousands of manuscripts. Other collections are known to exist in Cairo, Damascus, Mosul and Baghdad, as well as in Persia, India and North Africa. On this side of the Atlantic the most impressive collection of Arabic and

Islamic manuscripts is the Garrett Collection at Princeton University. Only few of the collections in Arab and Moslem countries have been officially listed, much less technically described or edited. Even the catalog of the Escurial Library in Spain, which comprises a large segment of the wisdom of Western Arab thought, is not yet complete. In recent years, the mass of material recovered has radically undermined the former faulty conceptions of critics regarding the nature, scope and virility of Arab thought. It has flashed a strong beam of light upon the early part of the history of the Arab world, revealing more than ever before the sources of its creative flexibility. With the new bearings at our disposal, new readings are being taken. Therefore at the moment, any outline of Arab scientific thought and achievements has perforce to be tentative, pending the new disclosures of vigorous investigation.

The first bona fide institute of advanced learning in the Arab world was the Baghdad House of Wisdom (*bayt al-ḥikmah*) initiated by al-Ma'mūn in A.D. 830. Forthwith Baghdad assumed progressively increasing fame and prestige as a most conspicuous center of higher learning through which the enriching streams of Greek and Eastern thought began to flow into the farthest ends of the Arab world. The multifarious ingredients assembled at the capital city were quietly analyzed and clothed with caliphal sanction, thus simplifying the task of assimilation. Insofar as medicine was concerned, the vital assets and resources of the one-time Persian Sassanid studium at Jundishapur were held as models of the highest order. In addition to its strategic function as a translation bureau, the Baghdad institute also became the envy of scholarship by reason of its academy, public library and the observatory attached to it. Here the caliph's astronomers not only made systematic observations of the celestial bodies in the starry heavens, but also verified with remarkably precise results all the fundamental elements of *Almagest*: the obliquity of the ecliptic, the precession of the equinoxes and the length of the solar year. To this observatory al-Ma'mūn soon added another on Mt. Qāsiyūn outside of Damascus. The equipment in those days consisted of quadrant, astrolabe, dial and globes.

That affiliation in Baghdad of library, academy, translation bureau and observatory is the most notable development in the domain of thought since the foundation of the Alexandrian Museum in the first half of the third century B.C. Be that as it may, the first full-dress academy in the Arab world was still largely in the future. It was bound to come, as it finally did on the occasion of the foundation of the Niẓāmīyah school in A.D. 1065-1067 by the enlightened Niẓām-al-Mulk, the Persian vizier of the Saljuq sultans, Alp Arslān and Malik Shah, and the patron of 'Umar al-Khayyām—also in Baghdad. It outlived the fatal debacle that befell the mother city when Hulagu annihilated the last vestige of 'Abbāsid authority, as it also survived the later onslaught of the Tartars. It was ultimately merged with its younger sister, al-Mustanṣirīyah, about two years after Tamerlane captured Baghdad in 1393.

In Cairo, one of the remarkable foundations of the Fatimids was the Hall of Wisdom or of Science (*dār al-ḥikmah* or *dār al-'ilm*), established by al-Ḥākim in A.D. 1005 for the teaching and propagation of the extreme Shī'ite doctrine. In conjunction with it al-Ḥākim set aside a fund of which the income was to be expended on the copying of manuscripts, the repair of books and general maintenance. The Hall was connected with the royal palace and contained a library and conference rooms. Its curriculum offered, in addition to the specifically Islamic subjects, astronomy and medicine. Al-Ḥākim's court was graced with the presence of 'Ali ibn-Yūnus (d. A.D. 1009), the greatest astronomer Egypt ever produced, and abu-'Ali al-Ḥasan ibn-al-Haytham (Alhazen), the leading Arab physicist and student of optics.

Anterior to the rise of intellectual life in Baghdad, Cairo and elsewhere were several Eastern, non-Arab, homes of creative thought which in many respects anticipated the swelling Arab tide. Of these the most active was in the city of Jundishapur of the province of Khūzistān in southwestern Persia. In the early part of the fourth Christian century, in the reign of the second Shapur, the city became a royal residence and to it the monarch called the Greek physician Theodosius or Theodorus, whom he made royal physician and whose system proved a major inspiration to Arab medicine. This physician, who was a Christian, received the unqualified admiration of the Persian court. Shapur caused a church to be built for him and at his request set free a number of his captive countrymen.

The great development of the school of Jundishapur was, however, the unforeseen and unintended result of that Byzantine intolerance which in the fifth century drove the Nestorians from their school at Edessa and forced them to seek refuge on Persian soil. In the following century the enlightened and wisdom-loving Khusraw Anusharwan, protector of the Neo-Platonist philosophers (*ca.* A.D. 531), sent his physician Burzuya to India, who together with the game of chess and the celebrated book of *Kalīlah wa-Dimnah*, brought back Indian works on medicine and also, apparently, Indian physicians to Persia.

At the time of Muhammad's birth the intellectual fame of Jundishapur was at its zenith. There converged Greek and Eastern learning, the former transmitted in part directly from Greek, but mostly through the industrious and assimilative Syrians. Sergius of Rās al-'Ayn (d. in Constantinople, A.D. 536), who flourished sometime earlier, was one of those who translated Hippocrates and Galen into Syriac. Of this intermediate Syriac scientific literature—which was a steppingstone on the road leading to Arabic translations—little remains.

The medical school of Jundishapur withstood like a rock the world-shaking events attendant upon the seventh century Arab invasion. Far from undergoing gradual decline its importance was enhanced, especially in the latter half of the eighth century when the foundation of Baghdad shifted the focus of the Arab world eastward. In A.D. 765 the second

'Abbāsid caliph al-Manṣūr, being afflicted with an illness that was the despair of his medical advisors, summoned to his court the Nestorian medical authority, Jurjis the son of Bakhtīshū', chief physician of the great hospital at Jundishapur.

Jurjis rose in favor with the caliph. Though court physician and a high dignitary in the Islamic capital, he clung unswervingly to the Christian faith in which he was sired. The caliph took pains to invite this medical celebrity to embrace Islam. But Jurjis avowed that he rather chose the company of his forebears, be they in heaven or hell. His career was not thus interrupted. On the contrary his power was multiplied manifold. He became the head of an eminent family which for six or seven generations—over a period of two centuries and a half—exercised, despite adversity and vicissitudes, monopoly of the court medical practice.

That the physicians of Jundishapur should have been characterized by a certain exclusiveness, claiming as they did to be the pundits of medical science, is perhaps understandable. They guarded their professional techniques jealously against possible contamination from outside. The existence of this intellectual snobbery is evidenced by the cruel treatment, at the outset of his career, experienced by the would-be renowned translator of Greek medical works into Arabic, Ḥunayn ibn-Isḥāq, to whom earlier reference has been made. A native of al-Ḥīrah in Iraq, he too was a Christian with burning thirst for knowledge.

We first meet Ḥunayn in the humble role of understudy to Yuḥanna ibn-Māsawayh whose lectures he also followed. But he was prone to ask too many troublesome questions. One day his master, losing patience, exclaimed, "What have the people of al-Ḥīrah to do with medicine? Go and change money in the marketplace," and drove him forth in tears. Says al-Qifṭi (d. A.D. 1248), the distinguished historian of Arab philosophers and physicians: "These people of Jundishapur used to believe that they only were worthy of this science, and would not suffer it to go forth from themselves, their children and their kin." But Ḥunayn, more resolved than ever on pursuing knowledge to its source, went away for several years to learn Greek.

During this period one of Ḥunayn's former acquaintances, Yusuf the physician, ran across a man, with long hair and unclipped beard and mustache, reciting Homer in the street. In spite of his changed looks, Yusuf recognized the stranger by his voice as Ḥunayn. Being questioned, he divulged his identity and enjoined silence on Yusuf, saying he had sworn not to continue his medical studies until he had perfected himself in knowledge of the Greek language. When he finally returned, Jibrīl ibn-Bakhtīshū', to whom he attached himself, was delighted with his high Greek scholarship and hailed him a miracle of learning. Ibn-Māsawayh, who had formerly despised the man, sought Yusuf's good offices to effect a reconciliation with the indomitable Ḥunayn.

When Ḥunayn had attracted the attention of the caliph, there was yet one other exacting test to which he must submit before his admission to full royal confidence. The caliph bade him concoct a poison to be employed in the elimination of an enemy. A rich reward was held out as bait, but Ḥunayn strongly resisted the temptation. The whole idea was revolting to his noble spirit and training. As a penalty for his open refusal to enforce the royal will he was given a year in jail. When his case came up before the caliph for review he was summoned again and offered another opportunity to make up his mind. Again he voiced an unqualified preference to die rather than allow the compromise of his personal integrity. "I have already told the Commander of the Faithful," he declared, "that I have skill only in what is beneficial. In my studies I have mastered nothing else." All attempts to intimidate him by the threat of capital punishment having failed, he went on: "I have a Lord who will give me my right tomorrow in the Supreme Uprising. If the caliph would injure his own soul, let the choice rest with him." Whereupon, it is reported, the caliph's face brightened and he told the severely tried Ḥunayn that his desire to ascertain the physician's probity had been amply satisfied.

This is no place to catalog exhaustively all the active centers in the powerhouse that supplied the future Arab thought with energy. Included in any such a presentation would be the names of Edessa (al-Ruhā'), the principal intellectual armory of the Christian Syrians; Antioch, one of the many Greek colonies; Alexandria, the meetingplace of Occidental and Eastern philosophy; and the busy cloisters of Syria and Iraq, where not only ecclesiastical but scientific and philosophical studies were cultivated with avidity.

Consider also the valiant efforts made at Harran, stronghold of the heathen Syrians. Here, too, forces were at work that in time came to be woven into the warp and woof of Arab scientific thought. As a nerve center the significance of Harran hinges on the prodigious task performed by its able translator who eventually brought about that phenomenal infiltration of Greek patterns into Arab science. Down to the thirteenth century, Harran remained pagan. Owing to the high degree of Greek culture long promoted there, it became known as a stronghold of Hellenism. Of all the learned Harranians the most magnificent figure was undoubtedly Thābit ibn-Qurrah (d. *ca.* A.D. 901). The pagan Ṣābians of Harran as star-worshipers had early been fascinated by astronomy and mathematics.

In the days of the 'Abbāsid caliph al-Mutawakkil (A.D. 847-61), Harran shone as the seat of a school of philosophy and medicine which had previously been transferred from Alexandria to Antioch. That was the unusual atmosphere where Thābit ibn-Qurrah and his cohorts flourished. They are worthily credited with the translation of the bulk of Greek mathematical and astronomical lore, including the compends of Archimedes (d. B.C. 212) and Apollonius of Perga (b. *ca.* B.C. 262). They also improved the earlier translations. The work done on Euclid by Ḥunayn was now revised by Thābit, who found another patron in the caliph al-Mu'taḍid (892-902). To him Thābit soon became a personal friend and table companion.

Those in broad outline were the general characteristics of the substructure on which the rising libraries, hospitals, universities and other diffusion agencies in Arab scientific thought were based. We may suppose, furthermore, that the establishment of hospitals in Europe during the thirteenth century which were no longer under clerical supervision alone proceeded partly under the influence of the crusades. They may have been imitations of such splendidly established bimaristans (Persian, *bīmār*, sick + *stān*, place), as that of the contemporary Saljuq ruler Nūr-al-Dīn in Damascus, and the Mamlūk sultan al-Manṣūr Qalāwūn in Cairo.

Qalāwūn, whose rule (A.D. 1279-90) over Egypt and Syria, in the line of the Baḥri Mamlūks, consolidated Moslem power and endowed it with impregnability against its deadly Mongol adversaries of Persia as well as aided it to withstand the recurrent Frankish onslaughts of the crusaders, achieved another less dubitable title to enduring fame. Not only was he the builder of citadels renovated on a large scale in Aleppo, Ba'labakk and Damascus, but also of the Cairo hospital, connected with a school-mosque and mausoleum. His hospital, whose remains constitute the earliest relics of a Moslem hospital extant, is the most famous of his buildings. The sultan is said to have felt the need for this humanitarian enterprise while lying ill in the Nūri hospital at Damascus. There he vowed to establish a similar institution in Cairo in the event of his recovery. The main structure—hospital, annexes, school and mosque—was completed in 1284. It comprised special wards for the segregation of infectious diseases, such as fevers, ophthalmia and dysentery, and was provided with laboratories, a dispensary, bath, kitchens and storerooms. The chief officer of its medical staff gave instruction in a properly equipped lecture hall. The principal endowment yielded about a million dirhams annually, and the hospital employed male and female attendants, its doors being open to the sick of both sexes.

European travelers visiting Cairo paid this hospital their highest tribute of praise and commendation. After a period of decline it has seen a renaissance in our own days. The Arabs who came in contact with Frank physicians during the crusades frequently expressed scorn for their professional skill. This appears, for instance, from anecdotes related by the Syrian prince Usāmah based on the reports of his Christian Arab physician Thābit. The latter, about A.D. 1140, observed two cases which ended fatally owing to the barbarous surgery of a Frank.

It is now generally understood, in certain specialized circles of competent historians of medicine, that the early patterns of hospitalization and hygiene in Europe received their energizing impetus from Arab medical science. In this way was progress finally made in the spheres of surgery, hygiene and practical medicine. Guy de Chauliac (d. 1368), the surgeon of Montpellier, adopted the scorned operations of Arab physicians for rupture and cataract. Lanfranchi of Milan, who established himself in France (1295), introduced advanced methods in ligature of blood vessels and suture of wounds. For some time in northern Italy, the non-suppuration treatment of wounds with wine-compresses was practiced. In all these and numerous other instances the influence of Arab medication was paramount.

Less traceable, though no less real, is the link of the early European university with the Arab diffusion centers. From the twelfth century onward, universities in Europe were established in numbers. The new learning crystallized in them. Such were Bologna, Padua, Montpellier and Paris. As in Byzantine Alexandria and in Baghdad of the caliphs, education revolved around the reading of ancient authors, at last accessible in Latin. Experimental science was hardly known as yet; and botany, zoology, physics and alchemy, as well as astronomy, mathematics and medicine took their cue from the Arab masters.

Only towards the close of the sixteenth century were human bodies publicly dissected at Bologna, and at first strictly in connection with the gathering of evidence for legal process. No purely scientific service was thereby rendered and the correction of the anatomical and physical blunders of Galen, as transmitted by Avicenna, had to wait indefinitely. Tradition overrode autopsy. Natural science in those days made its home in the University of Paris. Aristotelian science as introduced from Toledo, with Averroës' commentaries, was bedrock for all branches of learning.

The English philosopher and man of science, Roger Bacon (*ca.* 1214-92) and the German scholastic philosopher, Albertus Magnus of Bollstädt, were among the many leaders of European thought attracted to Paris where Aristotelianism as expounded by the Arab scientists was the chief object of interest. Roger Bacon, who was by no means friendly towards Albert, refers to him as "the first master of philosophy," and "the most noted of Christian scholars." Just as Roger Bacon's *Optics* was based on Alhazen's (ibn-al-Haytham's) *Thesaurus Opticae*, so Albert repeated the alchemical teachings of Geber (Jābir ibn-Ḥayyān) and other Arab writers, in his zoological and botanical studies where he relied greatly on translations from Arabic. The influence of Geber was far-reaching in the encyclopedic *Speculum Naturale* by Vincent de Beauvois. Arabic alchemy, associated as it was with astrology, predominated throughout the thirteenth and fourteenth centuries.

When the complete picture of Arab science is contemplated in retrospect it seems to extend with few serious setbacks over almost five hundred years. The works of speculation and technology possessed by the many Arab libraries may be reduced to the six classes of philosophy, mathematics, astronomy, physics, chemistry and medicine. The sages of Greece had formulated much of this heritage. Now it was the turn of the Arab mind to illustrate and to perpetuate. Plato wrote for the Athenians, and his allegorical genius is too closely blended with the language and religion of Greece. After the fall of that religion, the Peripatetics, emerging from their obscurity, prevailed in the controversies and wranglings of the Eastern Church. Long afterward their founder was restored, particularly by the Arabs of Spain, to the Latin schools.

The physics both of Plato's Academy and Aristotle's Lyceum, as it was built not on observation but on argument, retarded the progress of real scientific knowledge. It is to be deplored that the metaphysics of the Infinite has often been enlisted in the service of superstition. Yet undeniably the human faculties are fortified by the art and practice of dialectics. The ten predicaments of Aristotle collect and methodize our ideas, and his syllogism is the keenest weapon of dispute. These too were dexterously wielded by the Arab thinkers. The study of mathematics and its affiliate, astronomy, is distinguished by the peculiarity that in the course of the ages it may always advance, and can never recede. The Arabs cultivated with brilliant success the sublime science of astronomy which elevates the mind of man to disdain his diminutive planet and to look beyond his transient existence upon it. The costly instruments of observation were supplied by the caliph al-Ma'mūn, and the land of the Chaldaeans still offered the same unclouded horizon. In the plains of Iraq, his mathematicians accurately measured a degree of the meridian at fifty-six and two-thirds miles—a remarkably close result, only exceeding the real length of a degree at the place by about 2877 feet. The astronomical tables of Baghdad, Spain and Samarqand corrected some minute errors in the Ptolemaic hypothesis, without, however, actually renouncing it.

The science of chemistry owes its very inception to the tireless industry of the Arabs. They described scientifically the two principal operations of calcination and reduction. They improved on the methods for evaporation, sublimation, melting and crystallization. They knew how to prepare crude sulphuric and nitric acids and mix them so as to produce aqua regia, in which gold and silver would be dissolved. In general they modified the Aristotelian theory of the constituents of metals in a way that survived, with slight alterations, until the beginning of modern chemistry in the eighteenth century. They first invented and named the alembic for the purposes of distillation, analyzed the substances of the three kingdoms of nature and converted the poisonous minerals into soft and salutary medicines. In medicine, as elsewhere submitted in this chapter, they have been deservedly applauded. The names of Māsawayh, Jābir, al-Rāzi and Avicenna are deservedly to be classed with the Greek masters. The first, a Christian physician and pupil of Jibrīl ibn-Bakhtīshū', failing to obtain human subjects for dissection, a practice discouraged by Islam, had recourse to apes. Arab interest in the healing science found expression in the Prophetic tradition: science is twofold, theology and medicine.

The physician combined the functions of philosopher, theologian and healer. The title *ḥakīm* (sage) was applied to him in his many-sided office. In the curative use of drugs some remarkable advances were made by the Arabs. They established the first apothecary shops, founded the earliest school of pharmacy and produced the first pharmacopoeia. Like druggists, physicians were required to submit to a test. In A.D. 931 Baghdad had over eight hundred and eighty physicians, licensed to exercise their lucrative profession. In Spain the life of the Roman Catholic princess was entrusted to the skill of the Arabs, and the school of Salerno, their legitimate offspring, revived in Italy and Europe the forgotten precepts for the relief of suffering.

Enough facts have been marshalled in this survey regarding the size and substance of the Arab scientific contribution to justify a nod of agreement on the part of fair-minded readers. In determining this abiding heritage in specific terms one arrives at the focal point in the whole study undertaken here. Arab astronomy it will be noticed, transported by the Moslems into Spain, blossomed temporarily at Cordova and Toledo. From the latter city, the Toledan Tables, drawn by Arzachel (al-Zarqāli) in A.D. 1080, took their name. These tables, mainly based on Ptolemy and al-Khwārizmi, were rendered into Latin in the twelfth century by Gerard of Cremona. The astronomical canons of al-Zarqāli were similarly absorbed (*ca.* 1140) into the system of Raymond of Marseilles. Al-Zarqāli was the foremost astronomical authority of his time. He was the first to prove the motion of the solar apogee with reference to the stars. According to his measurements it amounted to 12.04″, whereas its real value is 11.8″. Copernicus quotes al-Zarqāli, together with al-Battāni in his *De revolutionibus orbium coelestium.*

Also at Toledo, the Alphonsine Tables were promulgated under the authority of Alphonso X of Castile in 1252. Their appearance heralded the dawn of European science, almost coinciding with that of the *Sphaera Mundi* as textbook of spherical astronomy, written by a Yorkshireman, John Holywood, known as Sacro Bosco (d. 1256).

Not until the Germany of the fifteenth century was the brilliant attempt made to doctor the discrepancies in the Ptolemaic doctrine. George Purbach (1423-61) was the first to introduce into Europe a method of determining time by altitudes, following the precedent of ibn-Yūnus. He lectured with applause at Vienna in 1450, and two years later was joined there by Regiomontanus. Purbach died prematurely at the age of thirty-eight when about to start for Rome to study a manuscript of *Almagest.* His labors lived on and bore fruit in the work of Regiomontanus and Bernhard Walther of Nuremberg (1430-1504), who constructed an observatory equipped with clocks driven by weights, and initiated various improvements in practical astronomy.

What was transmitted to the West only partially accounts for the legacy of science and thought bequeathed by the Arabs. There were, besides, those intangible yet imperishable possessions which live down the ages, regardless of their clinical or laboratory or museum value. In commenting on the high esteem in which the enlightened al-Ma'mūn regarded scholars and scholarships, Bar Hebraeus uses these words: "He was not ignorant that they are the elect of God, his noblest and most useful servants, whose lives are devoted to the improvement of their rational faculties. . . . The teachers of wisdom are the true luminaries and legislators of the world, which but for their aid, would once more sink in ignorance and barbarism."

In addition to mental virginity and their immense capacity for fresh reaction, the early Arabs owned a fabulous reservoir of zeal and curiosity. Al-Ma'mūn's fine example was emulated by succeeding princes of the House of 'Abbās, their rivals, the Fatimids of North Africa, the Umayyads of Spain and others. Together many of them were the patrons of the learned as well as the Commanders of the Faithful. The same royal prerogative was claimed by the independent emirs of the provinces. This emulation diffused the taste and rewards of science from Samarqand and Bukhāra to Fez and Cordova.

A continuous stream of slowly acquired wisdom unites the rich past with the living present, and enters effectively into the shaping of the future. Thus the destiny of the Arab is not without its peculiar potentialities. It is true that after the sixteenth century Arab scientific thought began to deteriorate. In Europe books of science begin to refer more and more to translation from Greek rather than Arabic Hellenism. Yet Arabic thought continued to bear the marks of distinction. Not until the period 1530-1550 did it suffer its greatest eclipse. Simultaneously with the revolution of astronomy by Copernicus (d. 1543), Paracelsus (d. 1541) reformed alchemy and medicine. He incessantly urged his students to abandon Galen and Avicenna and to return to the observations of nature. In 1543, the same year in which Copernicus published his famous work, Andreas Vesalius edited his fundamental new anatomy. This year marks the close of the Middle Ages insofar as Arab scientific thought was concerned. This was the end of a splendid era but not necessarily the withdrawal of the Arab forever from the world of thought.

The decline which had set in as far back as the second half of the eleventh century did not take Arab scientific thought by surprise, nor was it as abrupt as some would have us think. That was the time of ʻUmar al-Khayyām. That was the end of the golden age of Arab science but by no means the end of the Arab. By that time the scientific primacy of the Arabs had lasted more than four centuries—a period of sufficient duration to breed a civilization. Yet in spite of the fact that Christian Europe was beginning to awake, as evidenced by the appearance of Anselm, Psellus, Constantine the African and the Chanson de Roland, the Arabs were still in the vanguard of humanity. There was nowhere else in the world, in those days, a philosopher who could at all compare with al-Ghazzāli, an astronomer like al-Zarqāli nor a mathematician like ʻUmar al-Khayyām.

As late as 1520 in Vienna, and 1588 in Frankfurt on the Oder, the medical curriculum was still largely based on Avicenna's *Canon* and on the ninth book *Ad Almansorem* of Rhazes (al-Rāzi). Even in the seventeenth century in France and Germany some scholars kept to Arabic erudition, whilst the struggle between Hellenists and Arabists went on in northern Italy until both were crushed by the advent of the modern scientific method. Arabic pharmacology survived until the beginning of the nineteenth century. Parts of the Latin version of ibn-al-Bayṭār's *Simplicia* were printed in 1758 at Cremona. Serapion and Mesuë the Younger were studied and summarized for the use of European pharmacopoeias until about 1830. An old German treatise (1838) on Zoology from al-Damīri's *Life of Animals* reproduces the legends relating to the poisonous nature of the *abu-burayṣ* (gecko)—a harmless Eastern house lizard. The native druggists from Morocco to India habitually compose their remedies in accordance with the short treatises of medieval Arab physicians.

Above and beyond the visible course taken by Arab science are those changeless and timeless qualities of mind and spirit that made such an achievement possible. It is largely due to their capacity for erudition and scientific acumen that the Arabs came to occupy the position of honor that was theirs. As one surveys the present one may well entertain the hope that they who did so much before can and will do much again.

BIBLIOGRAPHY

Edward G. Browne. *Arabian Medicine.* Cambridge, 1921.

Philip K. Hitti. *History of the Arabs.* 2nd ed. (London, 1940).

Lucien Leclerc. *Histoire de la medicine arabe.* 2 vols. (Paris, 1876).

Max Meyerhof. "Science and Medicine," *Legacy of Islam,* ed. Thomas Arnold and Alfred Guillaume. Oxford, 1931.

George Sarton. *Introduction to the History of Science.* Vol. I (Washington, 1927).

H. Suter. *Die Mathematiker und Astronomen der Araber und ihre Werke.* Leipzig, 1900.

THE CHARACTER OF ISLAMIC ART

RICHARD ETTINGHAUSEN

Compared with the history of Western art, and certainly with that of classical archaeology, research in the field of Islamic art is of very recent date, and is today undertaken only by the second and third generation of scholars in the field. Many of the outstanding monuments were discovered during the past few years, and we can still hope to find major monuments in the near future. The study of iconography and literary sources is in its initial stages. We would like to know more about the special conditions under which the arts and crafts were executed. Still we have a large amount of material available, and, thanks to the researches of Professor Louis Massignon and of the late Sir Thomas Arnold, we have at least some means of understanding the problem as a whole. Therefore, although a general survey of the characteristic features of Islamic art is premature, it seems permissible to make a preliminary statement, superficial and eclectic as it may be, about what we have so far learned of the peculiar character of Islamic art.

There is no doubt that art in Islamic countries is a derivative of the classical traditions followed in various Oriental countries preceding the Arab conquest. Sometimes this inspiration is rather pure and direct; in other cases the influence came by way of Sassanian or Coptic art. There are also extraneous influences, such as those from India. But this paper does not intend to deal with steminas showing the sequences and interrelations of styles, forms and single motifs. The question of the "what" and "how" are dealt with in a general fashion; and there is also an endeavor to reply to the question of the "why," though the answer must necessarily remain inconclusive and subjective.

The first factors to be considered in such an evaluation are the social, economic and religious conditions in Arabia at the time of the Prophet. As Muhammad was subject to native and foreign influences even in his major religious concepts, we are entitled to assume that he was the child of his age and society as far as art was concerned.

We find a rather primitive society in which the bulk of the population are nomads. Only a minority of the people lived as traders in cities, where we can assume that the prerequisites of a more abundant life were not much beyond the scope of the hunter and shepherd in the desert. The latter, of course, could only surround himself with coarse, unbreakable simple objects which would not be destroyed by frequent transportation on the backs of camels. For instance, there would not be much room for glass vessels. Indeed, as is vividly demonstrated by the names given to them, all the finer material things of life in Arab society around A.D. 600 were foreign importations. The Arabic words for "tailor," "carpenter," "potter," "armor-maker," to mention a few, came from the Aramaic. One of the words for "book" (*miṣḥaf*), and words such as "window," "bracelet" and "smith" are from Ethiopic; terms for "silk" were originally Persian. Because the Arab is physically and mentally remote from the visual arts his poetry alludes only rarely to it, as, for instance, when the poet 'Amr in his contribution to the *Mu'allaqāt* compares the legs of a beautiful woman to marble columns, or her breasts to ivory boxes. This is all the more striking as poetry was the great art of the people of pre-Islamic Arabia.

Furthermore, the objects used in daily life could never achieve a higher physical form on account of their ignoble origin. Men decided the fate of their families, took care of the wealth—that is to say, the herds—provided food by hunting, and if necessary took part in the exigencies of war. These very men spurned the making of any kind of objects to be accomplished by the tedious work of the hands. This was left to the women, to the slaves, to foreigners and to the Jews. The social standing of the arts was therefore much lowered. If one wanted to deride somebody, one called attention to the fact that one of his ancestors worked with bellows, that is to say, was a smith; or one spoke of another as a "weaver, son of a weaver." There is no more vivid demonstration that the frescoes of Quṣayr 'Amrah belong to a foreign, non-Arab civilization—in spite of the fact that they are executed for the palace of an unknown prince of the Umayyad period—than the fact that these pictures show various craftsmen at work. According to one of the latest travelers to Yemen even today the Jews of Ṣana'ā' are the craftsmen of the region.

The religion of primitive Arab society, which might have offered possibilities for artistic activities, contributed nothing. The pagan Arabians of the Jāhilīyah worshiped near wells, trees and especially near stones, the abodes of the gods. There was hardly ever an actual piece of sculpture used in connection with the divine worship. The very names of such stone figures (*dumyah*, *ṣūrah*, *ṣanam*) were foreign. The goddess al-Lāt was worshiped at a square piece of rock in al-Ṭā'if. The god al-Fals was connected with a red projection of somewhat human appearance in the middle of an otherwise black mountain, while the god al-Jalsad had a body of a large white stone with a black one on top as his head, the human aspect of which was only visible if one cared to look with close attention. The Ka'bah was a very modest building in Mecca. When it burned down in the year 605, the Meccans called in a Greek carpenter who was then on board a ship passing through Juddah. This foreigner rebuilt the shrine with the assistance of a Coptic craftsman.

This describes in brief the artistic heritage handed down to the Prophet. There is nothing in Muhammad's career which might have mitigated or improved this picture. How strongly dependent he was on the material culture of his age is shown by the fact that his simple house in Medina was used as the place of worship by the Moslem congregation throughout his life, and even in the decades after his death. This very building is a clear proof of how decisively the material conditions in his time influenced the later periods.

All later mosques are derivatives of this simple house with its shade-giving portico for the prayer meetings on one side and its columned shelter on the opposite side of the large square courtyard.

While Muhammad accepted the general attitude of his age toward arts and crafts more or less in wholesale fashion, he gave it however a new, peculiar character which was of paramount importance for the later development of the arts.

Muhammad centered his divine revelation on the forthcoming Day of Judgment on which everyone was to be called upon to give evidence of his deeds, a day on which one was either punished by everlasting hellfire or rewarded by the pleasures of Paradise. The judge at this terrible event was Allah, the creator of everything in the universe, who was so all-powerful that no other god could be thought to share divine honors. The facts about the Day of Judgment and the omnipotence of God were brought to the Prophet from a book preserved in heaven. The same content had, according to the concepts of Muhammad, been revealed to the prophets of the other great religions. Now it had come in an Arabic version to the Arab people through an Arab prophet. This new prophet was not like Moses, who performed miracles before Pharaoh and who smote the rock to bring forth water. Nor was he like Jesus who raised Lazarus of Bethany from his grave after he had been there more than four days, who healed the sick, or who fed the five thousand with five loaves and two fishes. Muhammad disclaimed at all times having supernatural powers at his disposal, or being a worker of miracles. He wanted to be nothing but an ordinary human being who happened to be chosen as the messenger of God to promulgate the knowledge of the heavenly Book to his Arab compatriots.

These four basic concepts—the fear of the forthcoming Day of Judgment, the submission to the all-powerful Allah, the basic importance of the Koran as the Arabic manifestation of the heavenly Book, and the human aspect of Muhammad—were of paramount importance, not only for the development of Islam as a religion, but also of Islamic art.

The idea of the Day of Judgment has always imbued Islam with a humbling spirit. In view of the pending hour of reckoning, moral deeds seemed to be better than earthly goods with which to embellish life. Furthermore, the artfully made objects of daily life were nothing but symbols of worldly splendor, or even of ostentatious luxury, which only too easily could make the owner the victim of the vices of haughtiness and vainglory. Islam as a religion was always adverse to luxury. There was no use for jeweled, gold or silver vessels even within the mosque, for the greater glory of God. There is no parallel to the sumptuous objects in the church treasuries of the Christian Middle Ages, which are just as representative of the age as the cathedrals. Such accumulations of wealth as in the treasuries of the Fatimids were an exception, and ample evidence for the ebbing morale of the gradually declining dynasty. The religion itself was satisfied with the humblest materials, such as brass, clay, plaster and brick.

The result of this attitude is evident for instance in the use of such cheap material as stucco to decorate even the *miḥrāb*, the focal point of the mosque, when the wealth of the community could have provided the most costly material. Another aspect is that whole crafts had to be reoriented. As the *ḥadīth* states that "he who drinks from gold and silver vessels, drinks the fire of hell," no beakers of precious metal could be used at the courts of the Moslem state, which otherwise would have liked to imitate the customs of the Byzantines or Sassanians. Earthenware was suddenly called to the fore to fulfill the needs of the highest ranks of Moslem society.

Luxury is too human to be suppressed. And this was certainly not possible in an immensely wealthy society which had taken over some of the most luxury-loving kingdoms of history. Some rulers did not hesitate to transgress the religious laws of society, but others rather encouraged "luxury substitutes." As soon as the process of Islamization had created an integrated society and art, in the ninth Christian century, a make-believe art can be found, one which used "disembodied gold" in the form of a luster film to be applied on pottery. Later on the inlaying of thin pieces of silver and gold on bronze or brass objects served the same purpose. Such substitutes were also cheaper than gold.

Another far-reaching effect on the development of Islamic art was the human aspect of Muhammad's activities. As he disclaimed any miracles and any supernatural power, there was no possibility for developing a sanctified iconography of Muhammad paralleling that of Christ in the Western world. If one considers the representation of the life and especially the passion of Christ, of the Holy Family, and of the saints, within the iconographic repertory of the Roman Catholic or the Greek Orthodox Church, one realizes how the lack of representation of the founder of Islam drove the Moslem artists in entirely different directions. If there are figures within the Islamic world, they can only be of secular interest.

The greatest effect exercised by any of Muhammad's new religious concepts was, however, in connection with his views on the nature of Allah. For Muhammad he is the all-powerful creator of everything, who does not admit any companion to whom he might delegate any of his powers. The direct development of this basic idea by the later theologians had far-reaching effects on arts. The prophet himself had not taken any definite stand on the use of art objects, as it was only a minor concern within society—a fact which we have already discussed. His attitude toward art can only be learned from inference, and it is then mainly a part of his anti-Jāhilīyah point of view: he forbade the use of idols at the same time when he forbade the drinking of wine, the use of games of chance and divining arrows.

There is no book on Islamic art which does not quote the famous *ḥadīth* telling us that the artist will be called upon on the Day of Judgment to breathe life into the figures which he created, and that he will be condemned to eternal hell if he is not able to accomplish this. There is usually also a reference to another of the *ḥadīths* in which it is said that the angels will not enter the house of a Moslem where there are images. Both traditions attack the arrogant and deceptive assumption of the artist that he is able to imitate something which might have a likeness to the achievements of the real creator, Allah. As the artist achieves only a caricature of the true work of God, he will be doomed on the final day of reckoning, and for the same reason the angels will not enter the house of a Moslem decorated with figures.

The result of this attitude was the severe degradation of figure art, especially painting. We have such outspoken statements as "Those who will be most severely punished on the Day of Judgment are the murderer of the prophet, one who has been put to death by a prophet, one who leads men astray without knowledge, and a maker of images or pictures." Another grouping of the wicked is given by 'Awn ibn-abi-Juḥayfah: "The prophet forbade men to take the price of blood or the price of a dog, or the earnings of a prostitute, and he cursed the tattooing woman and the woman who had herself tattooed, the usurer, and the man who let usury be taken from him, and he cursed the painter."

It is worthwhile noting that this attitude toward figure painting was valid when the social condemnation of the arts and crafts, a heritage of the old Arab society, was overcome by an integrating and democratizing social process in the second and third century of the Hijrah and thus represents the "Islamic" point of view. Crafts ceased to be the nearly exclusive occupation of slaves; more and more craftsmen in the conquered country of the caliphate forswore the religion of their forefathers and accepted Islam, while members of the Arab ruling class, especially in the cities, sank lower in the Moslem society. This changed social attitude is expressed in a line of the diwan of the poet abu-al-'Atāhiyah, a contemporary of the caliph Hārūn al-Rashīd:

"When a pious man fears God in the right way,
It does not matter, even if he should be a weaver or cupper."

Also, the armorers and blacksmiths, once so despised in Arabic society, could now claim the biblical kings David and Solomon as their illustrious forerunners.

The condoned forms of figure art show how degraded pictorial representations were. Carpets dared to show figures because one tread upon them, while figured textiles used for cushion covers could pass because one sat on them, and the scissors cut through some of the pattern. In the dark entrance passage of a house and in bathhouses paintings were tolerated, as their very position excluded any possibility of esteem, the prerequisite for the worship of an idol. Especially the nudity of the human body in the bathhouses depreciated the importance of the murals and any claim of sanctity which the pictures might have had. Shadow figures were the only type of figural representations one was allowed to see for didactic purposes, although the making of them was officially forbidden. The Spanish philosopher ibn-'Arabi saw in them a vivid symbol of the universe. The puppets are seen only through the screen in a shadowy way, not in reality; they thus resemble human beings who live in the same shadowy existence and they are ruled, as is mankind, by the manipulation of one single force. This antagonistic attitude toward figure painting can be discerned in two characteristic instances: negatively in the emptiness of the *miḥrāb*, and positively in the unlawfulness of attendance at a wedding banquet when pictures are present. It is mainly in connection with the wedding banquet that the Islamic law books, regulating the whole life, speak of art. There they discuss the conditions under which one should decline an invitation to a wedding banquet when under other circumstances it should be attended. These unlawful conditions exist, when men and women sit together, when intoxicating drinks are served, when musical entertainment is given, when gold or silver is used or when pictures are present.

Figures, or three-dimensional forms, have to be transformed in a peculiar way in order to be acceptable to Moslem society. They must not show the "six directions or five senses," the prerequisite of living forms. Every representation has to be changed from the living aspect to a purely mechanical one. Characteristic examples are provided by the first well-developed Islamic style of the tenth Christian century. All figure forms are absolutely flat, and the parts look as if they were cut out of thin sheets of metal or cardboard and then fixed together. The elephants in the famous Saint-Josse textile in the Louvre give clear indication of that (*Fig. 1*). Most figures in this style have a definite "jumping-jack" appearance. One could easily visualize them as made of flat pieces and moved by the manipulation of a string. This mechanical appearance is preserved throughout the Islamic period by the usual severe juxtaposition of strongly contrasting, unnatural colors.

In the earlier periods of Islam before this flat style was invented, and in the periods after the tenth century when the artist reverted again to the three-dimensional form, another method was used to counteract it. In this instance, the massive solidity of an ordinary or zoomorphic vessel was overcome by decorating it in a fashion which was contrary to the idea of the vessel. This phenomenon is best visible in the seventh or eighth century bronze hawk in the Berlin Museum (*Fig. 3*), or in the famous bronze griffin in the Campo Santo of Pisa (*Fig. 2*). In both instances we have an engraved design which has nothing whatsoever to do with the animal itself. The Berlin piece shows on its breast floral stems and circles, into which are inserted smaller animals such as birds or hares (*Fig. 4*), while the Pisa monster shows engravings of small animals, Arabic inscriptions and all-over patterns. In these two cases the decorations are not very conspicuous and are only of secondary nature; still they demonstrate that the creature—whether it was an aquamanale, an incense burner or part of a base for an enormous fountain—cannot be counted as among the living. In the case of the Bobrinski bucket (*Fig. 5*) the very heavy mass of the vessel is entirely overcome by five registers of inlaid figures which not only have no direct connection with the vessel, but are so varied, bright and lively that they attract immediate attention and distract the onlooker from noticing the shape itself. An even more outspoken way of dissolving form as such was the use of luster painting on vessels. The unreal glittering and sheen of the metal surface leads necessarily to the dissolution of the solid body in a piece like the large jar with tile pattern in the possession of Doctor Hirsch (*Fig. 6*).

All of the objects just cited negate their forms by means of the surface decorations. But these surface decorations are in themselves rendered in Islamic fashion, that is to say, the figures belie their three dimensionality. And again, the decorative medium is in the case of the luster jar "disembodied gold" and in that of the bucket with its thin inlays "disembodied silver and copper."

If one would dare to generalize, one might say: in its visible aspect Islamic art usually consists of a humble base; this is often covered with some sparkling or evanescent surface decoration which purports to be of precious material and presents forms divested of corporeal substance. A thin layer of bright tilework or of faïence mosaic over a brick building, a luster film enveloping a glazed earthenware vessel, a network of enamels on a glass lamp, thin pieces of silver and wires of gold inlaid on a brass ewer, lustrous wool or silk pile knotted in a cotton base fabric—all these with abstract or unnaturalistic two-dimensional designs are characteristic creations of Islamic artists.

The camouflage of forms can be paralleled by features discernible in Islamic ornament. We have here the same sensation of contradiction and unreality. It manifests itself first in three unexpected transformations of one form into another: 1) of animal forms into flowers; 2) of animals into arabesques; and 3) of round geometric lines into straight ones, or vice versa. The griffin pottery plate in the Louvre Museum (*Fig. 7*) not only shows an absolutely flat animal painted in luster, but this animal is furthermore partly turned into floral forms, as demonstrated by the arabesque tail and the floral spray which seems to be a continuation of its beak. Even more characteristic is the famous eagle plate found by Professor Herzfeld in Sāmarra (*Fig. 8*). Here the animal is not only absolutely abstract and painted in luster, but partly converted into floral forms and set against the background in which the designs submerge. In this instance the main design is so formalized that, when turned upside down, it has definitely the appearance of a stylized, large, dentated leaf. This particular piece recalls the often-cited tradition in which a Persian painter, who formerly had not lived under such prohibition, asks ibn-ʿAbbās (d. A.H. 68) whether he would have to stop painting animals; how could he then make his living? The pious traditionist answered that he could go on painting animals, but he would have to cut off their heads and give the figures the look of flowers. The Fatimid wood panel from the Musée Arabe in Cairo (*Fig. 9*) shows two horse protomas turned into arabesques. There are thousands of examples in which very ingenious geometric patterns are created by suddenly converting straight lines into round ones (*Fig. 12*).

There is a definite unwillingness to create just one main pattern which is of individual, self-contained character and which is shown as the only design on the object. Instead we have an evasion of this closed form by making the pattern indefinite. This leads to one of the most characteristic Islamic decorations; innumerable examples of endless arabesque patterns (*Fig. 10*) and geometric configurations (*Fig. 12*). Into this category also belong the Saljuq animals running behind each other on a floral background (*Fig. 11*), designs which have no beginning or end. Another group of characteristic examples are provided by the medallion pattern in book bindings and carpets (*Fig. 13*). The quarter medallions in the four corners more or less imitate the center medallion, indicating that the pattern could continue in all directions, if it had not been incidentally cut away by the framing border.

One of the results of the investigations of Islamic art so far has been the discovery that artists tried to introduce a certain amount of unreality to dispose of the living aspects of figure paintings or of three-dimensional forms. The use of luster was of especial significance in this respect. But there were other ways to increase the sense of unreality and impermanence. As Professor Massignon has shown, this particular feature is of great importance, since the evanescence of art is necessary in view of the permanency of God. It is indeed through the transitory quality of everything that the stability of the deity is proven. The koranic story which tells of Abraham's finding of God after he had seen that the stars, the moon and the sun were only passing phenomena (Sūrah VI, 75-78) is only the first demonstration of the permanent quality of Allah. It goes on in Islamic theology and also in art. A vivid example is the mausoleum in which the great conqueror Tamerlane is buried, and which has as its main decoration a large Kufic inscription stating "*li-'llāh al-baqā'*" (Permanence is Allah's).

Under this aspect the use of materials such as plaster, brick, clay, wool, etc., is not only an indication of certain ascetic qualities as was pointed out above, but also an indication of the consciousness that everything in this world, and certainly the artistic creations by the human hand, are of transitory character.

The denial of causal interrelations in natural events seems to have had its effect not only in Moslem theology, but also in Islamic art. Instead of laws of nature we have only a customary course of things achieved by "the creation of a series of universes or actions with a certain regularity from time-atom to time-atom," but still with arbitrary sequence. Ever so often we find the decoration on objects split up in a great many single units which are applied in an arbitrary fashion and could be just as well reversed or exchanged. There is no connection between the units and even if the split-up compositions reproduces a scene, like the apotheosis of a king in a sixteenth century tapestry (*Fig. 14*), each single section leads a life of its own. The luster painted jar of Dr. Hirsch (*Fig. 6*) or the famous Mosul ewer from the collection of the Duke of Blacas in the British Museum (*Fig. 15*), are characteristic examples, in which the single units have no direct connections. This atomistic tendency can be paralleled in literature. For instance, in the *Maqāmāt* of al-Ḥarīri we have the same sequence of disconnected scenes—which in this particular work happen to be fifty, but could have been another number—whereas the single *maqāmah* has no definite place within the whole book. Only the leading characters of abu-Zayd and al-Ḥārith ibn-Hammām are the connecting links within the whole, just as is the representation of the king (or of a member of his family) the connecting link within the pictorial representation on the Blacas ewer.

The analysis of the various features of Islamic art has so far shown the means by which a severe handicap was overcome in various ingenious ways. All forms were created in spite of initial interdictions. There remains the question of whether there is a manifestation of art which was not born out of a prohibition. The answer to this leads us to the one form which has positive qualities, and can therefore be truly called an Islamic art: the various styles of Arabic writing. This art form is derived from the unique position of the Koran which, as we have seen, is the Arabic version of the heavenly Book. It is the instrument of divine revelation to the Arabs, and its style is believed to be inimitable. According to the later dogma, the Koran was thought to be immanent in God and, therefore, uncreated and eternal. The use of passages, long or short, from this Book, within the mosque or in a secular building, on large or small private or official objects, occupies the place which is taken by the pictorial cycles of the Old and New Testament, and especially of the life of Christ in the Christian world. The abstractness of this type of decoration in contrast to the pictorial representations in the West shows the rigid monotheism of Islam.

The special position of Arabic writing as an Islamic form of decoration is shown in the highest and lowest types of monuments. In the latter we have Arabic writing even when the humble craftsman was illiterate; he uses only a few letters which make a pleasant decorative combination, and applies them again and again (*Fig. 16*). On the other hand, in a Saljuq mosque or madrasa it is the large band of Kufic writing which runs in unobstructed sequence along the four inside walls just below the zone of transition that keeps the manifold architectural and decorative forms of the upper and lower part of the dome chamber together (*Fig. 17*). The same function was served by similar bands of writing in monuments of the Fatimid period, for instance, on the façade of the al-Aqmar Mosque in Cairo (*Fig. 18*); here, too, the inscription is the link between all the varied niche forms into which the outside walls are divided. Like a magic belt the inscription bands in both types of buildings give unity and stability to the whole.

It is clear that Arabic writing is the appropriate decoration for a *miḥrāb*. If this part of the mosque is executed in luster tiles, the inscriptions are given in dark blue relief which, in contrast to the luster design of the background, never changes its visible aspect. As the word of Allah it has to have a permanent appearance. As such, it is also protected against too much artistic interference beyond the allowed forms of floral, geometric or arabesque terminations. Zoomorphic or anthropomorphic letters customary in the West since Merovingian times are found only in very rare cases, and then on some secular metal objects. There is even, characteristically enough, a theory according to which we should interpret human forms as imitations of Arabic writing. Muhammad al-Tihāmī ex-

FIG. 1. Silk. East Iran, about A.D. 950. Paris, Louvre (After Migeon)

FIG. 2. Bronze Griffin. Egypt, XI cent. Pisa, Campo Santo (After University Prints)

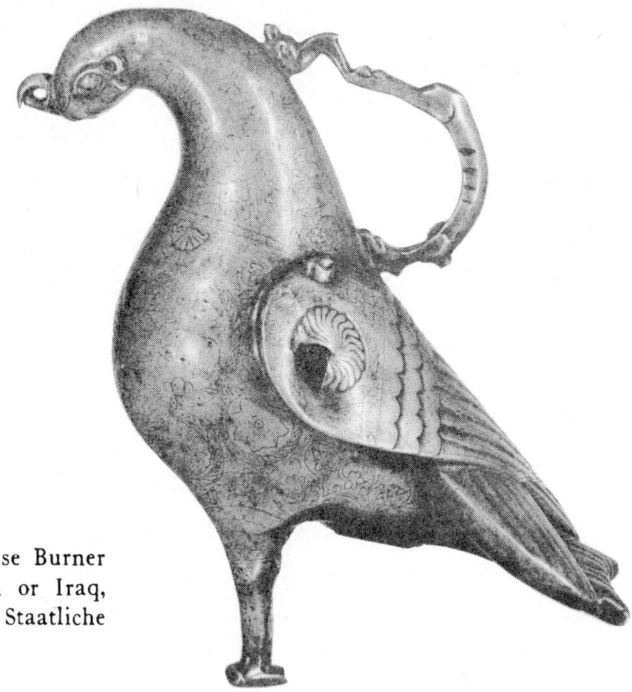

Fig. 3. Bronze Incense Burner or Aquamanale. Iran or Iraq, VIII-IX cent. Berlin, Staatliche Museen

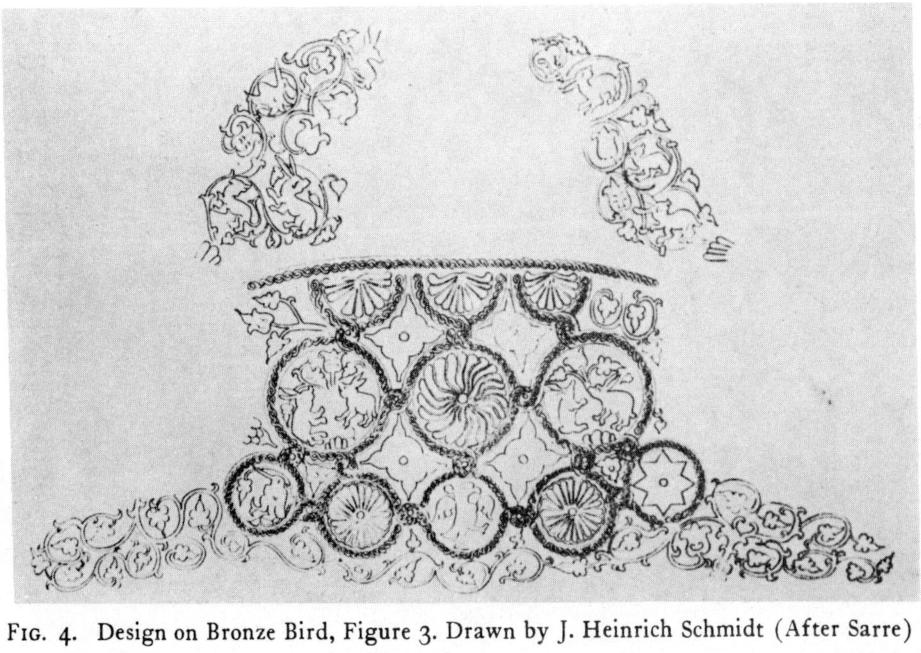

Fig. 4. Design on Bronze Bird, Figure 3. Drawn by J. Heinrich Schmidt (After Sarre)

Fig. 5. Inlaid Bronze Bucket. Iran (Herāt), 1163.
Leningrad, Hermitage

Fig. 6. Luster Jar. Iran, Second Half of XIII cent.
New York, Collection of Dr. J. Hirsch

Fig. 7. Luster Plate. Iraq, ix-x cent. Paris, Louvre (After Kühnel)

Fig. 8. Luster Plate from Sāmarra (Reconstruction). Iraq, ix cent. Berlin, Staatliche Museen (After Kühnel)

Fig. 9. Wooden Panel from a Door. Egypt, ix cent. Cairo, Musée Arabe (After University Prints)

FIG. 10. Glazed Terracotta Tile from the Mausoleum of Bayān Quli Khān. Būkhāra, *ca.* 1358. Paris, Musée des Arts Décoratifs (Photo Giraudon, after University Prints)

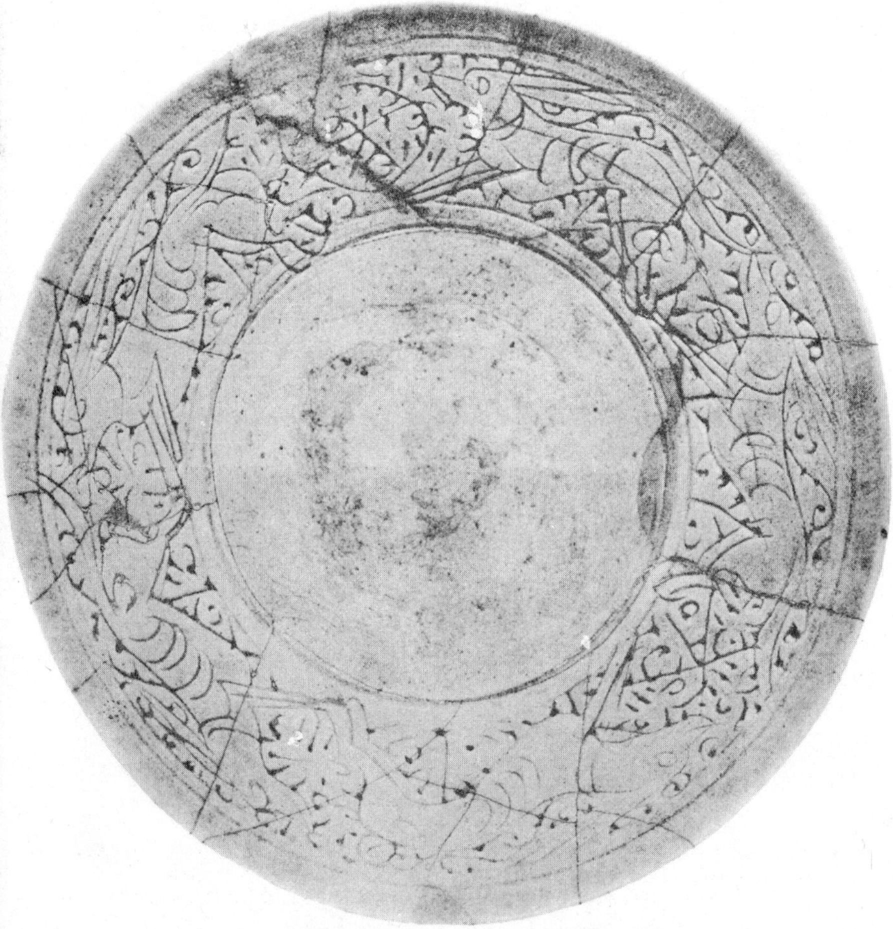

FIG. 11. Glazed Pottery Bowl. Iran, XII cent. Unknown Collection (Photo Chevojon)

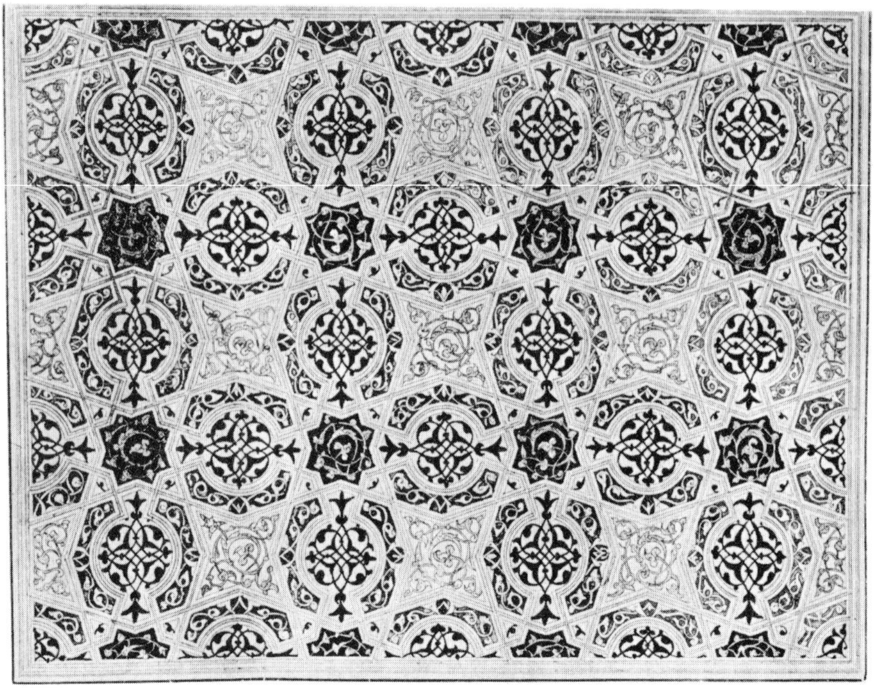

FIG. 12. Illuminated Page from Koran for Ūljāytu Khudābanda. Iran (Hamadān), 1313. Cairo, Royal Egyptian Library (Photo A. U. Pope)

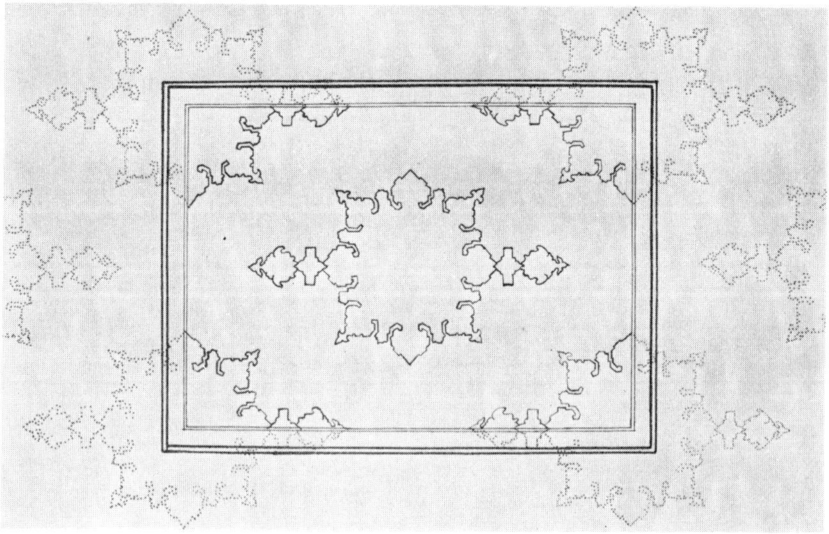

FIG. 13. Layout of Medallion Carpet. Iran, 1542. Milan, Museo Poldi Pezzoli. Drawn by Doreen Voiles

Fig. 14. Section of Tapestry. Iran (?), xvi cent. Cracow, Czartorysky Museum (After Ackerman in *A Survey of Persian Art*)

FIG. 15. Inlaid Brass Ewer. Mesopotamia (Mosul), 1232. London, British Museum

FIG. 16. Glazed Pottery Plate. Turkestan, x cent. New York, Formerly Demotte Collection (After Pézard)

FIG. 17. Haydarīyah Mosque, Qazvīn. Iran, Early XII cent. (Photo A. U. Pope)

FIG. 18. Façade of the al-Aqmar Mosque, Cairo. Egypt, 1125 (Photo K. A. C. Creswell, after University Prints)

presses in his *Hidāyat al-Muḥibbīn* the idea that man is created after the likeness of the name of Muhammad, written in Kufic: "The prophet said: God created Adam and his descendants after the letters of my name. The head corresponds to the *mīm*, the outstretched hands to the *ḥā'*, the belly to the second *mīm*, and the feet to the *dāl*."

Within the tremendous expanse of the Islamic world, it was, of course, natural that certain regions of very individual character should develop a style of their own, especially after the caliphate had broken down into single units. In the well-integrated and mature Persia of the thirteenth to the sixteenth centuries, we notice a kind of romantic and mystic escapism which found its expressions in many ways. The most obvious are the illustrations to the poems of Niẓāmi of the Timurid period. The most beautiful princes and princesses are placed in enchanting landscapes in many noble attitudes. They live in a kind of magic world which is usually separated from us by a brook in the foreground and by a range of hills towards the back, from which only a few happy people are allowed to look onto the scene. Another form of creating a romantic escape world is the large carpet, which seems to have as its main theme of decoration a Paradise complete with attentive houris amongst verdant shrubbery; or formal flower gardens within a rocky, arid landscape.

These creations are quite different from those of Egypt. It is in the Ayyūbid and Mamlūk periods that we find the full integration of the arts and crafts, which represent there not so much the spiritual, but rather the political aspect of the Islamic life. Colorful symbols of the feudal state show the self-glorification of the emirs who have risen from the lower ranks. The main monuments are the madrasas, a large important section of which is the mausoleum of the sultan erected during his lifetime. Here we find rather hard, solid material like marble for the decoration, instead of the preference for plaster in the more mystically inclined Persia. Pottery is neglected for inlaid bronzes. If ceramics are used, they are executed in the graffito technique in imitation of incised metal work. Instead of the flowery and graceful style of Iran, we have a rigid, geometric or palaeographic type of decoration which fitted better into the hieratically organized state.

These special national features present, however, only variations of the general Islamic aspect. Whatever these slight modifications in the various countries may have been, the general scheme has not been touched. Even closer contacts with Europe at first hardly interfered with the "Islamic" appearance of this art as a whole. But when some basic factors were changed—for instance, when the Koran was translated and exclusively published in the vernacular without reference to its Arabic, that is to say divine, prototype, or when naturalistically rendered or photographlike pictures were introduced on carpets, penboxes and on other places—only then the umbilical cord, so to speak, seemed to have been cut. Then a real transformation took place, radical and fateful.

LITERATURE CITED

T. Andrae. *Die Person Muhammeds in Lehre und Glauben seiner Gemeinde.* Stockholm, 1918.

T. W. Arnold. *Painting in Islam.* Oxford, 1928.

F. Buhl. *Das Leben Muhammeds*, tr. by H. H. Schaeder. Leipzig, 1930.

K. A. C. Creswell. *Early Muslim Architecture.* I (Oxford, 1932).

S. Fraenkel. *Die aramäischen Fremdwörter im Arabischen.* Leiden, 1886.

I. Goldziher. "Die Handwerke bei den Arabern," *Globus.* LXVI (1894), 203-5.

———. *Vorlesungen über den Islam.* Heidelberg, 1910.

E. Herzfeld. *Die Malereien von Samarra.* Berlin, 1927.

P. K. Hitti. *History of the Arabs.* 2nd ed. (London, 1940).

T. W. Juynboll. *Handbuch des islāmischen Gesetzes nach der Lehre der schāfi'itischen Schule, nebst einer allgemeinen Einleitung.* Leipzig-Leiden, 1908-09.

A. von Kremer. *Culturgeschichte des Orients unter den Chalifen.* Wien, 1875.

H. Lammens. "*L'attitude de l'Islam primitif en face des arts figurés,*" *Journal asiatique.* XIe serie, Vol. VI (1915), 239-79.
I. Lichtenstädter. "Das Nasīb der altarabischen Qaṣīde," *Islamica.* V (1931), 18-96.
L. Massignon. "Les Méthodes de réalisation artistique des peuples de l'Islam," *Syria.* II (1921), 47-53, 149-60.
———. "The Origins of the Transformation of Persian Iconography by Islamic Theology," *A Survey of Persian Art*, ed. Arthur U. Pope and P. Ackerman. III (London-New York, 1939), 1928-36.
T. Nöldeke. "Lehnwörter in und aus dem Äthiopischen," *Neue Beiträge zur semitischen Sprachwissenschaft.* (Strassburg, 1910), 31-66.
J. Sauvaget. "Observations sur les monuments Omeyyades, I: Châteaux de Syrie," *Journal Asiatique.* CCXXI (1939), 1-59.
M. Schapiro. "Review of K. A. C. Creswell, *Early Muslim Architecture, I,*" *Art Bulletin.* XVII (1935), 109-14.
C. Snouck Hurgronje. "Kusejr 'Amra und das Bilderverbot," *ZDMG.* LXI (1907), 186-91.
J. Wellhausen. *Reste Arabischen Heidentums.* 2nd ed. (Berlin-Leipzig, 1927).
A. J. Wensinck. *The Muslim Creed.* Cambridge, 1932.

INDEX

'Abbās, ibn-, 261
'Abd-al-Ḥamīd, 20
'Abd-al-Malik, Bishr ibn-, 67
'Abd-al-Raḥmān III, 12, 134
'Abd-Manāf, abu-Qays ibn-, 67
'Abd-Rabbihi, ibn-, 134
'Abduh, Muḥammad, 21
Abrahah, 44, 45, 64
Abraham, 64, 74, 79, 80, 81, 84, 90, 93, 97, 111, 113, 262
Abraṣ, 'Abīd ibn-al-, 126, 136
Abyssinia, 61, 64, 71
Abyssinians, 45, 61, 217
Acrab, 2
Acre, 163, 188, 193, 195, 196
'Ād, 27
'Adawīyah, Rābi'ah al-, 133, 139
Aḍḥa, al-, 206
Ādharbayjān, 233
'Āḍid, al-, 176
'Adn, Gardens of, 104
Aegean Sea, 33, 38
Afghāni, Jamāl-al-Dīn al-, 21
Afghanistan, 20, 142, 233
Africa, 3, 7, 15, 23, 29
Agada, 80, 94, 96, 100, 103, 105, 110, 112, 115
Aghāni, al-, 135
Aḥmad, 117
Aḥmad, al-Khalīl ibn-, 122
Aḥnaf, al-'Abbās ibn-al-, 132
'Ajjāj, al-, 129
'Ajjāj, Ru'bah ibn-al-, 129
Akhṭal, al-, 129, 134
Ākil-al-Murār, banu-, 47
'Alā', abu-'Amr ibn-abi-al-, 129
Alamūt, 192
Albategnius, *see* Battāni, al-
Albertus Magnus, 244
Albright, W. F., 54
Albumasar, *see* Ma'shar, abu-
Aleppo, 163, 164, 165, 168, 169, 170, 171, 178, 184, 192, 193, 242
Alexander the Great, 25, 35, 222
Alexandria, 148, 176, 196, 210, 213, 219, 241, 243
Algedi, 2
Algiers, 6
Alhazen, *see* Haytham, ibn-al-
'Ali (caliph), 67, 133
Allāhā, 52
Almagest, 236, 247
Alp Arslān, 142, 163, 237
Alphonso X, 247
Alphonso of Castile, 194
Altair, 2
Amaury, 174, 175, 177
Ambroise, 167
America, 12, 13, 18, 19
American Council of Learned Societies, 18, 19
American Oriental Society, 12, 13, 16, 18
Americans, 13, 22
American School of Oriental Research, 36
American University of Beirut, 22
Āmidi, al-, 135
Ammonites, 34, 36
'Ammūrīyah, 134
'Amr ibn-Kulthūm, 252
Amurru, 34
Anar, 171, 172
Anatolia, 163
Anbār, al-, 67
Anconitani, 188
Andalusians, 1
Andreas Vesalius, 248
Anglure, 200, 203
Anglure, baron of, *see* Ogier
Anglure, Dame d', 201, 202
Annas, 207
Anselm, 249
Anthony, St., 217, 218, 219
Anthony-in-the-Deserts, St., 213
Anthony-on-the-Nile, St., 213
Antioch, 97, 163, 165, 172, 174, 177, 188, 190, 193, 194, 232, 241
Antonius, George, 21
Anusharwan, Khusraw, *see* Khusraw Anusharwan
Apollonius of Perga, 241
'Aqabah, Gulf of, 36
Aqmar, al-, 264
Aqṣa, al-, 206
Āqsunqur al-Bursuqi, 169
Aquinas, Thomas, 4, 156
Arab Awakening, 21
'Arabi, ibn-, 258

Arabia, 9, 25, 26, 27, 28, 29, 30, 34, 38, 40, 41, 42, 43, 44, 48, 49, 50, 54, 55, 56, 59, 60, 64, 128, 216, 222, 233, 251, 252
Arabian Nights, 18
Arabians, 1, 27, 28, 33, 34, 35, 40, 46, 47, 48, 50, 51, 60, 65, 71, 72, 89, 91, 92, 253
Arabic English Lexicon, 18
Arabs, 2, 12, 16, 29, 38, 47, 61, 65, 92, 131, 135, 224, 230, 231, 234, 245, 246, 247, 248, 263
Aramaeans, 1, 34
Archer, John C., 6
Archimedes, 241
Aribi, 33
Aristotle, 4, 228, 229, 235, 245
Armenia, 174, 183, 188, 193
Armenians, 164, 169, 217
Arnold, Thomas W., 18, 251
Arsūf, 194
Aryabhata, 232
Arzachel, *see* Zarqāli, al-
Ascalon, 164, 173, 174, 190
A'sha, al-, 125, 126, 128
Ashraf, al-, 186
Ashraf Khalīl, al-, 196
'Ashtart, 31
Ashurbanipal, 33, 34
Asia, 7, 15, 23, 24, 28, 142, 169, 190, 191, 234
Asia Minor, 1, 142, 233
Asiatic Society of Bengal, 18
Asín, 4
Aṣma'i, al-, 135
Assassins, 178, 192, 194
Assemani, *see* Sam'āni, al-
Assyria, 35
Assyrians, 34, 39
Asti, 203
'Atāhiyah, abu-al-, 131, 132, 133, 140, 257
Athena, 160
'Athtar, 31
Atiya, A. S., 217
Atlantic Ocean, 1, 7, 221, 235
Averröes, *see* Rushd, ibn-
Avicenna, *see* Sīna, ibn-
'Awn ibn-abi-Juḥayfah, 257
Axum, 40, 41
Ayman, umm-, 63
'Ayn Jālūt, 193
Ayyūb, 190
Ayyūbids, 180

Baal, 159, 160
Babylon, 217
Babylonia, 61, 64
Bacon, Roger, 244
Baghdad, 1, 2, 20, 131, 136, 142, 143, 144, 148, 155, 169, 170, 176, 178, 192, 229, 230, 231, 233, 234, 235, 236, 237, 238, 243, 245, 246
Bahrain, 66
Bakhtīshū', Jibrīl ibn-, 240, 246
Bakhtīshū', Jurjīs ibn-, 239
Bakr, abu- (caliph), 63
Baktāsh, 168
Ba'labakk, 242
Balādhuri, al-, 67
Baldwin III, 173, 174
Baldwin de Burg, 168, 169
Baldwin of Edessa, 169
Balkh, 231
Bampton Lectures, 10
Bar Hebraeus, 157, 221, 247
Barkiyāruq, 145, 164
Barsbāy, 196
Baṣrah, al-, 134
Batrūn, 188
Battān, 232
Battāni, al-, 232, 247
Bayazid I, 220
Baybars al-Bunduqdāri, 194, 195
Bayṭār, ibn-al-, 3, 249
Bayt-Jāla, 209
Becker, C. H., 25
Beirut, 24, 193, 196, 204
Beirut, American University of, 22
Berbers, 1, 194
Bernhard Walther, 247
Bethany, 209
Bethfagé, 206
Bethlehem, 209
Bethzel, 209, 210
Bhaskara, 231
Bileam, 123
Bīrūni, al-, 233
Blacas, Duke of, 263
Black Stone, 53
Bobrinski, 260
Bohemond VII, 195
Bohemond of Tarento, 162
Bologna, 3, 243
Boniface VIII, 182
Book of the Dove, 157

Book of Idols, 48, 49
Bostra, 36
Botron, 188
Brahmagupta, 231
Brindisi, 186
Britain, 20
British Isles, 9
Brockelmann, 19
Broun, Heywood, 151
Buda, 219
Buddhism, 12
Buḥturi, al-, 135
Bukhāra, 248
Burd, Bashshār ibn-, 132, 139
Burgundy, 203
Burton, Sir Richard, 216
Burzuya, 238
Buṭlān, ibn-, 152
Buwayhids, 142
Byblos, 188
Byzantine Empire, 163, 183
Byzantines, 131, 142, 164, 174, 175, 255
Byzantium, 8, 50, 61, 71, 174

Caesarea, 194
Caetani, 28
Cairo, 1, 24, 33, 148, 155, 163, 170, 175, 184, 194, 209, 210, 212, 213, 215, 216, 217, 235, 237, 242, 243, 261, 264
California, University of, 16
Cambridge, 10
Cambridge Medieval History, 12
Campo Santa, 259
Canon, 3, 249
Carlyle, Thomas, 10
Carthage, 159
Carthaginians, 160
Casanova, Paul, 6
Catalans, 188
Categories, 229
Catholic University of America, 16
Cenis, Mont, *see* Mont Cenis
Central Arabia, 33, 35, 36, 37, 38, 39, 41, 44, 47, 51, 53, 54, 55
Central Asia, 231, 233
Chalandon, 174
Champagne, 200
Champagne, Count of, 200
Chanson de Roland, 249
Characene, 39
Charles I, 232
Charles of Anjou, 189, 194, 195, 234, 235
Chateau du Thoult, 201
Chaucer, 207
Cheikho, 19
Chicago, University of, 16
China, 1, 7, 221, 233, 234
Christianity, 7, 13, 44, 46, 54, 58, 59, 60, 61, 64, 67, 68, 78, 92, 93, 95, 96, 103, 112, 157, 215, 217, 226, 228
Christians, 1, 9, 63, 67, 69, 70, 71, 78, 79, 80, 81, 83, 85, 88, 89, 90, 91, 92, 93, 96, 97, 98, 103, 104, 118, 146, 156, 161, 166, 168, 169, 170, 176, 180, 181, 182, 187, 188, 192, 193, 196, 197, 205, 213, 215, 220
Christians, Abyssinian, 218, 219
Christians, Indian, 217
Christians, Malabar, 218
Christians, Syrian, 228
Christians of the Girdle, 209, 210, 216, 217
Christians of St. Thomas, 209
Chronicle of the Cid, 11
Church of Notre Dame, 207, 217
Church of Saint Saviour, 207
Cilicia, 164, 165
Clermont, 160
Cocheca, 212
Cœur de Lion, *see* Richard Lion Heart
Colette, 201, 202
Collège de France, 6
Colonna, 182
Columbia University, 16, 18
Comnenus, Emperor John, 174
Conrad de Montferrat, 180
Constantine (emperor), 160
Constantine the African, 249
Constantinople, 183, 194, 200, 238
Continens, 235
Contra Gentiles, 156
Cook, Thomas, 205
Copernicus, 247, 248
Cordova, 1, 12, 199, 246, 248
Crac des Chevaliers, 195
Cromer, 23
Cyprus, 183, 188, 189, 196, 219

Damascus, 6, 36, 46, 47, 144, 148, 155, 163, 164, 165, 168, 169, 170, 171, 172, 173, 175, 184, 185, 186, 188, 189, 190, 192, 193, 200, 210, 235, 237, 242
Damietta, 175, 184, 191
Damīri, al-, 249
Daniel, 104

Dānishmands, 164
Dante, 4
David, King, 258
Dead Sea, 36, 209
De Animalibus, 235
De Arte Venandi, 235
Dedan, 32, 37
Delos, 33
De Motu Stellarum, 232
Deneb, 2
Denmark, 42
Department of State, 11
Dharīḥ, Qays ibn-, 132
Di'bil, 135
Ḍirghām, 174, 175
Diyār-Bakr, 164
Dome of the Rock, 206
Dominican Order, 156
Dominico Gundisolvi, 234
Dorylaeum, 164
Dougherty, 30
Doughty, 29
Dropsie College, 16
Dryden, John, 232
Dubays ibn-Ṣadaqah, 169, 170
Duqāq, 164, 165, 168
Dura, 39

East Africa, 40
Ecchelensis, *see* Ḥāqilāni, al-
École des Langues Orientales Vivantes, 11
Edessa, 39, 163, 164, 165, 169, 170, 171, 173, 238, 241
Edib, Halide, 22
Edomites, 34, 36
Edward I, 195
Egypt, 1, 20, 21, 31, 32, 38, 93, 142, 148, 167, 172, 174, 175, 176, 177, 178, 181, 184, 188, 189, 190, 191, 194, 195, 199, 217, 237, 242, 265
Egyptians, 110, 111, 163, 173, 174, 176, 184, 186, 189, 190, 192, 193, 196
El, 52
Emesa, *see* Ḥimṣ
Encyclopaedia Britannica, 12
England, 19, 195
Enguerrand de Coucy, 219
Epernay, 200, 201
Epinal, 203
Ethiopia, 40
Euclid, 2, 241
Eudes Pelechin, 195
Euphrates River, 39, 51, 171
Europe, 1, 2, 4, 7, 8, 9, 12, 13, 19, 44, 172, 180, 182, 184, 187, 192, 199, 221, 225, 243, 246, 247, 248, 249
Europeans, 182
Ezra, 93

Fabri, 208, 209
Fals, al-, 253
Fārābi, al-, 233
Faragut of Girgenti, 235
Farazdaq, al-, 43, 129
Farghāni, al-, 231
Fārisi, 'Abd-al-Ghāfir al-, 144, 145
Farmer, Henry G., 5
Fatimids, 142, 163, 164, 237, 248, 255
Fayṣal, King, 20
Fazāri, Ibrāhīm al-, 230
Fertile Crescent, 1, 33, 34, 233
Fez, 248
Firās, abu-, 133, 134
France, 10, 11, 183, 190, 191, 213, 220, 243, 249
Frankfurt, 249
Franks, 166, 168, 169, 170, 171, 172, 173, 174, 177, 178, 179, 181, 184, 188, 196
Franks, Eastern, 167, 191
Franks, Syrian, 167, 182, 190, 193, 195
Frederick II, 185, 186, 187, 192, 195, 234, 235

Gabriel, 77, 84, 95
Galahad, 191
Galen, 2, 238, 244, 248
Galilee, Mount of, *see* Mount of Galilee
Ganges, River, 232
Garrett, Robert, 17
Garrett Collection, 236
Gaza, 32, 189, 210, 216
Geber, *see* Ḥayyān, Jābir ibn-
Gehenna, 104
Genoese, 188
George Purbach, 247
Gerard of Cremona, 234, 247
Gerash, 36
Germans, 160
Germany, 12, 19, 247, 249
Geshem, 35
Ghassamians, 46, 61, 64
Ghazzāli, Aḥmad al-, 144, 145, 148

Ghazzāli, al, 143, 144, 145, 147, 148, 149, 150, 151, 152, 154, 155, 156, 157, 233, 249
Gian Battista del Porta, 231
Gibbon, Edward, 11
Gibelet, 188
Gindubu, 34
Girard de Ridefort, 178
Glaser, 31
Glueck, Nelson, 36
Godfrey, 161
Gomorrah, 110
Graf, 19
Graves, Mortimer, 17
Greece, 1, 183, 227, 228, 244
Greeks, 36, 168, 169, 219, 223, 224, 234
Gregory IX, 186
Grimme, 31, 55
Grousset, 167, 193, 194
Guy de Chauliac, 243
Guy de Lusignan, 178, 180

Hadramautians, 30
Ḥafṣah, Marwān ibn-abi-, 129
Ḥajar, Aws ibn-, 124
Ḥakam, Marwān ibn-al-, 92
Ḥākim, al-, 237
Ḥallāj, al-, 133
Hamadhān, 169
Ḥamāh, 170, 178, 189
Ḥamāsah, al-, 130
Hammām, al-Ḥārith ibn-, 263
Ḥāqilāni, al-, 19
Ḥarīri, al-, 263
Ḥārith, al-, 230
Harran, 46, 65, 170, 225, 241
Hārūn al-Rashīd, *see* Rashīd, Hārūn al-
Harvard University, 12, 16, 18
Ḥaṭṭīn, 179
Hauran, 38
Haverford Symposium, 5
Haytham, ibn-al-, 237, 244
Ḥayyān, Jābir ibn-, 244, 246
Hebrews, 225
Hejaz, 22, 32, 51, 52, 62, 64, 65, 66, 67, 68, 69, 70, 73, 76, 85, 91, 92, 96
Hellenism, 1
Henri de Bar, 219
Henry IV, 183
Heraclius, 65
Hermeneutica, 229
Herodotus, 35
Herzfeld, Ernst, 261
Hibbert Lectures, 11
Hidāyat al-Muḥibbīn, 265
Ḥijr, al-, 38
Ḥillah, al-, 169
Ḥimṣ, 39, 168, 169, 170, 171, 189, 195
Ḥimyari, al-Sayyid al-, 132
Himyarites, 37, 44, 61
Hind, 'Amr ibn-, 66
Hinduism, 12
Hippocrates, 23
Ḥirā', Mount, 64, 83
Ḥīrah, al-, 46, 47, 60, 61, 66, 67, 126, 239
Hirsch, 263
History of the Church, 121
History of the Saracens, 11
Ḥizām, 'Urwah ibn-, 132
Holy Land, 182
Holy Roman Empire, 8, 185
Holy Sepulcher, 181, 191, 205, 206, 207, 208, 217, 218
Holywood, John, *see* John Holywood
Homer, 240
Hommel, 30, 31
Hospitalers, 167, 174, 186, 188, 189
Hrosvitha (nun), 12
Hubal, 53
Hudhali, Dhu'ayb al-, 125
Hudhalites, 127
Hugh of Cyprus, 195
Hulagu, 192, 233
Hungary, 184, 215

'Ibād, al-, 61
Iconium, 163, 164, 173, 174, 177
Idrīsi, al-, 3
Iḥyā' 'Ulūm al-Dīn, 148, 152, 154
Īl-Ghāzi, 169
Īl-Khāns, 194
Imām-al-Ḥaramayn, 143, 144
Imru'-al-Qays (king), 46, 47, 65, 67
Imru'-al-Qays ibn-'Amrah, 125
Imru'-al-Qays ibn-Ḥujr, 126
India, 1, 7, 162, 233, 235, 238, 249, 251
Indian Ocean, 51, 64
Indonesia, 233
Introduction to the History of Science, 19
Iran, 20, 192
Iranians, 1
Iraq, 20, 61, 192, 232, 233, 239
Isaac, 90

Isabelle de Brienne, 185
Isagoge, 229
Iṣfahāni, abu-al-Faraj al-, 135
Isḥāq, Ḥunayn ibn-, 229, 234, 239, 240, 241
Isḥāq, ibn-, 62
Ishmael, 90, 222
Isis, 19
Islam, 1, 6, 7, 8, 9, 10, 11, 13, 20, 22, 23, 25, 26, 28, 36, 39, 41, 48, 49, 51, 54, 56, 58, 59, 60, 63, 64, 65, 66, 67, 68, 69, 70, 71, 72, 83, 91, 110, 112, 114, 119, 128, 142, 143, 144, 146, 155, 156, 157, 162, 163, 170, 171, 176, 180, 181, 187, 188, 192, 194, 215, 217, 221, 226, 227, 247, 256, 259, 264
Israel, 32, 82, 87, 90, 103, 109, 111
Israelites, 34, 73, 79, 85, 87
Istanbul, 24, 235
Italians, 160
Italy, 230, 243, 246
Iti'amar, 34
Iturea, 39
Iyādi, Du'ād al-, 126

Jabal Kātrīn, 210
Jabal Mūsa, 210
Jābiyah, al-, 92
Jabr w-al-Muqābahah, al-, 230
Jaccopites, *see* Jacobins
Jacob, 90
Jacobins, 219
Jacob of Florence, 230
Jacques de Vitry, 167
Jadīs, 27
Ja'far, Qudāmah ibn-, 135
Jaffa, 174, 189, 190, 194
Jāḥiz, al-, 135
Jalandah, banu-, 51
Jalsad, al-, 253
Jamāl-al-Dawlah, 168
James of Aragon, 194
Japanese, 160
Jarīr, 43, 129
Jazlah, ibn-, 152
Jean d'Ibelin, 184
Jerusalem, 35, 36, 65, 148, 155, 163, 164, 165, 167, 168, 173, 174, 177, 178, 179, 180, 181, 183, 184, 185, 186, 187, 190, 191, 193, 195, 196, 202, 204, 205, 208, 209, 213, 215, 216
Jesus, 78, 79, 81, 85, 87, 90, 91, 92, 94, 97, 104, 116, 117, 254
Jewett, James Richard, 18
Jews, 1, 62, 63, 67, 68, 69, 70, 71, 72, 73, 76, 77, 79, 80, 81, 82, 83, 85, 88, 89, 90, 91, 92, 93, 96, 97, 98, 100, 103, 104, 111, 114, 118, 217, 225, 234, 252, 253
Joannitius, *see* Isḥāq, Ḥunayn ibn-
John, St., 207
John the Evangelist, 217
John de Gibelet, 193
John d'Ibelin, 193
John Holywood, 247
John of Damascus, 229
John of Piano Carpini, 192
Johns Hopkins University, 16
Joinville, 191
Jones, William, 18
Joppa, 204
Jordan, River, 209
Joscelyn de Courtenay, 169, 179
Joseph, 93, 212
Jubayl, 188
Judaism, 7, 13, 44, 54, 58, 59, 60, 61, 64, 68, 73, 76, 77, 79, 83, 91, 92, 93, 95, 96, 103, 106, 109, 110, 112, 157, 226
Juddah, 253
Judhām, banu-, 62
Juḥayfah, 'Awn ibn-abi-, *see* 'Awn ibn-abi-Juḥayfah
Julian of Sidon, 193
Jumaḥi, al-, 135
Jundishapur, 230, 236, 238, 239
Jundub, 34
Jurhum, 27
Jusham, 35
Justinian, Emperor, 230

Ka'bah, 43, 52, 53, 64, 253
Ka'b al-Aḥbār, 63, 70
Kaladah, al-Ḥārith ibn-, 229
Kalb, 45
Kalbi, Hishām ibn-al-, 48, 49
Kālīkūti, al-, 131
Kalīlah wa-Dimnah, 130, 238
Kāmil, abu-, 231
Kāmil, al-, 184, 185, 186, 187
Kamāl-al-Dīn, 170
Kamālist Turks, 22
Karaji, al-, 231
Karak, 190
Karbuqa, 164, 165

Katherine, Monastery of St., 209, 210
Katherine, St., 210
Kazan, 6
Keyserling, Count, 215
Khadījah, 64
Khaldūn, ibn-, 3
Khālid, Yaḥya ibn-, 133
Khalīl, al-, 130
Khansā', al-, 124
Kharijites, 133
Khaybar, 51
Khayyām, 'Umar al-, 230, 237, 249
Khilāṭ, 171
Khusraw Anusharwan, 238
Khūzistān, 238
Khwārizmi, al-, 2, 230, 231, 246
Khwārizm Turks, 185, 190
Kindah, 47, 50, 126
Kindi, al-, 231
Kitbugha, 192, 193

Labīd, 128
Lāḥiqi, Abān-al-, 130, 133
Lakhmids, 61, 62, 64, 67. *See also* Lakhmites
Lakhmites, 46, 50, 51
Lane, Edward William, 18
Lanfranchi of Milan, 243
Lāt, al-, 53, 253
Latins, 166, 168, 170, 173, 174, 175, 176, 177, 178, 179, 182, 184, 188, 189, 190, 193, 194, 195, 196, 228, 234
Lazarus, 209
Lebanon, 20, 21, 194
Leonardo Fibonacci, 230
Le Saint Voyage, 208
Library of Congress, 18
Liḥyān, 37
Liḥyānites, 37
Livy, 42
Lot, 110
Louis, St., 182, 190, 191, 195
Louvre, 259, 261
Ludolph von Suchem, 214
Lull, Raymund, 215
Lu'lu', 169
Luther, Martin, 9, 232
Lyall, Charles, 18

Macaulay, 222
Madrid, 232
Magians, 98
Mahavira, 231
Mahdi, al- (caliph), 132, 138
Maḥmūd (Great Saljuq), 145
Maimonides, *see* Maymūn, ibn-
Makki, abu-Ṭālib al-, 154, 157
Malabar, 131
Malaya, 233
Malik Shah, 142, 163, 164, 237
Mamlūks, 191, 193, 242
Ma'mūn, al-, 229, 234, 237, 245, 247, 248
Manāt, 53
Mandaeans, 60, 71
Manfred, 234
Manṣūr, al-, 229, 239
Manṣūrah, al-, 185, 191
Manzikert, 163
Maqāṣid al-Falāsifah, 156
Maraghah, 221, 233, 234, 235
Margoliouth, D. S., 11, 34
Ma'rib, 45
Māridīn, 169
Marie of Antioch, 195
Marne, 200
Martin, Raymund, 156
Mary, 79, 84, 93, 97, 117, 205
Mary Magdalene, 217, 218
Māsawayh, Yūḥanna ibn-, 239, 240, 246
Ma'shar, abu-, 231
Massignon, Louis, 251, 262
Mas'ūd, 172
Mas'ūdi, al-, 233
Matī', Ka'b ibn-, *see* Ka'b al-Aḥbār
Mawdūd, 169
Maymūn, ibn-, 4, 156, 227
Mecca, 7, 21, 43, 44, 49, 52, 53, 54, 60, 63, 64, 65, 67, 69, 174, 179, 222, 253
Mecca, Sharīf of, 21
Meccans, 113, 253
Medieval and Modern Times, 12
Medina, 7, 51, 60, 62, 63, 64, 68, 69, 78, 90, 91, 131, 179, 222, 253
Mediterranean Crescent, 233
Mediterranean Sea, 32, 36, 64, 204, 221
Meek, Theophile J., 13
Melanchthon, 232
Melissende, 173
Melkites, 71
Memoirs (Usāmah's), 166
Mesopotamia, 29, 30, 31, 33, 35, 39, 71, 142, 168, 172, 178, 186, 194
Metz, 203

Michael, St., 217
Michael Palaeologus, 194
Michael Scot, 235
Michigan, University of, 16, 18
Midian, 38
Midrash, 91, 96, 101, 102
Milan, 243
Minaeans, 30
Mingana, 19
Mishnah, 79, 101, 102, 111
Mīzān al-'Amal, 157
Moabites, 34, 36
Mohammedanism, 11
Mohammedans, 12
Mongols, 190, 191, 192, 193, 195
Monophysites, 61, 70, 71, 97
Mont Cenis, 203
Montgomery, James A., 5
Montpellier, 3, 243
Morocco, 7, 249
Moses, 73, 74, 75, 77, 78, 79, 81, 83, 85, 86, 87, 88, 90, 91, 92, 93, 94, 110, 112, 113, 216, 254
Moses of Palermo, 235
Moslems, 1, 2, 12, 62, 63, 70, 93, 98, 119, 146, 155, 162, 166, 167, 168, 169, 171, 179, 182, 183, 187, 188, 196, 222, 246
Mosque of Omar, *see* Dome of the Rock
Mosul, 164, 165, 169, 171, 172, 177, 178, 179, 235, 263
Mount of Galilee, 206, 215
Mount of Olives, 206, 215
Mount Zion, 205, 206
Mu'āwiyah, 67, 133
Mu'aẓẓam, al-, 185, 186
Mubarrad, al-, 135
Mueller, D. H., 37
Muhammad, 7, 8, 10, 11, 20, 25, 27, 48, 53, 54, 55, 56, 58, 60, 62, 63, 64, 65, 66, 67, 68, 69, 70, 71, 72, 73, 74, 75, 76, 77, 78, 79, 80, 81, 82, 83, 84, 85, 86, 87, 88, 89, 90, 91, 92, 93, 94, 95, 96, 97, 98, 99, 100, 101, 102, 103, 104, 105, 106, 107, 108, 109, 110, 111, 112, 113, 114, 115, 116, 117, 118, 127, 128, 152, 160, 229, 238, 252, 253, 254, 256, 265
Muḥammad ibn-Malik Shah, 169
Muḥāsibi, al-Ḥārith al-, 154
Mukarribs, 31
Mundhir, al-Nu'mān ibn-al-, 67
Murtaḍa, al-Sayyid al-, 147
Musée Arabe, 261
Musil, A., 38
Mustanṣirīyah, al-, 237
Mustarshid, al-, 170
Mu'taḍid, al-, 134, 242
Mutalammis, al-, 66
Mutanabbi', al-, 133, 141
Mutawakkil, al-, 241
Mu'tazz, ibn-al-, 131, 134, 135

Nabataeans, 35, 36, 37, 38, 39, 40, 52, 53, 55, 62
Naḍīr, banu-, 62
Naḍr, al-, 230
Nafīs, ibn-al-, 3
Najrān, 61
Namārah, al-, 45, 47, 65
Naples, 3
Napoleon, 21, 222
Navarre, 189
Nawawi, al-, 154
Nawfal, Waraqah ibn-, 64, 67, 69
Nazism, 160
Near East, 16, 19, 25, 26, 35, 96, 228, 233
Nebuchadnezzar, 222
Nehemiah, 35
Nehemiah, Book of, 35
Nejd, 22
Neo-Platonists, 223
Nestorians, 70, 71, 229, 238
Newman, John Henry, 151
New Testament, 59, 73, 78, 94, 98, 108, 228, 264
New York, 18, 20, 22
New York Public Library, 17
Nicea, 164
Nicopolis, 196, 220
Nielsen, D., 33, 55
Nile River, 3, 175, 184, 185, 191, 213, 217
Nilus, St., 121
Nisapur, 143, 148
Niẓām-al-Mulk, 143, 144, 237
Niẓāmi, 265
Niẓāmīyah (Baghdad), 143, 144, 145, 237
Niẓāmīyah (Nisapur), 143, 148
Noah, 111, 115
North Africa, 1, 136, 142, 155, 194, 230, 233, 235, 248

North Arabia, 32, 33, 34, 38, 44, 45, 47, 48, 61
North Arabians, 32, 34, 35, 222
Nubians, 194
Nufayl, Zayd ibn-'Amr ibn-, 63
Nūr-al-Dīn ibn-Zangi, 171, 172, 173, 174, 175, 176, 177, 242
Nuremberg, 232, 247
Nuwās, abu-, 132, 133, 134, 139
Nuwās, dhu-, 44, 61

Obermann, Julian, 16
Ockley, 11
Odenathus, 40
Ogier, 200, 201, 202, 203, 204, 205, 206, 207, 208, 209, 210, 211, 212, 213, 214, 215, 216, 217, 218, 219, 220
Old Testament, 59, 64, 94, 104, 264
Olives, Mount of, *see* Mount of Olives
Oman, 51
Optics, 244
Organon, 229
Ottoman Empire, 9, 20, 21
Ottoman Turks, 196, 222
Oxford, 10, 11

Padua, 204, 243
Palermo, 3, 234, 235
Palestine, 36, 62, 63, 64, 71, 148, 161, 163, 205, 215
Palgrave, 23
Palmyra, 39, 52, 61
Palmyrenes, 40
Paracelsus, 248
Paris, 3, 4, 11, 19, 243, 244
Parthians, 40
Pataliputra, 232
Paul, St., 151, 206, 213, 217, 218, 219. *See also* Saul
Paul of Aegina, 2
Pavia, 203
Pelagius, 184
Pennsylvania, University of, 16, 18
Perga, 241
Persia, 1, 40, 50, 135, 136, 142, 194, 221, 225, 233, 234, 235, 238, 242, 265
Persian Empire, 35, 40
Persian Gulf, 39, 51
Persians, 45, 46, 121, 222, 225
Peter, St., 204
Peter the Hermit, 161
Petra, 36, 39
Pherkad, 2
Philip de Novara, 167, 187
Philippine Islands, 233
Piedmont, 203
Pierre I, 196
Pilate, 205
Pillars of Hercules, 162
Pinnaforte, Raymond de, 156
Pirenne, Henri, 7, 8
Pisa, 230, 259
Pisans, 188
Plato, 244, 245
Plato Tiburtinus, 232
Pompey, 222
Porphyry, 229
Prester John, 219
Prideaux, Humphrey, 10
Princeton University, 16, 18, 19, 24, 236
Princeton University Library, 17
Psellus, 249
Ptolemies, 35
Ptolemy, 2, 221, 232, 246
Pugio Fidei, 156
Purbach, George, *see* George Purbach

Qalāwūn, 195, 196, 242
Qamī'ah, 'Amr ibn-, 125
Qār, dhu-, 51, 121
Qāsiyūn, Mt., 237
Qatabanians, 30
Qifṭi, al-, 239
Qilij Arslān, 164
Quraysh, 60, 63, 64, 65, 67, 68
Qurrah, Thābit ibn-, 233, 234, 241, 242
Quṣayr 'Amrah, 253
Quṣayy, 53
Qūt al-Qulūb, 154, 155
Qutaybah, ibn-, 60, 135
Quṭlumish, Sulaymān ibn-, 163
Quṭuz, 194

Rabelais, 11
Rabī'ah, 'Umar ibn-abi-, 131, 132, 138
Rama, 204
Ramaḍān, 7, 90, 206
Rameses II, 222
Ramlah, al-, 204
Ranke, Leopold von, 5
Raqqah, al-, 232
Rās al-'Ayn, 238
Rashīd, Hārūn al-, 20, 132, 257
Raymond III, 178, 179
Raymond, Archbishop, 234
Raymond of Aguilers, 168

Raymond of Marseilles, 247
Raymond of St. Gilles, 162, 169
Rāzi, al-, 3, 233, 235, 246, 249
Red Sea, 64, 179
Regiomontanus, 232, 247
Reland, Adrian, 10
Renaud de Châtillon, 174, 179
Rhazes, *see* Rāzi, al-
Rhodes, 204
Ribera, Julián, 5
Richard Lion Heart, 180, 181, 184, 200
Richard of Cornwall, 189, 190
Riḍwān, 164, 165, 168
Robert of Chester, 231
Robert of Flanders, 162
Robert of Normandy, 161
Robinson, James Harvey, 12
Roger I, 234
Roger II (Sicily), 3
Roger of Antioch, 169
Roman Empire, 8, 39, 40, 44, 45
Romans, 38, 39, 40, 45, 46, 121
Rome, 7, 19, 38, 39, 40, 247
Roosevelt, F. D., 17
Ross, E. Denison, 18
Ru'bah, 129
Ruhā', al-, 39, 241
Ruḥbah, al-, 169
Rūmi, ibn-al-, 134
Rummah, dhu-al-, 129
Rushd, ibn-, 4, 228, 244
Russia, 192
Rutebeuf, 183

Saba, 32, 34
Sabaeans, 30, 37
Sabas, St., 188
Ṣābians, 98, 241
Sacro Bosco, 247
Safa, 38
Ṣafad, 189
Ṣahyūni, al-, 19
Saint-Josse, 259
Saladin, 175, 176, 177, 178, 179, 180, 181, 183, 184, 194, 200
Ṣalāḥ-al-Dīn Yūsuf ibn-Ayyūb, *see* Saladin
Salām, 'Abdullāh ibn-, 62
Sale, George, 18
Salerno, 3, 246
Salisbury (professor), 13
Saljuq Turks, 142, 155, 161, 163, 164, 165, 168, 173, 174, 177, 190
Ṣalt, Umayyah ibn-abi-al-, 63
Sam'āni, al-, 19
Samaritans, 71, 216, 217, 218
Samarqand, 5, 245
Sāmarra, 261
Samaw'al, al-, 128
Sammāk, 62, 70
Ṣan'ā', 253
Ṣanawbari, al-, 134, 140
Saphadin, *see* Sayf-al-Dīn
Sapir, E., 5
Saracens, 9, 121, 210, 215, 216
Sargon II, 34, 222
Sarton, George, 19
Sassanians, 255
Saul, 144
Savoy, 203
Saxo Grammaticus, 42
Sayf-al-Dīn Ghāzi, 171, 172, 184
Schmidt, Nathaniel, 13
School of Oriental Studies, 11
Seleucids, 35
Semites, 29, 34, 55, 72
Sergius of Rās al-'Ayn, 238
Severus, 97
Shamash, 31
Shammākh, al-, 68
Shams, 31
Shanfara, al-, 126, 137
Shapur, 238
Shāwar, 174, 175
Shayzar, 169
Sheba, Queen of, 32
Shī'ites, 133
Shīrkūh, 175
Siberia, 192
Sibylle, 178
Sicilians, 1
Sicily, 2, 176, 185, 189, 194, 234, 235
Siddhantas, 230
Sidon, 193, 196
Simon of Sarrebruck, 219
Sīna, ibn-, 3, 233, 235, 244, 246, 248, 249
Sinai, Mt., 84, 121, 209
Sinān, Ibrāhīm ibn-, 233
Sionita, *see* Ṣahyūni, al-
Sitwell, Sir George, 203
Sīwān, 90
Sodom, 110, 111
Solomon, King, 32, 258
Solomon, Temple of, 206

South Arabia, 31, 32, 33, 35, 36, 37, 38, 40, 41, 44, 45, 51, 55, 61, 64, 222
South Arabians, 30, 31, 32, 37, 40, 55
Southern Palestine, 35
Southey, 11
Sozomenos, 121
Spain, 2, 12, 131, 134, 136, 142, 155, 226, 233, 236, 245, 246, 248
Speculum Naturale, 244
Sphaera Mundi, 247
Stephen, St., 206
Stevenson, W. B., 170
Suchem, Ludolph von, *see* Ludolph von Suchem
Sudan, 6
Sufyān, abu-, 65, 67
Sumerians, 30, 31
Summa Theologica, 4, 156
Suqmān, 164
Ṣūrah, 'Abdullāh ibn-, 62
Su'ūd, ibn-, 20
Su'ūdi Arabia, 20
Sweden, 182
Syria, 1, 2, 20, 32, 34, 35, 36, 38, 39, 40, 51, 52, 61, 64, 65, 71, 136, 142, 148, 160, 162, 163, 164, 165, 166, 167, 169, 171, 176, 177, 178, 180, 181, 183, 184, 186, 187, 189, 190, 191, 192, 193, 194, 195, 196, 200, 232, 233, 241, 242
Syrian Desert, 34, 39, 45
Syrians, 1, 122, 225, 238, 241

Ta'abbaṭa Sharran, 126
Ṭabari, al-, 233
Tabitha, 204
Tadmur, 39
Tahāfut al-Falāsifah, 156
Ṭā'if, al-, 63, 253
Ṭalḥah, 67
Talmud, 100, 103, 114
Tamerlane, 237, 262
Tamīm, 43
Tammām, abu-, 130, 132, 134, 135
Tancred, 168, 169
Taqwīm al-Abdān, 152
Taqwīm al-Ṣiḥḥah, 152
Ṭarafah, 66, 126
Targum, 80, 96
Tarsus, 144
Tartars, 237
Taymā', 68
Ṭayyi', 45
Templars, 167, 186, 188, 189, 190, 193, 195
Ten Rules, The, 149
Thābit (physician), 243
Thābit, Zayd ibn-, 68, 91
Tha'labah, Qays ibn-, 126
Thamūd, 38, 112
Theodorus, 238
Theodosius, 238
Thesaurus Opticae, 244
Thibaut of Champagne, 189, 190
Thomas, Bertram, 29
Thoreau, 214
Thoros, 164, 165
Thoult, le, *see* Chateau du Thoult
Thutmose III, 222
Tigre, 40
Tigris River, 131
Tihāmi, al-, 264
Toledo, 234, 235, 244, 246, 247
Tomkis, Thomas, 231
Torrey, Charles C., 62
Tortosa, 196
Trajan, 39, 222
Transjordan, 36, 39, 45
Tripoli, 180, 193, 195, 196
Troyes, 200
True Nature of Imposture, The, 10
Tughril Beg, 142
Ṭughtigīn, 169
Tunis, 191
Turanians, 1
Turkestan, 6
Turkey, 17, 20, 21, 22, 233
Turks, Kamālist, *see* Kamālist Turks
Turks, Ottoman, *see* Ottoman Turks
Turks, Saljuq, *see* Saljuq Turks
Ṭūs, 149
Ṭūsi, Naṣīr-al-Dīn al-, 234
Tutush, 163, 164
Tyre, 180, 188, 190

'Ubaydah, abu-, 43
'Udhri, Jamīl, al-, 132, 138
'Ula, al-, 32, 37, 38
'Umar (caliph), 63, 67, 70, 132
Umayyads, 248
Umayyah, Sufyān ibn-, 67
United States, 12, 16, 21, 22, 23, 24, 28
University of London, 11
'Uqaylids, 164
Urban (pope), 160, 161
Urmiyah, Lake, 233

Urtuqids, 164, 169, 170
Usāmah, 166, 243
'Uthmān (caliph), 67
Utrecht, 10
'Uzza, al-, 53

Venetians, 188
Venice, 203, 204, 219
Vesalius, Andreas, *see* Andreas Vesalius
Veth, 10
Vienna, 247, 249
Vincent de Beauvois, 244
Voltaire, 222

Wā'il, Qays ibn-, 126
Walīd, al- (caliph), 134
Walīd, Muslim ibn-al-, 129
Waterman (professor), 13
Western Asia, 1, 58
White, Joseph, 10
William of Malmesbury, 161
William of Rubriquis, 192
William of Tyre, 167
Winckler, 28, 30, 31
Winnett, F. V., 37, 52
Wüstenfeld, F., 5

Yaghi-Siyān, 164
Yaḥya, Imām, 20
Yale University, 13, 16
Yemen, 22, 61, 63, 64, 71, 253
Yethrib, *see* Medina
Yūnus, 'Ali ibn-, 237
Yūsuf (physician), 240

Zabad, 46, 65, 66
Zangi, 'Imād-al-Dīn, 170, 171
Zanj, 134
Zarqāli, al-, 233, 246, 247, 249
Zayd, abu-, 263
Zayd, 'Adi ibn-, 66, 67, 126, 134
Zenobia, 40
Zīj al-Ṣābi, al-, 232
Zion, Mount, *see* Mount Zion
Zoroastrians, 225